Detroit:

I Do Mind Dying

A Study in Urban Revolution

Please, Mr. Foreman, slow down your assembly line.
Please, Mr. Foreman, slow down your assembly line.
No, I don't mind workin', but I do mind dyin'.

A Detroit blues song by Joe L. Carter

Dan Georgakas/Marvin Surkin

Detroit:
I Do Mind Dying

A Study in Urban Revolution

St. Martin's Press   New York

To Our Fathers and Mothers—

Xenophon   *Abraham Jack*
Sophia   *Betty*

Library of Congress Catalog Card Number: 74-81262
Copyright © 1975 by St. Martin's Press, Inc.
All Rights Reserved.
Manufactured in the United States of America.
For information, write: St. Martin's Press, Inc.,
175 Fifth Avenue, New York, N.Y. 10010

Photo Credits

pp. 8, 14, 158, 182, 226   United Press International Photos.
p. 28   From the film *Finally Got the News.* Reproduced by permission of the film's present distributor, Tricontinental Film Center, 333 Sixth Avenue, New York, N.Y. 10014.
p. 100   Detail of "Body Presses and Assembly of Chassis" by Diego Rivera (Mexican, 1886-1957). Reproduced by permission of the Detroit Institute of Arts. Gift of Edsel B. Ford.
p. 210   Photo by Ira Rosenberg, from the *Detroit Free Press.*

Acknowledgments

pp. ii, 130   Excerpts from the lyrics of "Please, Mr. Foreman" by Joe L. Carter. Reprinted by permission of Joe L. Carter.
p. 75   Excerpt from "Father" by Abdeen Jabara, from the book *Z: An Anthology of Revolutionary Poetry* (New York: Smyrna, 1968). Reprinted by permission of the author.
p. 144   Excerpt from the poem "Coming Home, Detroit, 1968," from the book *They Feed They Lion* by Philip Levine. Copyright © 1968, 1972 by Philip Levine. Reprinted by permission of Atheneum Publishers and the author. Appeared originally in *The Hudson Review.*
p. 148   Excerpt from "Booker T. and W.E.B." by Dudley Randall. Reprinted by permission of the author.
p. 153   Excerpt from untitled poem by C. G. Johnson, from the book *Only Humans with Songs to Sing* (New York: Smyrna/Ikon, 1969). Reprinted by permission of the author.
pp. 156-57, 239   "The Ceremony" and excerpt from "Freeway Series/1" by b. p. Flanigan. Reprinted by permission of the author. "The Ceremony" was produced by Changeover Productions as a poster poem for From The Ground Up.

Material quoted from the film *Finally Got the News* is printed by permission of the film's present distributor: Tricontinental Film Center, 333 Sixth Avenue, New York, N.Y. 10014.

The authors are deeply grateful for a research grant from the Louis M. Rabinowitz Foundation, Inc., which allowed them to begin the study that ultimately resulted in this book.

Contents

Introduction   1

James Johnson—A Prologue   9

Chapter One   Inner City Voice   15

Chapter Two   Our Thing Is DRUM   29

Chapter Three   We Will Take the Hard Line   53

Chapter Four   The League of Revolutionary
Black Workers   83

Chapter Five   Niggermation at Eldon   101

Chapter Six   Finally Got the News   129

Chapter Seven   Black Workers Congress   159

Chapter Eight   Stop the Robberies, Enjoy
Safe Streets: STRESS   183

Chapter Nine   Mr. Justin Ravitz, Marxist
Judge of Recorder's Court   211

Chapter Ten   The 54-Hour Week   227

Index   242

DETROIT

KEY

⊟ Area of greatest destruction during
the Great Rebellion of 1967

1. Ford River Rouge plant
2. South End immigrant community
3. Cobo Hall
4. Veterans Memorial Building
5. Renaissance Center
6. Wayne State University
7. Detroit Institute of Arts
(Diego Rivera murals)
8. Solidarity House
(UAW Headquarters)
9. Chrysler's Jefferson Assembly
plant
10. Briggs Manufacturing
11. Chrysler's Mack Avenue stamping
plant
12. Wall of Dignity and St. Bernard's
Church

13. Chrysler complex, including Eldon
Avenue Gear and Axle plant and
Chrysler Forge
14. Dodge Main complex
15. Algiers Motel
16. Shrine of the Black Madonna
17. New Bethel Church
18. Scene of Rochester Street
Massacre
19. Muslim Mosque #1
20. Black Star Bookstore and China-
Albania Bookstore
21. From The Ground Up Bookstore
22. Motor City Labor League Bookstore
and Office
23. General Motors Technical Center

Introduction

Detroit is the fifth-largest city in the United States, the major industrial center of the nation's heartland, the headquarters of the automobile industry which directly or indirectly employs one out of every six Americans. In 1972, Lawrence M. Carino, Chairman of the Greater Detroit Chamber of Commerce, made the observation that "Detroit is *the* city of problems. If they exist, we've probably got them. We may not have them exclusively, that's for sure. But we probably had them first. . . . The city has become a living laboratory for the most comprehensive study possible of the American urban condition." When Detroit burned in July 1967, in the most widespread and costly of hundreds of urban rebellions throughout the United States, the men who rule America knew they had to take immediate action to end the general crisis. In Detroit, they formed a self-appointed blue ribbon New Detroit Committee. This organization of the city's ruling elite intended to put an end to urban unrest with a vast building program designed to replace inner city squalor with the sleek new architecture of modern office buildings, banks, condominiums, hotels, convention attractions, and a host of related enterprises. The program was meant to stimulate economic development, create jobs, and provide social stability and confidence for a troubled city.

The New Detroit Committee was not operating in a social vacuum. Already embodied within the process of destructive violence represented by the Great Rebellion of July 1967 was a fresh surge of positive revolutionary energy. An attempt to organize the power of the Great Rebellion into a political force capable of restructuring American society began as soon as minimal order had been restored by the National Guard and police. Black-owned newspapers and organizations of black industrial

1

workers began to present a series of programs and revolutionary visions in sharp contrast to the ideas put forward by the New Detroit Committee. The revolutionaries combined the experience of the black liberation struggle with the radical tradition within the labor movement to speak of a society in which the interests of workers and their families would become the new foundation of all social organization. Even as the New Detroit Committee began to put its plans into action, black workers unleashed a social movement of their own which soon forced a series of organizational, ideological, cultural, political, and economic confrontations with established wealth and power.

The New Detroit Committee represented forces that were the social antithesis of the movement led by black revolutionaries. Its personnel were headed by Henry Ford II, Chairman of the Ford Motor Company; James Roche, Chairman of the General Motors Corporation; Lynn Townsend, Chairman of Chrysler Corporation; Walker Cisler, Chairman of Detroit Edison (Detroit's power and light utility); Joseph L. Hudson, Chairman of the J. L. Hudson Company (Detroit's largest department store chain); Stanley J. Winkelman, President of Winkelman Stores, Inc. (another major retail chain); William G. McClintock, Vice-President of the National Bank of Detroit; William M. Day, Vice-President of Michigan Bell; and Ralph McElvenny, President of Michigan Consolidated Gas Company. Other members included Max Fisher, Chairman of Marathon Oil and Chairman of the United Foundation (Detroit's united charities fund); Dr. William Keast, President of Wayne State University; Dr. Norman Drachler, a retired Superintendent of the Detroit Public Schools; Walter Reuther, President of the United Auto Workers; Robert Holmes, Vice-President of the Teamsters Union; and a number of local political figures. The committee was organized in such a way that it was able to bypass openly the elected government and to finance its projects directly from corporate and foundation coffers. Over fifty million dollars were immediately earmarked by some fifty Detroit firms for a massive waterfront rebuilding plan which led to the formation of a separate organization called Detroit Renaissance. Two hundred million dollars in short-term mortgage loans were arranged for Detroit Renaissance by a group of thirty-eight banks led by the National Bank of Detroit. This loan was designed to have a second phase beginning in 1977 when the financing would shift to the Ford Motor Credit Company and four insurance companies (Aetna Life and Casualty, Equitable Life Assurance Society of the United States, John Hancock Mutual Life Insurance Co., and Travelers Insurance Co.). An enthusiastic Governor Milliken described Detroit Renaissance as "a monument to the vision of a few men and the faith of many."

The rebuilding of the center of Detroit proposed by the New Detroit Committee would mean that eventually the blacks, Appalachians, and students who inhabited the area between the riverfront commercial center and the Wayne State University area would be removed to make room for a revitalized core city repopulated by middle- and upper-class representatives of the city's various racial and ethnic groups. Stopgap anti-poverty programs were to be used as a short-term solution to street violence as a new class of black politicians and businessmen were given a wider role in running the city. These individuals would take places in corporate boardrooms, on union executive boards, and in whatever elective offices their "bloc" vote could carry them to. The police, desegregated and strengthened, were to be a front-line force against "extremists of the right and left" who sought to upset the new dynamism.

The New Detroit Committee, for all its financial and political clout, represented little more than a recycling of pre-1967 Detroit. It sought to deal with the basic contradictions and problems which had produced the Great Rebellion with what amounted to a showcase public relations program. In the first six years of the New Detroit Committee's existence the quality of life in the city deteriorated to a new low. The industrial workers who made up over 35 percent of the population were the hardest hit. They found that the New Detroit meant working longer and faster and paying higher taxes in exchange for diminishing city services and for wage gains more than outpaced by inflation. "Runaway" factories, new managerial demands, and a declining automotive industry made the very existence of many of their jobs a real issue. Union leaders, humiliated time and again by corporate managers pursuing higher productivity and higher profits, found themselves fighting their own membership as vigorously and as often as they fought the company. Black workers continued to hold the most arduous, dangerous, and unhealthy jobs. Their moves toward job improvement, union office, and shop floor reform were resisted by the company, the union, and even their fellow workers. The black population also bore much of the burden of curtailed public services, especially the nearly nonexistent public transit and a school system on the verge of bankruptcy. Thousands of homes in the city proper were deserted as a result of corruption in public and private lending institutions, making a mockery of the multimillion dollar towers of Detroit Renaissance. The grievances of "invisible" minorities such as white Appalachians and the city's growing Arab population remained largely unheard and unresolved. Established ethnic groups such as the Polish-Americans and Italian-Americans worried increasingly about jobs, property values, and personal safety. The police department resisted desegregation of its ranks, created secret elite units, and organized to win direct political power in city government. The organized state violence and the unorganized street violence of 1967 became more and more institutionalized. Motor City became Murder City, leading the nation and perhaps the world in homicides and crimes of violence. In 1973 the number of homicide victims in Detroit was triple the death toll on all sides in the civil disturbances that took place in Northern Ireland during the same year. Head-in-the-sand reformers talked glibly of gun control while literally millions of guns were sold to Detroiters of every race and class who sought protection from social chaos.

In the pages that follow we have attempted to relate the history of the Detroit struggle from 1967 to 1974, taking the activities of urban revolutionaries as our point of departure. We begin with a small core of black revolutionaries who began their political work in this period by publishing a newspaper and organizing in the factories and then led a series of activities which inspired other insurgent forces within the city and beyond. More than anywhere else in the United States, the movement led by black workers defined its goal in terms of real power—the power to control the economy, which meant trying to control the shop floor at the point of production. The Detroit revolutionaries did not get sidetracked into a narrow struggle against the police per se or with one aspect of power such as control of education. The movement attempted to integrate within itself all the dissident threads of the rebellious sixties in order to create a network of insurgent power comparable to the network of established power. This movement, clearly in conflict with the wealth, power, and interests represented by the New Detroit Committee, generated an amazing sequence of separate but interlocked confrontations in the factories, in the polling booths, in the courts, in the streets, in the media, in the schools, and in the union halls.

What clearly differentiated the Detroit experience from other major social movements of the sixties and early seventies was its thoroughly working-class character. We have tried to ascertain exactly what this movement by working people meant in terms of the mass culture and the quality of life found in the factories, schools, and neighborhoods of the city of Detroit. Without minimizing the enormous tensions within the working class, tensions between blacks and whites, between men and women, and between competing ideologies and strategies, we have attempted to determine, from primary sources, what those involved in the struggle accomplished and what they had to say about their ultimate goals. At various moments in this effort by working people to gain control of their own lives, different individuals and organizations became more important than others. Our purpose has been to follow the motion of the class which supported them rather than to trace particular destinies or to speculate on the possible future importance of specific individuals, ideologies, or organizations.

We have used original interview material extensively. Most of these interviews were conducted in the summer of 1972. All of them were recorded on tape, and the majority were recorded in the privacy of the homes of the people being interviewed. Usually, the person interviewed responded at length to a few introductory questions and then answered in more detail specific questions arising from the general discussion. We also had access to the personal papers of several important participants and to numerous plant bulletins, organizational memos, newspapers, and similar documents. In the pages which follow, when reproducing those materials, we have not tampered with the original in any way; this means that some typographical errors, unusual spellings, and grammatical mistakes have been reproduced. We believe this approach is necessary to preserve the unique flavor and tone of the language. Likewise, when quoting speeches, we have retained slang expressions and awkward constructions in the original without using brackets and other devices to make the speech patterns conform to more standard conventions.

Our account concludes on what may seem to be a pessimistic note. That is not our intent and our conclusion is not a pessimistic one. Nothing fundamental has changed in Detroit because the forces that controlled the city prior to 1967 still control the city and the nation. The strategies and tactics that guided their actions prior to 1967 remain more or less unaltered. Neither the ruling elite nor the workers have been able to revive the Motor City. But hundreds of thousands of people have begun to question basic assumptions about the organization and purpose of their lives and about the institutions that control them. They have begun to accumulate valuable skills and experiences necessary to challenge those institutions and to create substitute or parallel structures of power.

Increasingly, groups of white workers have begun to voice the complaints and pursue the objectives that black workers began to voice and pursue in the late 1960s. Ideas once limited to Marxists, youth counterculturalists, and women's liberation groups can now be found on the shop floor in myriad demands and actions for a humane way of life. The capitalist work ethic has been discredited. Men and women no longer wish to spend forty to fifty years performing dull, monotonous, and uncreative work. They see that the productive system which deforms their lives for a profit of which they have less and less of a share is also one that destroys the air they breathe, wastes the natural resources of the planet, and literally injures or disables one out of ten workers each year. Their rebellion is expressed in extraordinary absenteeism, particularly on Mondays and Fridays, in chronic lateness, in the open use of drugs, in poor workmanship, in repeated demands for earlier retirement, in sabotage, and in the wildcat strike. At the same time, many members of the working class, especially young whites unable to find well-paying jobs, have found a solution to their employment woes by volunteering for the police and armed forces. White workers who can accept racial cooperation on the shop floor often remain hostile to similar cooperation in matters of housing, schooling, health care, and a whole range of social issues. Whether internal divisions will thwart the development of united class action is a question that remains to be answered.

The decade of the sixties with its assassinations, protests, riots, war, and violence has given birth to a decade that is deceptively quiet on the surface, while the forces of change move even more certainly toward the taproots of American society. Popular doubt about the ability of the dominant class to govern effectively has become increasingly widespread in the wake of the energy crisis, corruption in the highest elective office, and malicious corporate intrigues. The system no longer produces what was once touted as the "highest standard of living on earth." The people of the city of Detroit have been dealing with the crisis of power in a dramatic fashion, sometimes emphasizing race and sometimes emphasizing class, sometimes seized by fear and sometimes with vision. This book is about their experiences, a history of the contemporary United States in microcosm, an exemplary case of a social condition and conflicting social visions which stretch from one end of America to the other.

James Johnson— A Prologue

On July 15, 1970, one of those midsummer days when the most important thing in town is the baseball game, a black auto worker named James Johnson entered the Eldon Avenue Gear and Axle plant of Chrysler Corporation with an M-1 carbine hidden in the pant leg of his overalls. The factory had been the scene of a series of bitter wildcat strikes for most of the year, and during a two-week period one female and one male worker had been killed from on-the-job accidents. The noise, oil pools, and defective machinery that characterized the plant were all around Johnson when he spotted one of the foremen who had been involved in his dismissal earlier that day. He took out his carbine, and before he was finished shooting, one black foreman, one white foreman, and one white job setter lay dead on the factory floor.

Few of the Eldon workers knew much about James Johnson. He was not identified with the militants of the Eldon Avenue Revolutionary Union Movement (ELRUM), the Wildcat *group, or the Safety Committee. James Johnson didn't even go to union meetings. He was one of those thousands of anonymous workers who spoke little and laughed less. He did not drink in the bars near the factory, and he was not a ladies' man. James Johnson was a Bible reader, and his biggest source of pride was the small house he was buying for himself and his sister.*

Opposite page: James Johnson on his way to arraignment in Recorder's Court.

9

Some days later, word got around the factory that Johnson's attorney would be Kenneth Cockrel. A few of the workers knew that Cockrel was on the seven-man Executive Committee of the League of Revolutionary Black Workers; more had heard of him because of the New Bethel case, in which he had successfully defended members of the Republic of New Africa accused of shooting two policemen. Sympathy for James Johnson grew at the plant when workers learned that he had received a suspension the morning of the shooting after he had refused to participate in a work speed-up. Later, Eldon workers learned of other disputes involving lost pay and lost vacation time in which Johnson had been treated unfairly.

A few days after the shooting, ELRUM published a leaflet with the headline "Hail James Johnson." The leaflet gave a brief biography of Johnson and went into detail about the various incidents leading to the fatal events of July 15. ELRUM blamed the deaths squarely on working conditions at Chrysler and on Johnson's lifetime experience as a victim of racism. ELRUM argued that Chrysler had pulled the trigger and the United Auto Workers (UAW) was an accessory after the fact. Similar leaflets favorable to Johnson appeared as far away as the General Motors plant in Fremont, California, and the Ford plant at Mahwah, New Jersey.

The judge for the James Johnson murder trial was Robert Colombo, formerly an attorney for the Detroit Police Officers Association. The preceding year, Ken Cockrel, assisted by Justin Ravitz, one of his law partners, had challenged the jury selection which had resulted in an all-white jury for the New Bethel case. Cockrel and Ravitz had argued that given that the New Bethel case involved racial violence in a city with a black majority, the defendants, who were all black, were being denied a jury of their peers as guaranteed in the constitution. In the Johnson case, Cockrel, again assisted by Ravitz, argued that the criteria for a jury of Johnson's peers involved class as well as color. The final jury was just what Cockrel wanted. It was sexually and racially integrated. Ten of the twelve jurors had had direct work ex-

perience in the city of Detroit, two were auto workers themselves, and three were married to auto workers.

The defense's presentation was complex. Johnson's relatives and friends came from Mississippi to testify about his boyhood in one of the backwater regions of America. They told all the familiar Southland horror tales. These included an account of how a five-year-old James Johnson had seen the dismembered body of his cousin on a highway following a lynching. The jury learned that Johnson had enlisted in the Army, only to be discharged for psychological problems. They learned the details of a work history in which an inferior education and racism led from one poor job to another in a pattern characterized by emotional outbursts and threats from both Johnson and various employers. They learned, too, that Johnson had finally found a steady job at Eldon, where he had worked for three years, supporting members of his family as well as himself. His attorneys presented evidence that Eldon was one of the most dangerous plants in the United States and that the UAW was unable or unwilling to protect workers on the shop floor. As a climax to the defense, Cockrel took the entire jury to the scene of the crime so they could judge conditions for themselves.

When the jury found James Johnson not responsible for his acts, an irate Judge Colombo called a press conference at which he released a letter he was sending to the Ionia State Hospital. The letter recommended most vehemently that Johnson be kept in custody for the rest of his natural life. Judge Colombo stated that it was his opinion that if Johnson were ever released he would kill again.

On November 2, 1972, Justin Ravitz was elected to a ten-year term as a judge of Recorder's Court, Detroit's criminal court, thus becoming a colleague of Judge Colombo. His election indicated popular support for the legal principles advanced in the New Bethel case, the Johnson case, and other well-publicized judicial battles involving Cockrel and Ravitz.

On May 12, 1973, James Johnson, represented by Ron Glotta, a white lawyer who was a member of the radical Motor City Labor League, was awarded workman's compensation for the injuries *done to him by Chrysler. The courts ordered Chrysler to pay Johnson at the rate of $75 a week, retroactive to the day of the killing.*

At the end of 1970, the year in which James Johnson had reached his breaking point, the huge Goodyear computer, located where the Chrysler Expressway intersects the Ford Expressway, indicated that car production for the year reached a total of 6, 546,817. In Solidarity House, the international headquarters of the UAW, the research department records showed that injuries in the auto factories that year exceeded 15,000 with an unknown number of deaths. The Detroit Tigers had completed their 1970 season with 79 games won and 83 lost to finish fourth in the Eastern Division of the American League.

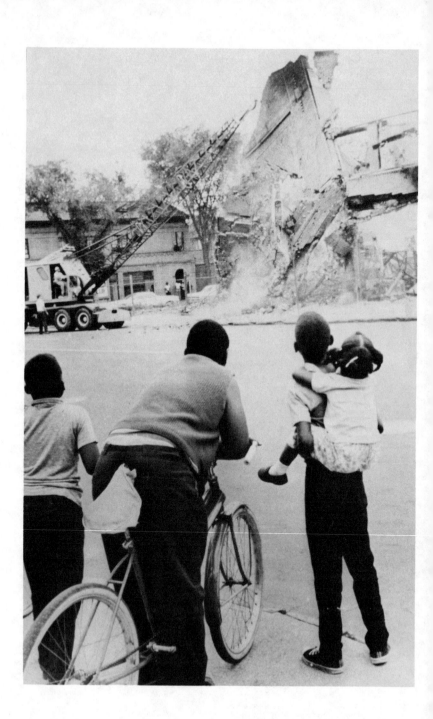

Chapter One

Inner City Voice

1

In the violent summer of 1967, Detroit became the scene of the bloodiest uprising in a half century and the costliest in terms of property damage in U.S. history. At the week's end, there were 41 known dead, 347 injured, 3,800 arrested. Some 5,000 people were homeless . . . while 1,300 buildings had been reduced to mounds of ashes and bricks, and 2,700 businesses sacked. Damage estimates reached $500 million.

Time Magazine, August 4, 1967

Less than thirty days after the Michigan National Guard lifted its occupation of the city of Detroit, H. Rap Brown spoke to an explosive crowd of some 5000 persons gathered in and around a theatre on Dexter Avenue just a mile or so from what had been the center of the Great Rebellion. Brown, who in August of 1967 was near the height of his influence as a revolutionary orator, delivered the kind of angry and militant speech for which he was famous. Later, he would be quoted as saying, ''There are people who can relate the struggle of black people better than I can. People in

Opposite page: A west-side street on the first day of quiet after the Great Rebellion.

Detroit, for instance." The sponsors of his appearance were some of those people. Their purpose had been to raise interest in their new monthly newspaper, the *Inner City Voice*.

The first issue of the newspaper appeared in October 1967. The headline was "MICHIGAN SLAVERY," and the focus on urban revolt was underscored in one of the first editorials:

> In the July Rebellion we administered a beating to the behind of the white power structure, but apparently our message didn't get over. . . . We are still working, still working too hard, getting paid too little, living in bad housing, sending our kids to substandard schools, paying too much for groceries, and treated like dogs by the police. We still don't own anything and don't control anything. . . . In other words, we are still being systematically exploited by the system and still have the responsibility to break the back of that system.
>
> Only a people who are strong, unified, armed, and know the enemy can carry on the struggles which lay ahead of us. Think about it brother, things ain't hardly getting better. The Revolution must continue.

ICV (Inner City Voice) carried two descriptive phrases astride its masthead—"Detroit's Black Community Newspaper" and "the Voice of Revolution." These reflected a belief that the paper's hard-hitting and revolutionary viewpoint was an accurate expression of the dominant mood of Detroit's black population. *ICV* was not like the alternate-culture newspapers of that period. Its editors did not see its function simply as one of a principled opposition to the dominant culture. Using their own resources, they tried to build their paper into a vehicle for political organization, education, and change. *ICV* was to be a positive response to the Great Rebellion, elaborating, clarifying, and articulating what was already in the streets. There seemed to be no reason why *ICV* could not supplant the weekly *Michigan Chronicle,* Detroit's largest-circulating black newspaper, and perhaps one day become a black-owned daily able to compete with the morning *Detroit Free Press* and the evening *Detroit News.*

The people who put out *ICV* were not newcomers to struggle and they were not underground journalists of the type which produced hundreds of periodicals during the late sixties. Their collective experience included every major black revolutionary movement of the previous decade. They had been active in SNCC (the Student Non-Violent Coordinating Committee), the Freedom Now Party (an all-black party which gained ballot status in Michigan), UHURU (a Detroit radical action group), RAM (Revolutionary Action Movement), and a number of additional formal and informal groupings. Some of them had been part of a group which defied the State Department ban on travel to Cuba in 1964, and some of them had had personal conversations with Ernesto "Che" Guevara.

ICV met its monthly publishing schedule for the next year with an average press run of some 10,000 copies. Each issue coupled a dynamic prose style with explicit revolutionary ideas about local, national, and international events. The first issue set the tone with three front-page stories concerning living and working conditions in the city of Detroit. The lead story was an expose of substandard conditions at Detroit General Hospital, an institution most poor people in the inner city had personal contact with. International problems were given a sharp local focus by *ICV*'s advocacy of massive black participation in the national anti-war March on Washington scheduled for October 21, 1967. Subsequent issues dealt with self-defense in the event of new fighting, with food and water logistics treated as seriously as overt military problems. Stories covering national events adopted a united front approach. Every figure or group actively engaged in struggle was given space, whether a white Catholic integrationist priest such as Father Groppi in Milwaukee, the emerging Black Panther Party of Oakland, California, or a black nationalist such as Imamu Baraka (Le Roi Jones) in Newark. Much of the paper dealt with revolutionary events on the national and international levels, but the front page and feature stories were rooted in Detroit conditions. Over the year the headlines included:

MICHIGAN SLAVERY

COPS ON RAMPAGE—14 YEAR OLD SHOT

GIRL LOSES EYE RUNNING FROM RATS

WHITE FOREMAN KILLED AFTER RACIST INSULT AT FORD'S

BLACK WORKERS UPRISING

The literary style and sensationalistic photographs of *ICV* were deliberately provocative. The editors of *ICV* wanted to present complicated revolutionary ideas in a popular and exciting format. The influences of Malcolm X and Che Guevara were strong, but there were many other currents. *ICV* regularly reproduced articles from the *Crusader,* a newsletter written by Robert Williams, an ex-marine whose advocacy in 1954 of armed black self-defense while head of the Monroe, North Carolina, NAACP had led to a kidnapping charge and self-exile, first in Cuba and then in China. *ICV* featured a regular column by Detroiter James Boggs, who had published *The American Revolution: Pages from a Negro Worker's Notebook* in 1963. Some of the *ICV* staff had worked with Boggs in political groups, and he was highly respected even when people did not agree with him. *ICV* also reprinted speeches by black Marxist C. L. R. James, best known for his book *Black Jacobins,* a study of the Haitian revolt led by Toussaint L'Ouverture. James had organized political groups in the city, and Martin Glaberman, the chairman of one of those groups, had once conducted a private study class on Marx's *Capital* for some of the individuals most prominent in producing *ICV*. Although a totally black owned and operated paper, *ICV* published a few stories by whites which were either written exclusively for the paper or taken from wire services. The unifying ingredient in all *ICV* material was the sharp emphasis on defining the strategy and tactics of the ongoing black liberation struggle and how it might prefigure and trigger a second American revolution.

Virtually all the individuals who later emerged as the leadership of the League of Revolutionary Black Workers worked on *ICV,* but the key person was editor John Watson, a slightly built man then in his early twenties. Watson already had a long political history. As early as 1960, he had been identified as too radical for CORE (Congress of Racial Equality). A few years later he was expelled from SNCC, along with the entire Detroit chapter, because the group had advocated direct action in the North as well as in the South. During the next few years he worked with NAC (Negro Action Committee), the Freedom Now Party, and UHURU. In 1963 Watson was part of a group accused of jeering at the American flag and booing the national anthem during a ceremony at City Hall staged to interest the Olympic Committee in selecting Detroit as a site for a future Olympiad. A year later he was part of a group that threatened a mass insurrection of 50,000 blacks if one of their number should be drafted, a pure bluff which brought about the mobilization of hundreds of troops around the Wayne County Induction Center. Instead of 50,000 demonstrators as promised, there were only eight. Nevertheless, the prospective inductee was found "unsuitable" for service.

Watson had been involved in so much activity and he had such a nonchalant personal manner that his power as an intellectual was sometimes underestimated. Watson had attended the Friday night forums of the Socialist Workers Party in the early sixties, and he had helped organize the all-black group that studied Marxism with Glaberman. He was a perennial university student, but most of his learning came from private reading, political activism, and contacts with people involved in political struggle. In contrast to some of the original SNCC and UHURU people who fell away from activism, Watson became increasingly important as an idea man, a public speaker, and a person who could get things started. A relatively poor administrator who was sloppy with details and time schedules, Watson was most effective when he had a colleague to handle day-to-day operations. He had almost unlimited energy when he was working on a project he considered important. At considerable cost to his health, his sheer energy pushed through project after project that others considered too bold for success. Watson had the ability to take an idea, shape it to Detroit reality, and somehow find funds to put it into action. Watson, more than anyone else, was responsible for the existence of *ICV* and for its characteristic ability to present complicated ideological analyses of capitalism in a popular style which made the leap from theory to practice seem almost automatic. An editorial of February 29, 1968, was typical:

> To struggle in our own interest means that the black people of the ghetto must struggle to overthrow white capitalism. The struggle against capitalism is world wide and the revolutionary struggle of the ghetto is crucial and essential in the over all world revolution. If the Koreans and Vietnamese can overthrow imperialism in Asia then Asia will be free. But if the Black Revolution can overthrow capitalism and imperialism in the U.S., then the whole world will be freed. This, then, is our role.
>
> With this understanding, let us praise the Vietnamese and Koreans, but let us pass the ammunition and do our own thing.

The paper's consistent anti-capitalist analysis transformed articles about hospitals, police, and housing from simple expressions of grievances capable of reform to a critique of the entire social order. While emphasizing caution, *ICV* continually evoked the liberating spirit of the Great Rebellion, which it referred to with the phrases "shopping for free" and "the general strike of '67." The *ICV* analysis of what was happening to blacks in the Detroit auto plants followed the same style. Other forces in the city spoke stridently of an abstract black power, but *ICV* raised the spectre of an uprising of black workers which not only would strike at the company but would totally bypass the United Auto Workers as well. A June 1968 front-page story laid out the problems of black workers and spoke of direct action on the shop floor:

> . . . black workers are tied day in and day out, 8-12 hours a day, to a massive assembly line, an assembly line that one never sees the end or the beginning of but merely fits into a slot and stays there, swearing and bleeding, running and stumbling, trying to maintain a steadily increasing pace. Adding to the severity of working conditions are the white racist and bigoted foremen, harassing, insulting, driving and snapping the whip over the backs of thousands of black workers, who have to work in these plants in order to eke out an existence. These conditions coupled also with the doublefaced, backstabbing of the UAW have driven black workers to a near uprising state. The UAW with its bogus bureaucracy is unable, has been unable, and in many cases is unwilling to press forward the demands and aspirations of black workers. In the wildcat strikes the black workers on the lines do not even address themselves to the UAW's Grievance Procedure. They realize that their only method of pressing for their demands is to strike and to negotiate at the gates of industry.

The first steps to stop such messages from reaching the streets of Detroit were taken by the American Legion and other well-organized groups of the Right who tried to use their influence in the state legislature and the mayor's office. They contended that *ICV* was calling for a resumption of the Great Rebellion, but, in fact, the paper stayed within the boundaries of the Bill of Rights and could not be legally suppressed. Breakthrough, a Detroit split-off from the John Birch Society which had terrorized peace marchers with physical assaults, began to attack *ICV* through its spokesman,

Donald Lobsinger. Breakthrough eventually attempted to disrupt a public meeting. An *ICV* article carried this terse information on the outcome: ''Lobsinger found one of his followers laying in the lavatory floor in a pool of his own blood.'' *ICV* omitted all details about its self-defense procedures. This was characteristic of those who produced the newspaper. While considering military matters to have a high priority, they always gave their specific apparatus a very low profile in all public pronouncements.

The enemies of *ICV* soon found more effective pressures than violence and open censorship. The FBI made a practice of visiting shops which produced the paper and of inquiring why the owners were supporting subversion. The usual result was an immediate refusal to print any more issues. An even more effective weapon was the typographers' union, which took the position that even if a printer was willing to publish *ICV,* the union would call a strike to prevent it. John Watson recalls with bitterness that one of the officials of the union had been a well-known member of the Communist Party. When personally asked to use his influence within the union, the official replied that nothing could be done. Other established radical groups and individuals associated with them as former or active members were likewise unwilling or unable to aid *ICV.* Their lack of support, rather than apparent ideological differences, was the basis for the generally poor opin- ion of the Left held by most of the *ICV* staff. As a result of the FBI and union harrassment, the *ICV* was never printed in the same shop more than twice. The consequence of the double attack was that copy had to be taken to Chicago, where it was printed by the same firm that printed *Muhammad Speaks,* the newspaper of Elijah Muhammad's Black Muslims. The printed papers were then trucked back to Detroit for distribution.

2

SENATOR [ROBERT] GRIFFIN: *Can you tell me what is the significance of General Gordon Baker? Is that really his given name?*
DETECTIVE SERGEANT PAUL CHAMBERS: *That is his name, sir. . . . It is not a rank.*

U.S. Senate Sub-Committee To Investigate Administration of the Internal Security Act and Other Internal Security Laws, hearings of August 6, 1970

The publishers of *ICV* were the core of a group of some thirty black activists who had organized themselves into an informal study/action group. Most of their time was spent exploring how revolutionary ideas might be implemented in their places of work. One of the most respected members of this group was General Gordon Baker, who was then working at Dodge Main, an assembly plant of Chrysler Corporation. Baker's radical background was extensive. He had been part of RAM, the *Capital* study group, UHURU, and the group that visited Cuba in 1964. In 1966, along with Glanton Dowdell and Rufus Griffin, he had been charged with carrying concealed weapons to a disturbance on the east side of Detroit. He and Dowdell had been convicted and placed on five years probation.

Baker was a powerfully built and amiable man who had often expressed his revolutionary views at work and in the streets, only to find them rejected as too militant. By the spring of 1968, the mood of workers had shifted. Mike Hamlin, another of the key figures at *ICV*, recalled the situation in an interview given to the authors on August 24, 1972: "Gradually he [Baker] began to pull together a group of workers who began to meet in the offices of the *Inner City Voice*. Usually, General and I would meet with them late at night. . . . One of the key persons in the plant was Ron March. It took him a long time to move from understanding that conditions in the plant were related to what was happening in Vietnam. Eventually he came to a sound analysis and with the rest of the group of workers decided to start agitation at Dodge Main.''

Hamlin's role as an intermediary between those most concerned with the publication of *ICV* and those who were involved in direct in-plant organizing was one he would repeat many times in the next years. A truck driver and Korean War veteran, Hamlin's special talent was to act as a mediator when serious disagreements arose. A soft-spoken man of great patience, Hamlin spent hours welding together elements that might otherwise have blown up at each other in fits of anger, frustration, and misunderstanding.

Nine months and five days after the Great Rebellion, the work of Baker, Hamlin, and March bore fruit when on May 2, 1968, 4000 workers shut down Dodge Main in the first wildcat strike to hit that factory in fourteen years. The immediate cause of the strike was speed-up and both black and white workers took part, but the driving force was the *ICV* group, which now named itself the Dodge Revolutionary Union Movement—DRUM. The activities and ideas of DRUM were to inspire black workers in factories throughout the United States. No less an authority than the *Wall Street Journal* took them very seriously from the day of the first wildcat, for the *Wall Street Journal* understood something most of the white student radicals did not yet understand: the black revolution of the sixties had finally arrived at one of the most vulnerable links of the American economic system—the point of mass production, the assembly line. And the DRUM militants were not simply another angry caucus of rank-and-file workers of the type that periodically sprang up in one plant or another. DRUM's anger was the anger of the Great Rebellion and its vision was that of a new society. In one of his rare public writings, General Baker, the soul of DRUM, spoke of being dismissed from his job for leading the wildcat strike. When Baker raised his voice against Chrysler Corporation, his words represented the feelings of many rank-and-file workers, and they reverberated throughout the plants. His views were a mixture of socialism and revolutionary black nationalism, but he was always consistent and forceful in supporting workers' grievances and in pushing confrontation forward. Using the device of an open letter to Chrysler Corporation published in the June 1968 issue of *ICV*, General Baker took the offensive—the DRUM road —against the company and the union:

OPEN LETTER TO CHRYSLER CORPORATION

Dear Sirs:

In response to my discharge on May 5, 1968 for violation of the 5th section of the agreement between Chrysler Corporation and the UAW, dated Nov. 10, 1967, which reads

"No Strike or Lockout"

(1) Strike prohibited (etc.)

In discharging me you have falsely placed the banner of leadership upon my shoulders. And in so doing you have denied two main things. Number one, you have denied me the right to receive any justice from this corporation. And number two, you have nullified the possibility of the real issues which caused the walkout of ever being aired. Even though you have falsely placed the banner of leadership of a wildcat strike upon my shoulders I shall wear it proudly. For what more nobler banner could a black working man bear. In this day and age under the brutal oppression reaped from the backs of black workers, the leadership of a wildcat strike is a badge of honor and courage. In discharging me you have attempted to belittle the racial overtones in this affair which will prove to be an impossible task on your behalf. Any confrontation between black and white men in this racist decadent society is a racial and therefore a political question. Let it be further understood in the wildcat strike that the harshest discipline was issued against black workers attributing further to your blatant racism. Also, Hamtramck Assembly Plant (old Dodge Main) has a long history of trampling upon the rights of black people. It was as late as 1952 while black men were shedding their blood in the dirty unjust war of aggression against the Korean people that black men were allowed to work on the assembly lines, in the trim shop, and final assembly. And even then, many white workers stormed off of the line refusing to work next to black men. Some of the same outright white racist policy makers of this corporation are still in control of this racist corporation today. Black people are expected by the Chrysler Corporation to purchase Chrysler finished products, but are brutally oppressed and overworked and harrassed on the production lines.

Yes, the struggle between black workers and white racist Corporation owners and operators is the most vicious of all existing struggles in the world today. It is sometimes opened and sometimes closed, it is some- times hot and sometimes cold. It is, nevertheless, in the final sense a vicious struggle. Let it be further un- derstood that by taking the course of disciplining the strikers you have opened that struggle to a new and higher level and for this I sincerely THANK YOU. You have made the decision to do battle with me and therefore to do battle with the entire black community in this city, this state, this country, and in this world of which I am a part. Black people of the world are united in a common struggle which had its beginning with the exploitation of non-white people on a world wide scale. To quote from W. E. B. DuBois, ''The emancipation of man is the emancipation of labor and the emancipation of labor is the freeing of that basic majority of workers who are yellow, brown, and black.'' You have made the decision to do battle, and that is the only decision that you will make. WE shall decide the arena and the time. You will also be held completely responsible for all of the grave consequences arising from your racist actions.

Thank you again
General G. Baker, Jr.
0290-170

p.s. You have lit the unquenchable spark.

Chapter Two

Our Thing Is DRUM

1

*There will always be people who are willing to work the
10-12 hour day, and we're going to look for them. . . .*

James Roche, President, General Motors Corporation,
quoted in William Serrin, *The Company and the Union*,
1973

Chrysler Corporation, Detroit's single largest taxpayer and employer, is among the seven largest corporations in the United
States. Since the end of World War II, like the entire auto industry,
Chrysler has experienced wild fluctuations of sales, profits, and
capital investments. Companies such as Hudson, Nash, Fraser,
Briggs, Kaiser, and Packard did not survive the boom-and-bust
cycle and were liquidated or bought out. Even GM, the patriarch of
the auto industry and the world's largest private employer, made
more capital investments in terms of real money in 1956 than it did
fifteen years later. More cars were produced by the industry in
1950, 1955, 1960, and 1965 than in 1970. Chrysler suffered more
from the roller-coaster economic pattern than the other auto
makers, for a number of reasons. Originally distinguished by
superior engineering, Chrysler let its standards fall, settled for

*Opposite page: A DRUM-led demonstration at the UAW convention, November
1969.*

being a style-follower instead of a style-setter, and made poor domestic and foreign investments. This poor corporate record was capped by a management scandal in the late fifties that nearly drove Chrysler into bankruptcy. In spite of these developments, Chrysler still had some outstanding profit years; and in Detroit, the prosperity of Chrysler was crucial to the prosperity of the city itself.

By the late fifties significant numbers of Americans had begun to buy well-built, small, inexpensive foreign cars, but the auto industry resisted the trend and continued its traditional policy of making big cars with high-priced (and highly profitable) accessories. Each new "compact" from Detroit tended to grow larger and less economical after its first year of sales. Instead of producing a single model that could be built for a number of years with increasing reliability, Detroit insisted on the annual model changeover, which put a premium on visual rather than engineering changes. Gas consumption per mile increased steadily. Cars were designed for quick obsolescence, and parts were designed to be replaced rather than repaired. The recall of cars for defects in production, a rare event in earlier periods, became routine in the sixties and was a symbol of falling standards. The industry began to suffer from a saturated American market and from a host of problems related to advanced middle age, yet it still directly or indirectly employed one out of six Americans. Auto production remained a cornerstone of the U.S. economy.

The difficult postwar decades had brought one tremendous advantage to the Big Three (GM, Ford, and Chrysler): a chance to counter the effects of unionism. Frightened by the radical spirit and mass actions of the late thirties, the Big Three made a deal with the UAW after the war. Their overriding managerial concern was maximizing profits, and the prime condition for doing that in the auto industry was control of the shop floor. All operations had to be evaluated in terms of worker-hour and worker-minute costs. Time-study experts investigated each job to eliminate wasted motion and to invent new procedures for increasing the work load. A worker at the GM plant at Lordstown explained the process in an interview printed in the September 9, 1973, issue of the *New York Times:* "They tell you, 'Put in 10 screws,' and you do it. Then a couple of weeks later they say, 'Put in 15 screws,' and next they say, 'Well, we don't need you no more; give it to the next man.' " This worker was giving a specific example of the way management tried to systematize speed-up on an unprecedented scale. Sometimes the entire assembly line was accelerated either on a permanent basis or for temporary periods. Sometimes the number of operations required of a single person was increased. And sometimes workers were forced to keep up with the precise rhythms of a new machine or tool. Management could not get back to the "good old days" of Henry Ford when workers were not allowed to talk during lunch; but washing-up times, rest periods, job-preparation periods, and other paid nonproduction times were reduced. The net result of all facets of speed-up was that more labor was extracted from each person during each working hour. This increased tempo of work was not confined to a forty-hour week. The companies discovered that the savings from not paying fringe benefits to additional workers made it cheaper for them to pay time-and-a-half rates for overtime than to increase the total workforce. Compulsory overtime was enforced throughout the industry during the fifties. Auto workers were made to work one to four hours overtime after finishing their regular eight-hour shift, and many were made to work on Saturdays and occasionally on Sundays.

The union acquiesced to company demands and was rewarded by support in dealing with its own internal problems. One form of support was that the companies collected union dues directly from the workers' paychecks, freeing the union from the worker's tactic of withholding dues if dissatisfied with union performance. Company and union amiability went so far that, during the GM strike of 1970, the company allowed the union to delay payment of $46 million into the health-insurance program because of the enormous financial burden that would place on the union. GM was paid 5 percent interest by the union after the strike was over. In effect, the company had floated the union a loan in the middle of the strike and thus financed a work stoppage against itself. Such cooperation found further expression in three- and five-year contracts with which the mutual interests of company and union were insulated from annual crisis. The chief consequence of the long contracts was that there would be no work stoppages of any kind. Any unauthorized (wildcat) strike could be punished by the courts as a breach of contract, pitting the offending workers against the union as well as the company. William Serrin, the Pulitzer-Prize-winning reporter of the *Detroit Free Press,* summed up union-management relations in his 1973 book, *The Company and the Union:*

> What the companies desire—and receive—from the union is predictability in labor relations. Forced to deal with unions, they want to deal with one union, one set of leaders, and thus they have great interest in stability within the UAW and in a continuation of union leadership. They also want to have the limits of the bargaining clearly understood and subscribed to. "GM's position has always been, give the union the money, the least possible, but give them what it takes," says a former negotiator." But don't let them take the business away from us." The union has come to accept this philosophy as the basis of its relationship with the companies: it will get money, some changes in work procedures, usually nothing more. "We make collective bargaining agreements," Reuther once declared, "not revolutions." Both the union and the companies, a mediator says, have one major goal: "They want to make cars at a profit."

The only weapon left to the worker was the grievance procedure. If a job was speeded up or an extra procedure added, if safety goggles or gloves were inadequate, if a machine malfunctioned, the worker could not fight it out on the factory floor in a direct confrontation with a supervisor. The worker could only write out the complaint, file it with the union "rep," and wait the complaint to be processed. Meanwhile, whatever the new procedures or safety violations might be, they remained in effect unless they were gross enough to trigger a walkout by all the workers. The grievance procedure became yet another device by which company and union eliminated worker participation in decision-making. The companies and the union had developed a division of labor. The companies looked after the machines, and the union looked after the workers. American auto workers were told by their mass media that they had one of the world's highest standards of living. They were not told that they also had one of the world's highest and most gruelling standards of work.

The company-union agreements meant that American factories remained unnecessarily noisy, unhealthy, and dangerous. Rather than retooling or rebuilding, the corporations, especially Chrysler, tended to just patch up. White-collar workers in management considered air conditioning in summer and heating in winter to be matters of course; but in the shop temperatures in summer could soar to 120° in some departments, while in the winter they fell to near freezing in others. Compulsory overtime meant that workers had to put in nine to twelve hours a day, six and seven days a week, at such factories. Safety infractions and contract violations mounted, but the grievance procedure was a joke. By 1970, there were 250,000 written grievances at GM alone, or one for every two workers. It didn't matter if a worker was employed at GM's new Lordstown plant, publicized as a model of progress and modernity, or at cranky old Dodge Main. Ultramodern Lordstown had a roof that leaked whenever there was a hard rain, and Dodge Main had been declared a fire hazard as early as 1948. Conditions in the auto factories of the sixties were as bad as they had been in the days before the union. George B. Morris, Jr., a GM Vice-President and Director of Labor Relations, explained the situation in *The Unions,* a 1972 book by Haynes Johnson and Nick Kotz, Pulitzer-Prize-winning reporters working for the *Washington Post:* ''I guess it was understandable when the unions were beginning to organize that they had to be militant and aggressive. And they adopted a vernacular vocabulary that was militaristic, aggressive, and inculcated into the minds of their constituents this idea of conflict, of war between the classes, between the worker and the employer. Hell, that day is gone. That's like nickel beer and button shoes. It's gone.''

2

Few industries, if any, can match the auto industry in terms of the vast array of poisonous chemicals, gases, and other health and safety hazards which its workers are exposed to daily.

Jannette Sherman, M.D., and Sidney Wolfe, M.D., *Health Research Group Study of Disease among Workers in the Auto Industry,* September 1973

A new explosive element in the factories of the late sixties was the presence of a quarter of a million black workers. Except for Ford, which had a special policy of using large numbers of blacks as an anti-union ploy, none of the auto companies hired many black workers until the labor shortages of World War II. At that time, blacks, mainly fresh from the South, were hired by the tens of thousands. Chrysler's number of black women employees went from zero in 1941 to 5000 by 1945. Detroit blacks often wisecracked that Tojo and Hitler had done more for the emancipation of black labor than Lincoln and Roosevelt. Many of these new jobs were taken away in the recessions of the fifties. To cite Chrysler again, there were years when no blacks were hired at any plants. The company's blue-collar force fell from 100,000 to 35,000 and its white-collar force declined by 7000. Other companies were in no better shape. In the General Motors Building in midtown Detroit there were two black workers out of a force of 3500.

When the auto industry staged a comeback in the early sixties, blacks began to be rehired. Since Ford and GM had moved most of their operations out of Detroit in various decentralization schemes, the bulk of the new black workers in Detroit were employed by Chrysler. They invariably got the worst and most dangerous jobs: the foundry, the body shop, and engine assembly, jobs requiring the greatest physical exertion and jobs which were the noisiest, dirtiest, and most dangerous in the plant. Blacks were further abused by the 90-day rule, under which workers could be dismissed at will before coming under full contract protection. The companies made it a practice to fire hundreds of workers per week, creating a rotating and permanent pool of insecure job seekers. The UAW was kept at bay on the issue because it received a $20 initial fee and $21 in dues for each 89-day worker. The companies also received poverty-program fees for the purpose of "training" parolees and welfare recipients. These individuals were often blacks and they were usually put on the least desirable jobs. Any protest could mean an end to government aid and possibly a return to prison.

The exploitation experienced by all workers was compounded for black workers by the institutional racism which pervaded every aspect of factory life. Dodge Main was typical: 99 percent of all general foremen were white, 95 percent of all foremen were white, 100 percent of all superintendents were white, 90 percent of all skilled tradesmen were white, and 90 percent of all skilled apprentices were white. All the better jobs were overwhelmingly dominated by whites, and when whites did have difficult jobs, there were often two workers assigned to a task that a black worker was expected to do alone. The company was not even subtle in its discrimination. Sick notes signed by black doctors were refused as inadequate. Organizations like DRUM emphasized how the company deliberately cultivated and institutionalized racism in order

that white workers and black workers would face their workaday
lives in racial conflict with one another rather than in class solidarity.

The large majority of white workers at Dodge Main were Polish-
Americans. They tended to dominate the union and to hold the
better jobs. Many of them were immigrants or first-generation
Americans who had acquired negrophobia as part of their
Americanization. The plant itself was located in Hamtramck, an
independent city totally within the city limits of Detroit, and a city
that had a Polish population larger than that of Poznan.
Hamtramck was run by a Polish-dominated city government and a
Polish-dominated police force. In addition, the Poles voted Democratic by margins of 70-90 percent, and their voter turnout was
very high. This gave them enormous power in the Democratic
Party, which needed to carry the Detroit metropolitan area heavily
in order to win elections in what was otherwise a Republican state.
The political power of the UAW was closely linked to its ability to
get out the vote in areas like Hamtramck. The Polish-Americans
did not like working conditions at Dodge Main any better than the
blacks did, but they had a power base in the union and in the local
government that made them concerned with the prosperity of
Chrysler as well. They had no apparent option but to view their
own vested interests as interlocked with the vested interests of an
already interlocked system of company, union, and government.

The Polish-Americans had the reputation of being a conservative force. This conservatism, like the so-called conservatism
of other white ethnic groups, was often a defensive response to
deteriorating social conditions in urban life. Seeing hard-won
gains threatened by increasing insecurity at work, inflation, and
crime in the streets, many white ethnics began to act defensively in
support of what they considered their own interests. In fact,
however, the Polish-American politicians in the Democratic Party
were often New Deal liberals who fought for progressive social
legislation, especially legislation affecting the working class.
Earlier in the century, the Polish-Americans and Eastern
Europeans had a tradition of being associated with the most

progressive social movements. Even in the 1960s, Hamtramck still had a Polish-language communist newspaper and a restaurant which was a well-known meeting place for leftists; but these were only remnants of a former activism that had been effectively submerged in a climate of fear and insecurity.

The only other identifiable groups of workers of significant size were the white Appalachians and the Arabs. The Appalachians had come to the North from the states of Kentucky, Tennessee, and West Virginia at pretty much the same time as the blacks. They too tended to cluster in ghettos, to attend inferior schools, and to move back and forth to the South as employment waxed and waned. Factory conditions were not much better for them than for blacks, but racist feelings kept the two groups effectively divided most of the time. The independent, individualistic hill people were un-predictable, however. They liked the liberal Kennedy brothers, and they also liked George Wallace and the Ku Klux Klan. They fought blacks all the time; but during the Great Rebellion, they had joined blacks for looting purposes, and an amazed Detroit Police Department had discovered that the majority of captured snipers were not blacks, but white "hillbillies."

Possibly the only group exploited more than blacks at Dodge Main was the recently immigrated Arabs. In 1968 they already numbered 500, and in the next six years that number would multiply fourfold. These workers were often totally confused by American conditions, and they were fearful of losing their jobs or being deported. The bulk of them were men who lived alone and sent most of their pay to relatives in the Middle East. A 1972 bulletin put out by Spark, a radical organization at Dodge Main, described the situation:

> Chrysler figures that no one will try to help an Arab worker when Chrysler attacks him. So now Chrysler is attacking. Foremen tell Arab workers to do more work than their jobs call for. Eventually the "extra" work is "officially" added to the job. Other Arab workers are kept as floaters and continually put on the worst jobs,

despite their seniority. Medical passes get put off. Reliefs are forgotten about. . . .

It's the same kind of shit they have pulled for years with black people. At first, black people were given work *only* when Chrysler was trying to break a strike. Chrysler consciously set white workers against black workers—both fighting for the same job, during the desperate high unemployment of the Depression, when there was no union.

Then when Chrysler finally did hire black workers regularly into the plant, it was *only* in the foundry (or the Body Shop a little later)—all the hot, heavy dirty work around. . . .

Then in the fifties, the company finally figured it could get a greater advantage by letting black workers go on the line in other parts of the plant. And most white workers in the plant were suckered into the company's plan—most of the whites sat down, to protest that black people were coming onto the line. . . .

Now today, Chrysler is trying the same thing again—bringing in still another group of workers. Chrysler hopes to make conditions worse for all of us by first attacking conditions for the Arab workers. And they count on turning us against each other so they can do this.

The composition of the workforce at Dodge Main was indicative of the workforce throughout the city. The older, established work group was made up of European immigrant stock, while the newer force contained blacks, white Appalachians, Arabs, and other, nonwhite minorities. Facile analysts often stated that the older force was conservative and the younger radical. While this was true as a vague rule of thumb, there were many serious exceptions and qualifications. The older workforce, for instance, tended to be far more union-minded and was less intimidated by corporate threats than some of the new force. Young white workers in the skilled trades could be just as socially conservative as their fathers and mothers. Yet Local 160 of the GM Technical Center, representing 4000 mainly white skilled workers with the highest-paying jobs, was among the most militant locals in the UAW. Its members dropped nails, snarled traffic, and formed car barricades during the 1970 GM strike, and it was the only unit to defy a UAW directive to allow certain technical personnel through the union lines. Local 160 was also the base of Belfast-born Pete Kelly, one of the two chairmen of the United National Caucus, a multi-plant organization opposed to the UAW leadership and advocating worker control of the shop floor. Conversely, some young blacks who were quick to clench their fists and shout "Right on!" proved less reliable and militant in the long run than some older black workers schooled in patience and in the skills of protracted struggle. Black or white, young or old, male or female, the workers on the shop floor were angry, yet the UAW offered no solutions. An agitational leaflet put out by workers at Chrysler's Eldon Avenue plant in March 1971 quoted UAW President Leonard Woodcock as having told reporters: "If some company says to us tomorrow, 'Okay, you take it, humanize the plant,' we wouldn't know where to start. . . . We don't have the answers."

3

I never went on a strike in my life, I never ordered anyone else to run a strike in my life, I never had anything to do with the picket line. . . . In the final analysis, there is not a great deal of difference between the things I stand for and the things that the National Association of Manufacturers stands for.

George Meany, President of the AFL-CIO, in a speech to the National Association of Manufacturers, 1956

By the late sixties, the UAW had lost touch with its mass base, especially its minorities. At least 30 percent of the UAW membership was black, yet the 26-person executive board had only two blacks, Nelson Jack Edwards* and Marcellius Ivory. In 1969, blacks filled only seven out of one hundred key staff positions. Fourteen percent of the UAW membership was female, yet women had even fewer posts than blacks and only one representative on the executive board, Olga Madar. Once considered the cutting edge of militant industrial unionism, the UAW showed little interest in organizing the numerous nonunion feeder shops in the industry, in moving for unionization in the South, or in fighting for substantial gains such as forty hours' pay for thirty hours' work. Walter Reuther, President of the union until a fatal plane crash on May 9, 1970, Vice-President Leonard Woodcock, and Secretary-Treasurer Emil Mazey had once belonged to the Socialist Party; but they had grown distant from dissident social movements, and they had come to power within the UAW by leading a purge of Communist Party members and sympathizers. Reuther, who had once run for Congress as a Socialist and who had worked in a Soviet auto plant, did not like the militants of SNCC, the white radicals of Students for a Democratic Society, or peace marchers who insulted the nation's President. Rather than honest-to-goodness slugfests with the corporations, Reuther staged elaborate rituals in which neither side was badly hurt. He enjoyed having his photo taken embracing nonviolent activists such as Martin Luther King and Cesar Chavez; but under his leadership the UAW did little to combat racism, anti-Semitism, or sexism, either within its own ranks or where it had influence. *Detroit Free Press* reporter William Serrin made the trenchant comment that the UAW was a right-of-center union with a left-of-center reputation.

Reuther died in a plane crash en route to the $23-million Black Lake educational and recreational center which was the obsession of his later years. The center's price tag had swelled enormously

*Edwards was fatally shot on November 2, 1974, when he tried to break up an argument at a west-side Detroit bar.

from original estimates, and most of the financing was arranged without the approval of the union membership or the executive board. Angry DRUM leaflets attacked the project as symptomatic of what the union hierarchy thought was important. DRUM pointed out that at maximum the complex could accommodate 600 people at a time. At that rate, it would be 7 1/2 years before all of the 1 million UAW members had a chance to spend one day at the resort, even if they went alone. Just one guest per member would double the time to 15 years. The center was obviously not intended for the workers' use at all, but as a hideaway for UAW executives and their inner circle.

Black Lake was only one gross example of how the UAW leaders acted like corporate executives. The executive-board members drew salaries comparable to those of industry officials, and they affected the lifestyles of their business counterparts, even though they had begun their careers as production workers. Corporate headquarters was the sleek Solidarity House, built on the Detroit River at a cost of over $6 million and having a healthy annual maintenance budget.

Like all business ventures, the UAW had labor troubles. In March 1971, custodial and secretarial workers went on strike, demanding pay increases of approximately $11 a week. The strike lasted three weeks; and just as important an issue as the wage increase, which was $3 more than the UAW wanted to pay, was the reputed paternalism of the UAW leadership. In *The Company and the Union* William Serrin quotes Emil Mazey as calling the striking women "little bitches." Other officials called the 400 strikers "greedy," "blackmailers," "unrealistic," "selfish," and "pea-brained women." The heads of the UAW crossed the picket lines every day. Their only concession to collective bargaining was to inform all nonstriking staff members and workers that they could honor the picket lines without fear of union retaliation, although, of course, they would receive no pay if they did so.

The UAW had a national reputation for having a progressive stance on racism, but the UAW looked good only when compared to the lily-white and stridently racist unions which composed so much of the organized labor movement. Racism had always been used as a weapon against unions in the auto industry, and Henry Ford had systematized the practice. Beginning in the late 1920s, Ford made it a rule to employ blacks in his factory at every job level in the same percentage as that of the blacks in the general population. Ford helped finance the all-black suburb of Inkster and always provided low-paying jobs to any unemployed residents. This new-style "plant-ation" owner also cultivated a select group of black clergy and professionals. Ford was called a humanitarian for some of these actions, but his motives were strictly business ones. His personal views on blacks, Jews, communists, and other "un-American" elements were expressed in the *Dearborn Independent,* a paper he owned and personally financed for more than a decade, even though it lost more than $5 million. Ford considered the Jews to be the world's major problem, and in 1938 he went to Nazi Germany to accept an Iron Cross from Adolph Hitler. Dearborn, the city which Ford built, the home of the mammoth River Rouge complex, and the headquarters of the Ford empire, prohibited black residents. As late as 1970, Orville Hubbard, Dearborn's Mayor since 1940, regularly used the word "nigger" in his public utterances.

Ford Motor Company was the last major auto firm to be unionized, and Ford's black policy was a factor in the delay. Most of the 10,000 black workers at Ford participated in the final organizing strike which began on April 1, 1941; but Ford's hand-picked coterie of black "leaders" agitated for black workers to break the strike. On April 3 one group of approximately 800 black workers made three serious physical assaults on the UAW lines in what was the only genuine worker resistance to the union. Racial antagonism and suspicion did not end with the strike. Two years later, Detroit erupted in the worst race riot in the history of the United States; and long after World War II had ended, white workers staged walkouts whenever a factory or a department hired its first blacks. The corporations had virtually no black officials, and the situation in the UAW wasn't much better.

The strongest organized attack on racism within the auto industry came with the formation of TULC (Trade Union Leadership

Conference) by angry black unionists in 1957. The major leaders were Horace Sheffield and Buddy Battle, activists from the giant Local 600 at Ford's River Rouge plant. Viewed with alarm by most of the union leadership at first, TULC eventually became part of the bureaucracy, although it often took independent political approaches, especially in the area of Detroit elections. TULC became instrumental in getting out a large vote for liberal Jerome Cavanagh in the 1961 contest in which Cavanagh unseated Louis Miriani, the latest in a series of conservative, police-oriented mayors. TULC had a membership of 9000 at times, and it was consulted by the mayor, industrial executives, and leaders of various unions. TULC hoped to win jobs for black apprentices in the skilled trades and otherwise to advance the cause of black job upgrading and equal pay for equal work. In 1963, in a totally peaceful March for Freedom, Martin Luther King led some 200,000 mainly black Detroiters in a mammoth walk down Woodward Avenue, Detroit's main thoroughfare. Twenty years after the bloody 1943 race riot, Detroit gave the appearance of a commitment to racial harmony. King, Cavanagh, Reuther, and a host of dignitaries locked arms to achieve a local victory in the land of the New Frontier.

But the New Frontier kept receding into a forever-deferred tomorrow. The all-white unions and the all-white skilled trades remained all white. Blacks were sent to die in Vietnam in the name of democracy when they couldn't buy a home in Dearborn, Grosse Pointe, Warren, or many other Detroit suburbs. The most minor reforms met resistance from the companies, the union, and white workers. When DRUM's first leaflets addressed the question of unresolved black grievances, the UAW viewed the group as another bellicose rank-and-file caucus, a more radical version of TULC. B. J. Widick, a former union official associated with progressive leadership in the UAW, wrote DRUM off in his *Detroit—City of Race and Class Violence,* as simply "an important symptom of frustration among black workers over the lack of progress within plants." He thought DRUM "allowed social steam to blow off harmlessly." Emil Mazey didn't think DRUM was quite so harmless. He said the black revolutionaries represented the most dangerous radical thrust since the 1930s, and he was instrumental in having 350,000 letters sent to Detroit-area UAW members accusing DRUM of being a hate organization whose purpose was to divide the working class along racial lines.

Both Widick and Mazey were mistaken in their major premise that DRUM was a caucus. DRUM was not a caucus, at least not a caucus of the type the UAW had dealt with for thirty years. Caucuses fought within the union for control of the union. The United National Caucus, led by Pete Kelly of the GM Tech Center and Jordan Sims, a black worker at the Eldon Avenue Gear and Axle plant, hoped eventually to supplant the Reuther-Woodcock machine with their own. DRUM was something else. It bypassed the UAW to organize workers directly into a structure dedicated to principles which went far beyond simple trade unionism. DRUM's earliest leaflets stated its goals of gaining direct representation of black workers. More like the IWW of an earlier generation of radicals than like a trade union, DRUM had many aspects of a popular revolutionary movement that could go in many directions. Although not always clear about its tactical methods or all of its strategic goals, DRUM was an illustration of what James Boggs had written in 1963 in *The American Revolution:* "Historically workers move ahead by the new. *That is, they bypass existing organizations and form new ones uncorrupted by past habits and customs.*" DRUM had no intention of sharing the economic pie with Chrysler, and it had no interest in making cars for a profit. DRUM wanted workers to have all the pie and to produce goods only for social needs. DRUM concentrated its organizing efforts on black workers, but it was conscious of the long-term necessity of organizing all workers. Its immediate program was a combination of demands for the elimination of racial discrimination and demands for workers' control, which would be beneficial to all workers, regardless of race, sex, or age. DRUM publications regularly stated that the organization was working in the best long-term interests of all workers and that the overall struggle must be fought on class rather than racial lines.

For years, Detroiters had heard conservative Fulton Lewis, Jr., spar in back-to-back newscasts with the UAW's Guy Nunn. Lewis made the union sound like a dangerous and radical threat to "the American way of life," while Nunn made it sound like the fearless champion of every righteous cause in America. The programs were on the same radio station which brought Detroiters adventure stories like "Captain Midnight" and "Sergeant Preston of the Canadian Northwest Mounted Police." Like these serials, the hoopla about the illustrious UAW was mostly a matter of sound effects. The business of the company executives had always been the business of maximizing profits. They viewed the city and its people as a corporate resource. The business of the union executives had become labor control. They viewed the city and its people as a union resource. In the auto industry, as in so many industries, the company was the senior partner and the union the junior partner. A worker with a decade of seniority in the plants wrote an article for the October 1970 issue of *ICV* explaining the formation of DRUM in the context of this company and union partnership:

> More than an opportunist officialdom, the working class suffers from the conversion of the institution of the union itself into a part of the boss' apparatus. The sacred contract, once viewed as the register of the workers' gains, has become the written record of their subordination to the power of capital. The seniority system, once a defense against favoritism and arbitrary firing, has been adapted to give legal force to the white male monopoly of the better jobs. The automatic dues check-off system has removed the union entirely from any dependence on its membership. The huge treasuries, originally conceived to stockpile ammunition for class warfare, have put the unions in the banking, real estate, and insurance business. The closed shop has become the token of wholesale selfishness.
>
> In this wasteland of labor's twisted hopes, where else could redemption come than from among those whose

interests were at every turn sacrificed so that another, more favored group could make its peace with the masters? Where else, indeed, but from among the black workers at the automobile manufacturing infernos of the city of Detroit?

4

Assuming control of the means of production essentially means that you are at the first stage of assuming state power.

John Watson, interview in *Fifth Estate,* July 1969

The wildcat of May 1968 at Dodge Main was followed by a flurry of plant bulletins put out by DRUM. A series of meetings, demonstrations, and actions attracted hundreds of workers from Dodge Main and surrounding factories. The May strike had involved both black and white workers concerned about speed-up, but the administrative punishments were directed primarily at blacks, causing a swelling of black support for DRUM. In the sixth week of its official existence, DRUM demonstrated its strength by calling for a boycott of two bars outside the plant gates that were patronized by blacks but did not hire blacks and practiced other, subtle forms of racial discrimination. Near-unanimous cooperation quickly brought the desired concessions without the use of pickets, signs, or violence.

Three weeks later, DRUM attracted over 300 workers to a rally held at a parking lot across from the factory. After speeches from DRUM leaders, the workers, accompanied by a number of neighborhood groups and a conga band, formed a line and marched to the headquarters of UAW Local 3, two blocks away.

The panic-stricken executive board opened the union auditorium and listened to criticisms aimed at the company and the union. Unsatisfied with the cliches that President Ed Liska and Vice-President Charles Brooks, a black, responded with, DRUM stated it would close Dodge Main in defiance of the union contract.

The following morning, a Friday, workers were met at the gates by DRUM pickets who told them the situation. No attempt was made to interfere with whites, and the majority of white workers entered the factory. Many others honored the picket line out of years of working-class savvy. Sympathetic or not, they went home. Some 3000 black workers did not go home or into the factory. They stood outside the gates as production all but halted. At noon, six DRUM members went to the local to meet with Liska and other officials. They presented their grievances a second time, emphasizing that having only 72 blacks out of a union-wide total of more than a thousand paid union representatives was unacceptable to black workers. The UAW was expected to change its ways and to change them rapidly. The demands were then read to the striking workers as police began to arrive in sufficient numbers to make trouble. DRUM dispersed the strikers after organizing a hard-core group of 250 into car pools. The cars then drove five miles to Chrysler headquarters in Highland Park. There the demonstration was repeated, and the demands read to the company as they had already been read to the union. The Highland Park police soon arrived with gas masks and riot weapons. Satisfied with having shaken company and union and having caused the mobilization of two departments of police, DRUM transported its demonstrators back to their homes.

That Sunday a dozen DRUM members were invited to the regular citywide meeting of black UAW representatives. Tempers flared. Even after guarantees were given that the black UAW officials would support specific DRUM demands, there was clearly a parting rather than a meeting of minds. The following Monday, picketing resumed at Dodge Main until John Doe injunctions were served by the Hamtramck police. DRUM felt it had done well with its limited forces in such a short period of time. Rather than continue the strike, the activists tore up their injunctions and either went in to work or went home for the day.

In the weeks that followed, DRUM organized parties, demonstrations, and rallies which were attended by workers, students, and people from church and neighborhood groups. DRUM also threw up a picket line at Solidarity House to publicize its demands, just as, a year later, it was to demonstrate at a special UAW national convention to reach delegates from all over the country. DRUM stressed that one of the major historical lessons of the black struggle in the United States was that it had failed because of "traitors" from within. The "traitors" had often been white leaders who capitulated to racism among white workers or who habitually postponed meeting specific black demands until there was a more "favorable" political climate. Just as often, however, the "traitors" had been blacks. They had subordinated the mass struggle to their personal careers or had gone along with the cowardice of the white leadership. As a consequence, DRUM was unsparing in its condemnation of "Uncle Toms, hoinkie dog racists, and knee-grows." DRUM lashed out at the hypocrisy of the supposedly infirm Chrysler Corporation, which donated over a million dollars to black-owned banks and gave away vans to the Detroit police department while crying poverty to avoid meeting the demands of its workers. DRUM stated that it would be pleased if whites and moderate blacks would support its demands, but it would offer no concessions for that support and was prepared to fight alone. In *Finally Got the News,* a film made in 1969-1970 by black and white revolutionaries about the struggles in Detroit, Ron March described DRUM's policy toward alliances with white workers: "White workers came to support us. Some wanted to work with us. But we found out that management knew how to divide the whites. We decided that we could work best by organizing alone. We told whites to do the same thing. Once they did that, we could work with them on a coalition basis."

The weekly DRUM leaflets covered every aspect of working-class problems: the unaccountability of UAW officials, discriminatory hiring, unsafe machinery, capricious time studies, the exclusion of blacks from skilled trades, speed-up, holdups in pay, short paychecks, harassment over sick leave, the need for job upgrading, and increasing regimentation at the plants. DRUM attacked the salaries of UAW officials, the UAW grievance procedure, the policies of the UAW credit union. It advocated worker rather than company control of production, but the rhetoric was often that of a revolutionary black nationalism, a fact which tended to confuse people about the major issues. A union election in September provided DRUM an opportunity to test its strength at the ballot box. In the film *Finally Got the News,* Chuck Wooten recalled the experience:

> Our man was Ron March. Most of the old-line guys told us that we didn't have a chance. They said we didn't have experience—we didn't have a platform. All that kind of crap. We went out anyway. Ron pulled 563 votes. The next highest guy was a white worker who had 521. There were other candidates, so we had to have a runoff election. Immediately after that, the Hamtramck police department began to move in a much more open way. They gave us tickets on our cars and just generally harassed us. One day about fifty of us were in the union hall, which is right across from the police station. The mayor of the city and the chief of police came in with guns in their hands. They told us to stop making trouble, and we said all we wanted was to win the election. We asked them why they weren't harassing the others. While we were talking, a squad of police came through the door swinging axe handles and throwing Mace around. That gave us an idea of the kind of repression black workers seeking to make a revolutionary organization would face. It tipped us off about what would happen when we tried to create a black labor struggle to be part of the black revolution.

March and other DRUM activists were candid in admitting that even if their entire slate of candidates won the election there would be no real improvements at Dodge Main. The major goal of DRUM was another demonstration of insurgent workers' power. All its resources were thrown into a similar campaign one year later. Leaflets were written in Arabic in hopes of picking up votes from the bloc of Arab workers, and an unsuccessful attempt was made to negotiate a compromise with a radical slate which was integrated; basically, however, DRUM relied on its ability to mobilize the black vote. John Watson recalled the results in *Finally Got the News*:

> DRUM suspected the union would cheat. We arranged observers for every candidate and machine. Black workers were incensed when the levers for our candidates would not go down. We were in a toe-to-toe battle with the bureaucracy just to make it halfway fair. When the local saw that it could not steal the election, it called for help. George Merrelli, the regional UAW leader, stormed into the hall with his entire fifty-man staff. They were armed and had the additional support of a contingent of police. They evicted the workers and occupied the hall. The voting machines had not even been sealed. The next day the union said Ron March had come in third with only 943 votes. There wasn't even a runoff election. Of thirty-five candidates, only two DRUM people were elected. A week before, in another factory in the city, the ballot boxes had been confiscated by the police and held in the police station overnight. These acts demonstrated the UAW would risk outright scandal rather than let blacks assume any power. It didn't matter whether DRUM won or lost in this election. What counted was that the enemy lost by being forced to provoke the anger and raise the consciousness of thousands and thousands of workers.

The struggle led by *ICV* and DRUM could not be contained

within one factory, much less within a single election. Although the leaders of DRUM had to cope with police harassments, union denunciations, and court injunctions, workers all over the city were forming RUM (Revolutionary Union Movement) units at their places of work. Students and other sympathizers continued to volunteer for picket lines and leafleting to minimize police, company, and union intimidation of plant militants. On the same day as the first Dodge election, a coalition of white and black supporters of DRUM took editorial control of Wayne State University's daily newspaper, the *South End.* The new editors immediately set about the task of transforming what had been a strictly student newspaper into a citywide daily voice for black and white revolutionaries, both on and off the university campus.

the south end

"One Class-Conscious Worker Is Worth 100 Students"

Volume 27 — Number 62　　　　　WAYNE STATE UNIVERSITY　　　　　Thursday, January 23, 1969

D.R.U.M.—VANGUARD OF THE BLACK REVOLUTION

Dodge Revolutionary Union Movement States History, Purpose and Aims

By LUKE TRIPP

Feature Editor, South End

HISTORY

DRUM's scope is not limited to the oppressive situation at Chrysler nor all t h e rest of the plants for that matter. Although most organizing activity will be in t h e plants, DRUM sees its long range goal as the complete and total social transformation of the society. This necessarily will take the effort of the whole Black community as well as other progressive sectors of the rest of the society.

In order to gain more support for black workers from the black community at large, DRUM established ties with the more radical section of the black clergy. They helped by putting us in contact with people who could aid DRUM in some way and also by publicizing their support of DRUM's program.

Several weeks after DRUM shut down Dodge Main this summer, both the UAW and Chrysler's were still reacting to DRUM's action. Both of these racist institutions got into the

act of confusing the public. The UAW tried to shift the attention away from itself to Chrysler. Chrysler did likewise. On August 20, 1968, a story appeared in the Michigan Chronicle (a "negro" newspaper) about the black worker's struggle. A UAW official was quoted as saying "DRUM's main thrust was towards the company and not the UAW." Over the weekend of August 16 through the 19 there had been several stories in the News and the Free Press which depicted DRUM as a group of flaming black nationalists who were trying to pit black workers a g a i n s t white workers.

On the question of pitting black workers, here is DRUM's answer which appeared in the 13th edition of their Newsletter:

"In the recent letter put out by the UAW, they accused DRUM of pitting Black against white. The purpose of DRUM is to unite black workers to fight the problems that black workers face, and that problem is racism. Now the white workers are not victims of racism. If any-

thing, they benefit from it. How do they benefit? It starts in the employment office. The white workers are usually sent to work in what is considered the easy areas. Now if one should happen to be unfortunate enough to get sent to the body shop, then the foreman will give him the easiest job he can find; even if it means moving a black worker. When it comes to taking disciplinary action against workers you will find that white workers are given all the breaks. Also, when it comes to advancement, the black workers are given all kinds of reasons why he is not qualified for the job, while a white worker, qualified or not, will get it. Now according to the UAW, pitting the black worker against the white workers makes a weak union. Either the UAW is too weak to fight racism, or it condones racism, for it is a fact that racism runs rampant throughout the auto industry. The pitting of black against white starts with the power structure, for it is the power structure that controls the jobs, and the job you get is based on the color of your skin, not your

background. If you are white you are in. If you are black and you want to get in, then you must first sell your manhood, because they don't want black men. They only want black boys. So who is pitting black against white?

To show what a sham the UAW's support for black people is, DRUM points to these facts. Black workers pay millions of dollars to the UAW headed by Walter Reuther the most coniving sell-out artist in the labor movement. He manages to pop up at the head of practically every grandiose civil rights jive-time demonstration. DRUM's protest against racism practiced by both the UAW and the company was as moral and legal as any demonstration in the history of the Black Man's Struggle. History slams in every phase of the struggle from the sit-ins to the March on Washington. Walter Reuther and our dues were there.

Further, in Memphis after Dr. King's assassination, Reuther and the black workers' dues were there. Now

(Continued on Page 2)

Chapter Three

We Will Take
the Hard Line

1

You can't talk to them. They don't speak the same language. The previous editor hated my guts and I had an abiding contempt for him. I was glad to see him go, but when this new one, this Watson, walked in, he had the look of cool hatred in his eyes.

Frank Gill, *South End* faculty adviser, quoted in *Detroit Free Press,* November 1968

In the autumn of 1968, Wayne State University had almost 35,000 students. Most of them lived at home and most of them worked. Classes began at 8:00 A.M. and continued until near midnight. The school was open year round and there were some classes on Saturday. The first colleges of the Wayne complex were old land-grant institutions of the nineteenth century. They had undergone a number of name changes until they became a state university in the early sixties. Wayne is located in the center of Detroit, midway between the downtown shopping area and the business district around the General Motors Building. It is

Opposite page: Front page of the DRUM issue of the South End.

surrounded by impoverished black and Appalachian ghettos dotted with some student housing. For years, blacks, immigrants, women, the working poor, and upwardly mobile first-generation white ethnics had found Wayne a convenient place to get an education. It was typical of Wayne that Walter Reuther and Leonard Woodcock had been students there and that the official UAW archives were housed in its Labor Relations Institute.

Wayne had a reputation for radicalism; but, in fact, the administration had driven all left-wing groups from the campus during the McCarthy period, as well as firing some professors. Even so, Wayne prided itself on its egalitarian and liberal traditions. There were between 2500 and 3500 black students at Wayne during the sixties, giving it a higher black enrollment than all the schools of the Big Ten and Ivy League combined. However, the tough municipal university, like so many Northern institutions, did not understand how far it had fallen short of black expectations. Many of the black students only attended part time and did not end up with a degree. The 10 percent black enrollment might compare favorably to the figures for conservative, "prestige" institutions; but Detroit's population was moving rapidly toward a black majority, and against that background a 10 percent enrollment in the city university was not impressive. A minor indication of Wayne's relative indifference to racism was the fact that the college newspaper had never been known to take up social issues. It functioned primarily as an extension of the journalism department and was run like a high-school paper. Few blacks wrote stories for the paper, and there had never been a black editor.

The police riot at the Democratic Convention in Chicago was fresh news in the frantic summer of '68, and much of America wondered if the armed uprisings of the previous summer would be repeated. The Weatherman faction of SDS (Students for a Democratic Society), with its dream of using bombs to open a military front within the borders of the United States, was about to become a household word. The revolutionaries of *ICV* and DRUM were thinking in far more practical terms. Through adroit electioneering and persuasion, they managed to capture a majority on the student committee responsible for selecting the editor of the *South End,* Wayne's daily student newspaper. The choice of the committee for the academic year 1968-1969 was John Watson. DRUM had scored an important victory, for editor Watson had virtually full control of a newspaper with a daily run of 18,000, a printing budget of $100,000, an editor's salary of $2400, and a staff payroll of $23,400.

Watson had a bold vision of how the *South End* could be used. His term as editor proved to be one of the most successful examples in the late sixties of how a black could lead a principled coalition of black and white forces struggling within a major institution. Watson took the position that the *South End* did not belong to the university, the state, or even the students as students. Wayne State University was a public resource that belonged to the entire population, and its daily newspaper was also a public resource that must speak to the needs of the entire population. This meant the *South End* would deal with the needs of students as workers, as slum dwellers, as potential draftees, as taxpayers, as parents, and as performers of any other role the society expected of them. The various university departments sent trainees into the neighborhoods, schools, industries, and clinics of the city as a matter of routine. It was only logical that the newspaper should also burst the boundaries of the campus and reach into those same places.

Luke Tripp and Mike Hamlin, two key members of *ICV* (which was published irregularly during this period), immediately came over to work as paid staff members of the *South End.* Tripp had been involved in most of the organizations in which Watson had figured. He was a quick-tempered man who had gained university notoriety in the early sixties when he and Charles "Mao" Johnson worked in the library mailroom, from which they enthusiastically spread news about China quoted directly from the *Peking Review.* Tripp spent several hours a day on a physical-fitness program, had been a participant in the 1964 Cuba trip, and was fond of explaining his attitude to the United States government by declaring,

"I oppose everything you support and I support everything you oppose."

Tripp summed up the general view of the university held by the *South End* staff when he told the authors in August 1972: "The university serves as the ideological and technological servant of the American ruling class." The *South End* rebels proposed to make their part of the university do just the opposite. They would be advocates for all those insurgent groups that were challenging the power of the old white men who ruled American society. They rejected the definition of objectivity used by the mass media, saying that it was only a pretext for perpetuating the viewpoint of the system. Mike Hamlin taunted one critic by saying, "There are two views, of course. The right and the wrong. You wouldn't want us to print the wrong one, would you?" The first editorial of the Watson term appeared on September 26, 1968, and spelled out the *South End*'s goals:

> The *South End* returns to Wayne State with the intention of promoting the interests of impoverished, oppressed, exploited, and powerless victims of white, racist monopoly capitalism and imperialism. . . . We will take the hard line. . . . Our position in each case will be demonstrated to be logical, just, and concrete and we will always be prepared to defend any position we take. . . . Our only enemies will be those who would further impoverish the poor, exploit the exploited, and take advantage of the powerless.

Readers of that first issue might have written off the editorial as part of the typical rhetoric of the black and student movements of that era. Even the two black panthers on either side of the masthead and the inscription "The Year of the Heroic Guerrilla" could be seen as brave posturing. Watson and associates soon put an end to such illusions. The most important person on the staff, next to John Watson, was a lean, tough white ex-paratrooper with a prison record named Nick Medvecky. Watson and Medvecky had met earlier that summer. Medvecky had belonged to the Young Socialist Alliance but had left after disputes over the group's rules on discipline, such as the one prohibiting the smoking of marijuana. The relationship between Watson and Medvecky was crucial to the action which swirled around the *South End*.

Most of the black radicals working on the paper were also involved in agitation at Dodge Main and other activities of the emerging League of Revolutionary Black Workers. Medvecky, heading a mostly white production staff of whom only a few were radical, was responsible for actually putting out the paper. Watson laid out its general strategy, looked over the stories that went in, made criticisms before and after the fact, and had the final word on everything; but Medvecky was the gruff managing editor who chewed out lazy reporters and saw to all the details of day-to-day production. When some radical new line emerged from the editorial office, Medvecky would often act as the buffer between uneasy white staff members and Watson. He would recall with amusement in 1972 how some of the whites would sometimes threaten "to go to John over this," as if he and Watson were not in complete accord to begin with.

The *South End* quickly became the voice of a de facto radical united front. Although articles on DRUM, the local Black Panthers, third-world guerrilla movements, women's liberation, and anti-war activities predominated, every progressive element on campus and in the city could get its views published. The situation was exactly the reverse of that in the daily press. Insurgent opinion set the tone of the paper and commanded the editorial columns, while conservative and status quo opinion was relegated to rebuttal articles and letters to the editor.

The cultural revolution at the *South End* was not without its minor compromises. Medvecky and Watson took a practical line on the questions of sports coverage, the reporting of social activities, and the use of questionable language. Very early in their regime, they informed the fraternities and sororities that they could write their own copy and would have unquestioned access to a full page of the paper whenever they wanted it. Wayne had de-emphasized sports for years, but the radicals allotted space and photos to whatever events the sports-minded students were interested in. Most importantly, they avoided obscene and blasphemous language. University President Keast, a liberal, saw this as a significant compromise in a day when the alternate-culture press was making nudity and profanity an important freedom-of-the-press issue. Medvecky and Watson had no personal or ideological objection to using obscene or blasphemous language, but they saw it as a side issue the university might exploit to shut them down. The important thing was the politics of the paper. About that, there could be no compromise.

Some days less than a thousand copies of the *South End* were distributed on campus, while several thousand were transported to school, hospital, and factory gates. Sometimes members of the staff would pick up copies of the paper from the stands after they had been distributed by the "straight" elements; more often, they simply arranged for the papers to be transported directly to a target community. The big twelve-page special issue about DRUM written by Luke Tripp was distributed in the thousands at factories throughout the city. New exposures of conditions at Detroit General Hospital continued the attack on that institution started in *ICV;* the issues were given away in and around the hospital and eventually brought action from the city government. Issues attacking the deteriorating conditions in the public schools were distributed at high schools; and, as the year went on, high-school students came to work in the *South End* offices to prepare centerfolds on education. These were often slipped out of the larger paper and distributed as broadsides.

Watson demonstrated his customary fairness and flexibility throughout the time of his editorship. Rather than holding the newspaper as a resource only for his own organization or solely for the black movement, he encouraged other forces to use it as much as possible. A striking example of this was the special issue put out by staff member Nick Boyias and other Greek-Americans who wished to agitate against the colonels who had seized power in Greece on April 21, 1967. For one day, the second anniversary of the coup, two Z's replaced the usual black panthers and the masthead inscription read, "One Greek Freedom Fighter Is Worth 100 Idle Greeks." The issue reviewed the revolutionary traditions of the Greek nation and called for armed struggle against the colonels. Some 10,000 copies mysteriously found their way to anti-junta organizations throughout the United States, Canada, Europe, and Australia. Similar consideration was given to other movements and causes which met the criterion of opposing "those who would further impoverish the poor, exploit the exploited, and take advantage of the powerless."

The *South End* was an important resource for insurgents in another fashion. Some members of DRUM drew *South End* salaries yet rarely appeared on campus, since they were busy doing work elsewhere. The editors never flaunted this or similar practices that the university might have been able to use against them. The paper appeared each and every day, so there could be no question of incompetency. All university rules and regulations were scrupulously followed—at least on paper. The legally selected editor and his legally selected staff had insulated themselves from any technical avenue of university attack.

President Keast had been finessed, and he knew it; but he was under increasing pressure from the UAW, business forces, and the state legislature to do something to stop the paper. As early as November 1968, suburban newspapers such as the *Southfield Sun* were making vitriolic attacks on Watson. The Wayne State Fund, an alumni group which contributed $300,000 a year to the university expressed its concern repeatedly. These people knew very well that special agitation issues running to tens of thousands of copies were being used to undermine the Detroit power structure. They understood that the state of Michigan had been put into the position of supporting an organ that called for revolution against that very state. President Keast had no easy options. The Great Rebellion was barely a year past and there was no telling what black reaction would be to the dismissal of the paper's first black editor by executive fiat. This was especially true given the power DRUM and its sister groups had recently demonstrated in the

factories. There was also the fact that Wayne had never had a
significant campus protest movement. As one faculty member
explained to a *Free Press* reporter in November, "[Keast] is
haunted by the examples of Berkeley and Columbia. That might
happen here if he clamps down. But at the same time, he's got
important people complaining and telling him he's got to do
something." Unfortunately for the enemies of the *South End,* they
had no recourse but to bide their time and hope that Watson would
make a mistake.

2

*The unions were born 100 years ago, and claim to be
free associations of the workers to defend themselves
against the bosses. But today, in every country in the
world, they have become one of the main instruments
that the bosses have to maintain their control over the
working class.*

An Italian Fiat worker, writing in *Lotta Continua,*
November 1970

Events in the Detroit factories were not unique, either in the United
States or in advanced industrial society as a whole. During the late
sixties, strong student and worker groups emerged throughout
Europe and became particularly powerful in Italy and France. Just
as the American workers challenged the UAW, the European
rebels challenged their traditional unions, despite the fact that the
unions were usually under socialist or communist control. The
new groups rejected the traditional political formations and liked
to call themselves *extraparliamentarians.* They searched the
American political landscape for comparable phenomena. Most of

them became attracted to the Black Panther Party, but others became interested in the revolt at Dodge Main.

The Italian Socialist Party of Proletarian Unity (PSIUP) was part of the movement against the established parties, even though it maintained a parliamentary role by electing deputies to the national and provincial parliaments. PSIUP planned an international anti-imperialist conference for December 1968 which would feature speakers from the South Vietnamese National Liberation Front and a representative of the American black-liberation movement. Many of the organizers wanted a Black Panther as the American speaker, while others wanted someone from Detroit. As chance would have it, John Watson was then a member of the Detroit Black Panther Party. His name satisfied both groups, and he was issued an invitation.

Watson's membership in two separate revolutionary organizations, DRUM and the Panthers, represented a short-lived compromise between black revolutionary forces in Detroit and California. *ICV* had given publicity to the Panthers when they first came to prominence. The Detroit group's original attitude had been positive, yet the Detroiters understood that the Panther label would be as attractive in their city as elsewhere and that the organization could be a rival of consequence for DRUM if allowed to develop an independent power base within the Detroit population. They tried to avoid a possible crisis by having Luke Tripp and John Williams organize the local Panther chapter; most of the people associated with *ICV* and DRUM became the initial membership. The effort was not grounded in duplicity. The Detroiters assumed that the Panthers would recognize that their long experience in the city qualified them to head the local struggle. They expected the national linkage to be flexible, so that their chapter could enjoy semi-autonomy. This arrangement quickly broke down, but dual membership was still possible during Christmas of 1968.

Watson's trip to Italy was no pleasure jaunt. He had less than $10 in his pocket when he arrived in Italy, and he had the flu. The major benefit of the trip was that he came to have firsthand knowledge of the dissident workers' movement in one of Europe's more industrialized countries. Watson was amazed at what he considered the tactical and ideological timidity of the Italian Marxists, especially given their enormous working-class base. After speaking at the conference in Naples, Watson made brief stops in Sardinia, Rome, and Turin, Italy's major automobile manufacturing center, a city often compared to Detroit. During this trip, Watson made the acquaintance of individuals from extraparliamentary groups and the radical wings of established parties. Many of these people followed up the contacts made that Christmas of 1968 with subsequent visits to the United States, where they made additional contacts and pursued mutual theoretical concerns with their fellow revolutionaries. Events in the Michigan plants were probably followed more avidly in Turin and other Italian industrial centers than anywhere in the United States.

Watson returned to Detroit with his flu worsened and his wallet flat. Within a short time, he was fired by the *Detroit News* for having taken a vacation while claiming sick leave. It was more than a little ironic that the editor of the *South End,* Detroit's third daily, was supporting his family by working in the delivery room of the paper which boasted of having the largest circulation of any evening newspaper in America. It was even more ironic that it was at the *News* that Watson had become good friends with Mike Hamlin and Ken Cockrel. Hamlin had been employed as a driver of a delivery truck, and Cockrel, then working his way through law school, had served as Hamlin's assistant. The *News* had a reputation among blacks of being "a racist rag," and in its delivery room were three of its angriest critics. One of their revolutionary aims was to put papers like the *News* out of business, and their activities soon carried them to the front page of the newspaper they had once stacked, tied, and delivered.

3

*When John Watson and myself, as the Editor-in-Chief
and Managing Editor of last year's* South End, *came
out with a front page news/editorial statement on Al
Fatah, little did we realize at the time what a Pandora's
Box had been opened.*

Nick Medvecky, *Inner City Voice,* November 1969

The *South End* masthead for 1969 declared, "One Class-
Conscious Worker Is Worth 100 Students," and the paper became
increasingly aggressive in its attacks on the UAW and the Big
Three. Although the *South End* was viewed by its editors as the
daily organ of the DRUM forces, it continued its policy of
publicizing all mass-based revolutionary movements. Special
issues dealt with the thought and the lives of Malcolm X and
Martin Luther King, as well as with local controversies involving
Judge George Crockett and attorney Ken Cockrel. The special
issue on Greece appeared in April, and articles on Marxism by
various authors were featured in numerous issues, along with
articles on women's liberation and the anti-war movement. President Keast made his first effort to remove Watson as editor by
saying that he had failed to register for winter classes; but Watson
had simply registered late and Keast was forced to make a frontal
assault. This major thrust began in late January, following an
article favorable to the Al Fatah guerrilla organization written by
Nick Medvecky. Keast charged that the *South End* was anti-Semitic and "reminiscent of Hitler's Germany."

Keast's attack was soon seconded by city, state, and union
officials, backed up by the *Detroit News,* the *Detroit Free Press,*
and the television stations. Many otherwise liberal people who
knew that criticism of Zionism often served as a cloak for anti-

Semitism did not understand that such was not the case with the *South End,* whose criticism was political and not racist or religious. Letters to the editor and rebuttal articles supporting Israel were printed as regularly as material supporting the Palestinian viewpoint. Similar articles on African guerrilla organizations had never generated such a reaction, and the editors were genuinely surprised at the storm brought down on them by the Al Fatah piece. They reaffirmed their own views, but emphasized that they would continue to provide ample space for opposing opinions, as had always been their policy. In spite of this reasonableness, the attacks on the *South End* mounted from every quarter, and on February 3 there was an arson attempt on the paper's offices.

The 24-year-old Watson stood his ground. He noted that the forces now raging against him had never spoken out against the institutionalized racial and religious discrimination found in Detroit and its suburbs, especially in Dearborn, where the Ford Motor Company could get anything it wanted, or in the five Grosse Pointe communities with their unique point system which effectively excluded Jews, blacks, and other "undesirables." The prestigious Detroit Athletic Club, to which many of Watson's critics belonged, had only one Jewish member, while the *South End* had an impeccable record of militant opposition to all forms of bigotry. Numerous Jewish writers had contributed guest editorials, plays, news stories, and columns to the *South End* throughout the fall of 1968, and the Jewish members of the staff unanimously supported the political criticism of Israel. Watson charged that the American Civil Liberties Union had attacked him because of the influence of the UAW and Max Fisher, the chairman of New Detroit. The state legislature, which threatened to cut off $100,000 in aid if Watson was not removed, had never taken such tough action to enforce civil-rights legislation. The Wayne State Fund, an alumni group which also opposed him, was in the same position. Watson questioned why those who were so outraged by the *South End* had never moved against Breakthrough's Donald Lobsinger, a city employee who went around organizing openly racist and anti-Semitic groups reminiscent of the Black Legion that had terrorized Detroiters in the 1930s. Watson further pointed out that the Detroit area and nearby Toledo had the largest Arabic-speaking communities in North and South America and that the *South End* was a voice for them as much as for anyone else. An article by Harry Clark which appeared in the February 7 *South End* summed up the feelings of most of the blacks on campus: "The furor is based on the fact that the black journalists refuse to religiously follow the inane routines and ceremonies necessary in the establishment media."

The tempest came to a dramatic head on February 10 in an incident involving Joe Weaver, a newscaster for WJBK-TV2, the CBS affiliate in Detroit. Weaver entered the offices of the *South End* to get a taped interview with the editor. John Watson responded with a curt "no comment" to all questions and closed the door to his office. Weaver promptly forced his way in, and even though Watson ordered him to leave, continued to ask his questions. When Watson and other members of the staff tried to block the cameras which were recording the entire scene, scuffling began. Weaver was considerably taller and heavier than Watson, but when he left the *South End* offices, he went to police headquarters, where he filed charges against Watson for assault and battery. "The mad editor" of the *South End* had irrationally attacked a simple newsman trying to get a story.

Watson's response to Weaver's charges was to take the offensive. Rather than defend his own actions, in a *South End* article published on March 5 Watson made Weaver defend his: "I was completely within my rights and was fulfilling my obligations and responsibilities as editor when I expelled Weaver from the office. He was trespassing, abusive, provocative, and disruptive to the operation of the office. . . . It is TV-2 and Recorder's Court which will really be on trial." Ken Cockrel represented Watson and developed the defense strategy. The film made by WJBK proved more helpful to Watson's case than to Weaver's. The jury had little difficulty in reaching a decision of acquittal for John Watson.

Mike Hamlin wrote an article at the time of the trial in which he said that the attack on the *South End* had opened the closet and let loose all the Detroit power-structure ghosts. He charged that the university and the UAW had entered into a conspiracy with Chrysler and the mass media to put the *South End* out of action. What the masters of Detroit were really upset about was not an article discussing a Palestinian guerrilla organization but the assault on their power in the factories. Just as Chrysler called out the Hamtramck police to try to stop DRUM, Chrysler and the UAW had called out President Keast, the *Detroit News,* and WJBK-TV to stop the *South End.*

4

If Crockett is right, we should change the law. If Crockett is wrong, we should change Crockett.

Carl Parsell, President, Detroit Police Officers Association, quoted in *South End,* April 3, 1969

Watson's position at the *South End* was shored up on March 29 by an incident, apparently unrelated to the university, which showed the importance of the newspaper as a resource against oppression and the need for a united response to legal and military pressures. The incident occurred at Reverend C. L. Franklin's New Bethel Baptist Church on Detroit's west side, where the Republic of New Africa (RNA) was holding its first anniversary meeting. Over two hundred people were at the meeting, which was protected by armed security guards, a practice fully within the Michigan law. The celebration had ended and people were starting home when a squad car pulled up to the security guards. Officers Michael Czapski, aged 22, and Richard Worobec, aged 28, came out of the car. The confrontation which followed resulted in Czapski being killed, Worobec being badly wounded, and four civilians being wounded. Police cars careened into the neighborhood from every direction and the church was surrounded by police, who began firing rifles and pistols. For a moment, it seemed the Great Rebellion would flare anew; but there was little return fire, and soon every black person in sight had been seized and taken to the nearest police station.

Republic of New Africa members would state in court that the police had drawn their weapons and begun to fire for no apparent reason. The RNA members stated that they remembered the Algiers Motel incident, in which defenseless blacks had been killed by police, and that three separate police attacks on unarmed civilians in the latter part of 1968 were fresh in their minds. They claimed to have returned the officers' fire in self-defense. Worobec contested this version of the incident. He testified that he and Czapski had come out of their car with their guns in their holsters and that the security guards had shot at them for no apparent reason.

Brother Gaidi (Milton Henry), who was then the leader of the Republic of New Africa, had left the area before the shooting began. When he heard what had happened, he contacted black State Representative James Del Rio, who in turn informed Reverend Franklin of the incident. These two men then called black Judge George Crockett, who proceeded to the police station, where he found total legal chaos. Almost one hundred and fifty people were being held incommunicado. They were being questioned, fingerprinted, and given nitrate tests to determine if they had fired guns, all without benefit of legal counsel, in total disregard of fundamental constitutional procedures. Hours after the roundup, there wasn't so much as a list of persons being held, and no one had been formally arrested. An indignant Judge Crockett set up court right in the station house and demanded that the police either press charges or release their captives. He had handled about fifty cases when Wayne County Prosecutor William L. Cahalan, called in by the police, intervened. Cahalan promised that the use of all irregular methods would be halted. Crockett adjourned the impromptu court, and by noon of the following day, the police had released all but a few individuals who were held on specific charges.

Crockett's action touched off a bitter controversy that was to engage Detroit for weeks. The Detroit Police Officers Association (DPOA) charged that Crockett's behavior sprang from racial feelings rather than legal principles and that he had given black paramilitary organizations a license to kill cops. The *Detroit News* concurred, calling Crockett's actions "unwarranted leniency." The DPOA launched a petition campaign to have Crockett impeached or removed. It took out a full-page ad in the *Detroit News* to present its case, and it set up picket lines around the Judge's court. Governor William Milliken and various state senators responded to the initial DPOA efforts by calling for a full legislative probe of Crockett's fitness to remain on the bench.

Crockett refused to repent his actions. He declared that the police had no right to declare martial law whenever it pleased them. The mass arrests and unconstitutional procedures were typical of the police lawlessness which had victimized Detroit blacks for years. The police actions, he said, might have set off massive counterviolence in the streets if he had not intervened on behalf of due process. The *South End* of April 10 quoted him as saying: "Can any of you imagine the Detroit police invading an all-white church and rounding up everyone in sight to be bussed to a wholesale lockup in a police garage?"

The black population in the city rallied behind Crockett by forming the Black United Front, a group which included sixty organizations ranging from Christian churches to a black policemen's organization to DRUM. The Black United Front was an extragovernmental response similar to the People's Tribune set up to investigate the Algiers Motel killings. Dan Aldrich, a radical intellectual who had been active in the People's Tribune, became the chairman of the Black United Front. He articulated the four major premises of the organization, saying that the police failed to respect religious institutions, that the police failed to respect black women and children, that the police failed to respect the rights of those opposing institutionalized racism, and that public

opinion was being misled by Governor Milliken, Police Commissioner Johannes F. Spreen, Mayor Cavanagh, Prosecutor
Cahalan, the DPOA, and the *Detroit News,* all of whom were
guilty of racism.

The *South End* devoted an entire issue to the New Bethel case. It
reprinted statements from all sides, including those of Crockett,
Del Rio, Franklin, the DPOA, and anti-Crockett reporters.
Lengthy attempts were made to reconstruct the events accurately,
and editorials probed the nature of the forces seeking to remove
Crockett from office. If there were any doubts about where the
South End stood editorially, a centerfold portrait of Judge Crockett
put them to rest. Once more, thousands of copies of the paper left
the university campus, reaching the streets, neighborhoods, and
schools of the city.

The jurist at the center of the storm was no newcomer to political
turmoil. George Crockett belonged to an earlier generation of
Detroit black radicals. He had been one of the defense attorneys for
the Communist Party in 1948 and 1949, when its leaders were
prosecuted under the Smith Act. During the heated trials, Crockett
had been cited for contempt of court by Judge Harold Medina, and
he had served four months in a federal prison. In the 1950s,
Crockett had defended Coleman Young and other blacks involved
in trade-union work when they were attacked by the House Un-
American Activities Committee. Through the years Crockett had
remained an active participant in a wide range of social
movements; but because of his radical past he had been unable to
gain elective office until 1966, when the surge of the black-
liberation movement had brought him to Recorder's Court. His
friend Coleman Young had been elected to the state legislature in
1964 and had begun to build the power base that would carry him
to the Detroit Mayor's office in 1973. In the April 10 *South End*,
Crockett spoke of the New Bethel problems as only the latest of a
long sequence. "The causes are steeped in racism—racism in our
courts, in our jobs, in our streets, and in our hearts."

On April 3, 1969, the Black United Front called for demonstrations in support of Crockett, and some three thousand people
responded. Among the cooperating groups were two white

organizations, the Ad Hoc coalition, led by Sheila Murphy, and People Against Racism, led by Frank Joyce. Two weeks later, the Detroit Commission on Community Relations issued a report which was generally favorable to Crockett. On the same day the report appeared, the *Detroit Free Press* published an unusual editorial apologizing for inaccurate information in earlier stories which had been damaging to Crockett. A short time later, the Michigan Bar Association and spokesmen for the UAW and New Detroit defended Crockett's legal positions. Governor Milliken and other officials reversed some of their original views and attacked the political opinions being expressed by the DPOA. The storm was passing for the 59-year-old judge, who was completely vindicated. The sensational New Bethel trials lay in the future; but the black community had fought for its judge, and some of the spillover aided the embattled John Watson at the *South End*. It did not take a political pundit to note that many of those who had opposed Crockett most vociferously also opposed Watson.

5

ONE QUESTION—The facts in this paper are in the hands of the news media—why do you not see them? THINK.

South End masthead, June 1969

Watson had committed the *South End* to the Crockett fight without any reservations. Crockett's subsequent victory, coupled with the court victory over Joe Weaver, strengthened Watson immeasurably. The paper's policy of printing pro-Israel articles, the support of students and faculty, and the general cooling of temperatures brought more people to the realization that a newspaper could criticize the state of Israel without being anti-Semitic just as an individual could be personally anti-Semitic yet support the domestic or foreign policy of the state of Israel for business or political reasons. Watson agreed to hold a weekly public coffee-hour meeting with President Keast in the Student Center cafeteria to keep communications open and promote student-body participation in the decision-making. Even so, articles favorable to the guerrilla organizations continued; and on May 15, a special eight-page issue dealt with the Palestinian question in much the same terms as had the issue of January 29 which set off the confrontation. The radicals had won.

The importance of Watson's editorship of the *South End* would be hard to overemphasize. A group of white and black radicals had consciously wrested an important resource from the state, and they had successfully warded off a serious attempt to dislodge them. The radicals had transformed a lifeless student publication into a daily mass-circulation paper. The principled use of the *South End* had strengthened the alliance of radical forces under black leadership, an alliance that did not indulge itself in sycophantism or appeals to white guilt feelings. The *South End* had worked because its readers had seen the journal as being written for them rather than against them. In a very real way, Watson, Medvecky, and the others had realized Wayne's often-expressed goal of being relevant to the larger Detroit community. Their sense of what was relevant, however, differed drastically from that of Keast, the university, and liberals. Watson had explained his views in an interview printed in the July-August 1968 issue of *Radical America*:

> We are no more for integrated capitalism than for segregated capitalism. Neither are we in favor of a separate state, based on the same class lines as in this society. We are against a separate state in which a black capitalist class exploits a black proletariat. We are opposed also to all sorts of haphazard talk which doesn't tell us what to do with the United States, capitalism, and imperialism. . . . We had studied the history of the Russian Bolsheviks and found a specific pamphlet by

> Lenin called *Where To Begin,* written in 1903, before
> he wrote *What Is To Be Done?,* where he described the
> role a newspaper could play. A newspaper was the focus
> of a permanent organization. It could provide a bridge
> between the peaks of activity. It creates an organization
> and organizes the division of labor among revolu-
> tionaries. Revolutionaries do something, not just a
> meeting on Sunday, making speeches, and passing
> resolutions. It creates the kind of division of labor
> needed not just for the newspaper but for a revolutionary
> organization.

Two years after his work on the *South End* finished, Nick
Medvecky evaluated the Watson editorship for the authors of this
book. He stated that the Trotskyist group to which he had belonged
had responded to the political stance of the pre-Watson *South End*
by proposing a critical newsletter to be distributed on campus.
Watson's response to the same situation had been the more
dynamic one of taking over the paper entirely. One view reflected
the oppositionist mentality which dominated most of the radical
and student movement, while the other assumed that a serious bid
for power might become a short-term objective. Medvecky noted
that although the *Fifth Estate,* Detroit's alternate-culture paper,
had done good work since being founded in 1966 and deserved its
reputation as one of the best underground papers, it was still
cemented in an essentially oppositionist framework. It had not
gotten its own production equipment and thus remained dependent
for survival on costly printers and other outside technicians. Its
goal was to be a perpetual weekly alternate-culture news and
''freak'' sheet rather than a widely read popular paper capable of
fomenting deep social change. Harvey Ovshinsky, the founder of
the paper, had said as much when asked to comment on the role of
the *Fifth Estate* for Robert J. Glessing's *The Underground Press in
America,* a book published in 1970: ''There are four estates, the
fourth of which is journalism. We are the fifth because we are
something different than . . . other newspapers. We hope to fill a
void in that fourth estate. . . . A void created by party news-

papers and the cutting of those articles which express the more liberal viewpoint. That's what we really are—the voice of the liberal element."*

The differing perspectives of Ovshinsky and Watson reflected a real division between advocates of an alternate lifestyle and hard-core political revolutionaries. Nationally, individuals such as Abbie Hoffman and Allen Ginsberg practiced a cultural revolution from above, based on the glorification of a few thumb-nosing superstars in a Hall of Fame conception of history. They mythologized the mammoth musical concert held at Woodstock, New York, in August 1969 into a political convocation of a youth nation. They believed the mass media could be infiltrated and manipulated into popularizing their views. William Burroughs, author of *The Naked Lunch,* summarized the possibilities of media manipulation as a cultural weapon in an interview given to one of the authors in 1970 and subsequently published in *Something Else Yearbook 1974*: "There's an extremely chaotic situation which revolutionaries can take full advantage of. For instance, there's a gap between the mass media and the administration. We're beginning to get an overlap between some liberal elements in the mass media and the underground press. I think this is an important development. It should be encouraged."

The forces around DRUM were never sympathetic to the notion of manipulating the established media because they believed that the media could publicize any number of revolutionary acts without threatening the established power structure. By giving some exposure to radical ideas, especially those which were moral and cultural rather than economic, the media solidified the liberal mystique of open debate and discussion of challenging ideas. Burning cities, guerrilla spokesmen, and gurus of every creed

---

*Ovshinsky's views dominated throughout most of the paper's history even though staff members such as Peter Werbe tried to take a more radical political line. The paper's policy changed slowly. Unlike most underground papers begun in the sixties, the *Fifth Estate,* under changing editors, survived into the seventies and in July of 1974 became a weekly. An editorial of June 8 expressed the politics of the paper at that time: "The *Fifth Estate* is simply a newspaper which is owned and operated by the people who work there. Our politics are simple: everybody's lives and tools for survival should be owned and operated by those who expend labor—not those who manage and take a cut (profit) of the labors of others."

could be and were reduced to a ten-minute spectacle on the evening news or a talk show.

Their struggles with the *Detroit News,* WJBK-TV, and other news vehicles had led the Detroiters to the conclusion that they needed total control of their own cultural apparatus if they were serious about contending for power. The problems in printing *ICV* and the attempted suppression of the *South End* had indicated the necessity of owning printing equipment and having trained personnel to operate it. DRUM was about the business of gaining power for its constituency, rather than merely acting as a moral witness for it. The sharpening conflict with the Black Panthers involved some of the same issues regarding the media. The black leather jackets and berets of the Panthers were good media fare, perhaps too good. The DRUM forces believed in keeping their membership under cover as much as possible, especially those involved in military operations. They felt that the masses should be presented with images that were realistic rather than those of superheroes whom they might admire but would be afraid to imitate. DRUM activists and their allies did not refer to themselves as "freaks" or "movement heavies." Rather than making a spectacle in the courtroom, they wanted to be in a position to control that courtroom, to control the judge, and to control the jury selection. Rather than shouting "Off the Pig!" as some others did, DRUM worked for the power to control the police department. Gestures made for a capitalist headline, even a "hip" capitalist headline, were perhaps counterproductive and in any case were secondary to amassing the resources, trust, and talent to promote a cultural revolution from below.

The major error made by the *South End* leaders concerned the continuity of control. Fighting off the charges of anti-Semitism and involved in one political struggle after another, Watson and his associates did not pay attention to the 1969-70 appointments. Since the paper was never used to organize the student body and the rules for selecting the editor had been changed in midyear, no candidate who could slip through the process was put forward until too late. There was, in fact, a revolt of part of the staff late in the year. Calling themselves the *South End* Revolutionary Union Movement, some whites on the staff, including the woman who would become summer editor and the man who would become editor for 1969-1970, asked for more collectivity in decision-making. The rebels supported the general editorial direction of the paper but complained that Watson and Medvecky operated in a dictatorial manner. When all efforts at compromise failed, Medvecky fired all the dissidents and Luke Tripp threatened to throw them out the window if they didn't vacate their offices. Most were quickly rehired, but the possibility of the Watson group's retaining control for another year had been lost. The summer editor got the paper closed down for obscenity after only a few days of publishing, and the 1969-1970 editor began a transition to safer ways. Even so, the *South End* would never quite return to its former political irrelevance. Periodically, the paper would fight as it had fought under Watson, and during the student agitation over the invasion of Cambodia Medvecky and the Watson stalwarts returned to the paper for a brief period of control. In retrospect, Watson saw that losing control of the *South End* was a costly mistake, but by the spring of 1969 the DRUM and *ICV* forces were involved in various funding projects that gave every indication of being able to finance a totally independent print shop which could produce *ICV* at will.

6

Father, I know you came
Out of a long mountain
Wide thumbed, brimming with mustache
Your shoulders stuck in a tight coat
Pieces of bread in your pocket. . . .

Abdeen Jabara, "Father"

The furor over the alleged anti-Semitism of the *South End* tended to obscure a far more substantial link developing between the black revolutionaries and Detroit's Arabs. The Detroit Arabs, like most of the Arabs in the United States, were a more or less invisible minority. The earlier, established immigrants tended to be white-skinned, 90-percent Christian, and involved in small business. Due to their relatively small numbers, they had been absorbed into the American melting pot more easily than most immigrant groups. A popular television comedy series starring Lebanese-American Danny Thomas was about as much play as their Arabness ever got. One of the mainstays of the program was a quaint old uncle still imbued with the customs and habits of the Middle East.

The Arab immigration pattern changed abruptly in 1966 when the federal laws were revamped to allow easier immigration of people who were relatives of American citizens. The new wave of Arab immigrants who took advantage of the change were primarily dark-skinned Muslims with little formal education. The new-comers invariably worked in heavy industry, where they got the same dangerous and arduous jobs as blacks. The Arab community in Detroit swelled to 85,000 and began to take on a dual quality. On the one hand, it was like the established European immigrant communities of an earlier epoch; and on the other hand, it was like the racially defined ethnic minorities such as Native Americans, Asian-Americans, and Hispanic-Americans.

The most coherent Arab community was in a section of Dearborn which had the same name as Wayne's newspaper, the South End. This area, immediately to the east of the Ford River Rouge complex, housed over 6000 people who were almost entire-ly immigrants or first-generation Americans of various nationalities. Approximately half of this population was Arabic, with a heavy proportion of Yemenites. In many cases 400-600 people from the same village in Yemen had come to the South End. Mayor Hubbard had never made it a secret that Dearborn was a "white man's town," and the Arabs were considered to be so many "white niggers." Beginning in the early sixties, Hubbard had harassed home-owners by restricting building and repair permits, strictly enforcing an onerous housing code, and scaring off federally guaranteed financing. These moves effectively eliminated the private real estate market and all but forced people to sell their property to the city, which promptly tore down all buildings in an effort to push out the immigrants and convert the South End to industrial use. The Mayor's actions had been challenged in a class-action lawsuit begun by a Community Council headed by Arab-American Alan Amen.

The personal history of Alan Amen's family illustrates the kind of lives Dearborn Arabs led. Amen's grandfather had been born in Lebanon and had worked forty-two years for the Ford Motor Company. His father was working in his thirty-fourth year as a janitor at Ford in 1973 and had never had the opportunity to learn to read or write English. Alan Amen's older brother Ron, a Vietnam veteran, had lost the use of his left hand when it was crushed by machinery at the Premier Steel Company. Like many of the working poor before him, Alan Amen tried to break his family cycle of factory work by taking courses at Wayne State University. His mother, Katherine, who had been a secretary and was active in community affairs, drew him into the struggle against the city. The Amen family, like many Arab-Americans, saw Dearborn's efforts as one more contemptuous act by a society that viewed Arabs as dirty illiterates without culture or commonsense. Alan Amen's personal dream was to see the South End become a center of Arabic life that would promote Arab culture in the way Chinese centers did in San Francisco and New York. His mother became the plaintiff in the class-action suit brought against the city of Dearborn, and the pressures on Alan Amen became so strong that his wife, Karen, a nurse, had to support the family.

Amen became Treasurer of the Community Council in 1968 and President in 1970. Other officers were Nick Kolcheff, a Greek in his sixties, Jerri Rallis, a Cherokee Indian in her thirties, and Helen Okdi Atwell, a mother of eight who, although a Muslim of Lebanese descent, hoped to become an anti-Hubbard member of the Dearborn City Council. Under their leadership, the community achieved a landmark victory on August 14, 1973, when federal Judge Ralph Freeman ruled that Mayor Hubbard had improperly conducted a ten-year campaign of harassment. The Judge gave 350 former home-owners affected by the class-action suit the right to sue the city for the difference between the price paid to them for relocation and the true market value of their property. Judge Freeman agreed with 28 of the plaintiff's 33 grievances in a decision that saved the South End community from further destruction. The Community Council was legally represented by Abdeen Jabara and by the Center of Urban Law and Housing at the University of Detroit Law School, a Jesuit institution. Zakhour Yousseff of the Psychology Department of Eastern Michigan University and Barbara Aswad of Wayne's Anthropology Department offered key testimony on the disruption of cultural vitality by the city's actions.

Attorney Jabara was representative of yet another new force in Arab-American life. Born in a small town in Michigan, he had served in a number of Arab cultural organizations and had been the Arabic-speaking lawyer on the defense team of Sirhan Sirhan, the Palestinian immigrant convicted of assassinating Robert Kennedy. Rather than seeking to further Westernize their lifestyles, Arab-Americans like Jabara took pride in their distinct political, culinary, literary, and musical heritage. They felt that Arabic culture, far from being a slave culture, was at least equal if not superior to Western culture. At Wayne, they sought to create an Arabic Cultural Room to be a showcase of Arab accomplishments, and they were active in a series of ethnic festivals held annually in the city of Detroit. One goal of the Arabs in Detroit was to establish an Arabic Community Center for Economic and Social Services with a bilingual staff to deal with the roster of labor, health, legal, and housing difficulties facing the Arabic community. Jabara was not as pleased with the court victory as might be expected. He told the authors in February 1974 that the lawsuit ''wasn't won on community rights, but on the constitutional principle of due process of law to protect the taking of private property.''

The problems of the Dearborn Arabs were reflected in the rest of the metropolitan area as well. In an article in the *Arab-American University Graduate Newsletter* of October 1973, Amen stated that 2000 of the 35,000 workers at Ford Rouge were Arabs. He was incensed that Ford Local 600, the largest local in the UAW, had bought $300,000 worth of Israeli bonds without rank-and-file approval. The UAW as a whole had bought over $750,000 of the 5 1/2% bonds, and by mid-1973 Arab members of the UAW were trying to organize a serious opposition to the union leadership, which they felt did not represent or respect them. They had many of the same on-the-job problems as blacks, and they asked blacks how they would feel if the UAW had bought the national bonds of the Union of South Africa or Rhodesia. The potential power of the dissident Arab workers was something to be reckoned with. An informal UAW count in three plants disclosed that Chrysler's Jefferson Assembly plant had 1400 Arab workers, its Mound Road plant had 800, and the Hamtramck complex that included Dodge Main had almost 2000. The UAW's national membership included at least 15,000 Arab workers, most of whom were in the Detroit area.

During the peak of activity of DRUM, many of the Arabs at Dodge Main had crossed DRUM picket lines for fear of losing their jobs. By 1973, they had gained in numbers and militancy, both in their neighborhoods and in their workplaces. On October 14, marching seventy abreast, 3000 Arabs staged a militant parade from the streets of the South End in Dearborn to the offices of Local 600, where they protested the UAW bond purchases. On November 28, when Leonard Woodcock was being presented the Humanitarian Award of B'nai B'rith at a $100-a-plate dinner attended by a thousand guests, 2000 Arabs and their supporters demonstrated outside. Most of the demonstrators were workers who had walked off their jobs and had agitated to get other workers to do the same. The result was that both lines of Dodge Main's afternoon shift were shut down that day for the first time since the DRUM wildcats. In the next issue of *Solidarity,* the union paper, Emil Mazey denounced the demonstration as communist inspired. He said that the disputed bonds had been purchased in the 1956-1966 period and had been converted in 1967 to bonds payable in 1986. He said that they did not indicate support for Israel against the Arabs but were simply a good investment, backed by "the only country in the Middle East with a free and democratic labor movement and a freely elected Labor Party government.''

The new Arab immigrant workers of the late 1960s felt that the UAW, like most American institutions, was hostile to them. The Arabs believed that they were regarded as so many transplanted ''camel jockeys'' who had the additional handicap of being not quite white and not quite black. They were like the Puerto Ricans, Chicanos, Filipinos, and West Indians employed in other American industries and localities. They were also part of a larger world pattern. Beginning in the 1950s, European capital had made massive use of cheap immigrant labor. Black Africans, Turks, Greeks, Arabs, Yugoslavs, Italians, and Spaniards had found work in northern Europe, France, Switzerland, and northern Italy. They frequently were forced to live in separate compounds and were paid wages inferior to those of domestic labor. In a French auto plant it was not uncommon to find five or six nationalities interspersed on an assembly line who literally did not speak the same language. Similarly, in the early 1970s, American capital began to import cheap labor for specific industries. In the East, along with Puerto Ricans, who had been immigrating for years, there were large influxes of South Americans and various Caribbean peoples, particularly Haitians, Jamaicans, and Dominicans, each with their own culture and language. On the West Coast, the cheap labor was primarily of Mexican and Asian ancestry.

The migrant-labor pattern was so invisible to most Americans that it came as a shock even to knowledgeable people that the first farm worker killed by police in the decade-long struggle to unionize the farm workers was not a Chicano but a young Yemeni immigrant named Nagi Daifullah. On August 17, 1973, 10,000 people marched in Delano, California, in a memorial service for the slain Daifullah and for Juan de la Cruz, a sixty-year-old Chicano killed one day later. United Farm Workers National Director Cesar Chavez called for a national three-day fast for the two men. At the memorial service for Daifullah, Chavez said, ''He came to this country seeking opportunity and fell into a trap of poverty and powerlessness that has enslaved so many migrant farm workers in our country. Nagi was not content to be a slave in a free country. He joined the United Farm Workers Union and gave of himself fully to the grape strike and the assertion of farm workers' justice. Nagi Daifullah is now dead at the age of 24, a victim of violence by a sheriff's deputy of Kern County.''

In Dearborn, the Arab community held two marches in honor of Daifullah. They learned from speakers that the thousands of Arabs working in the California fields were mostly men without skills or knowledge of English who lived in company ''camps'' often lacking the most basic sanitation. The workers were completely alienated men—alienated from their families, from their community, and from American society. Few of the Arab workers could even communicate directly with the Chicanos, Filipinos, and Portuguese who shared their lives in the fields and on the picket lines.

The killing of Daifullah in a California grape strike also reinforced the fear many Arabs had of the American government. They knew that an ''Operation Boulder,'' set up by the United States State Department in 1972, had brought federal pressure on all Arab travelers and visiting students. Everyone knew of people visited in their homes and places of work by the FBI and of students deported for their political views. In the harbor of Detroit, sailors from the ships *Kuwait Horizon* and the *Star of Kuwait* had not been allowed shore leave in the United States. In the latter case, the captain of the ship was emotionally unstable, and the vessel had to dock on the Canadian side of the river so that he could be dismissed and the seamen's needs met. Many Arab-Americans began to fear that if the Middle East wars should ever involve U.S. troops on a serious level, they might be treated as the Japanese-Americans had been during World War II. These fears, justified or not, combined with the problems facing Arab workers, paved the way for a working alliance with revolutionary black workers. From the standpoint of organizations like DRUM, the Arabs were only one example of several racial minorities that might be persuaded to work on a fraternal basis with blacks.

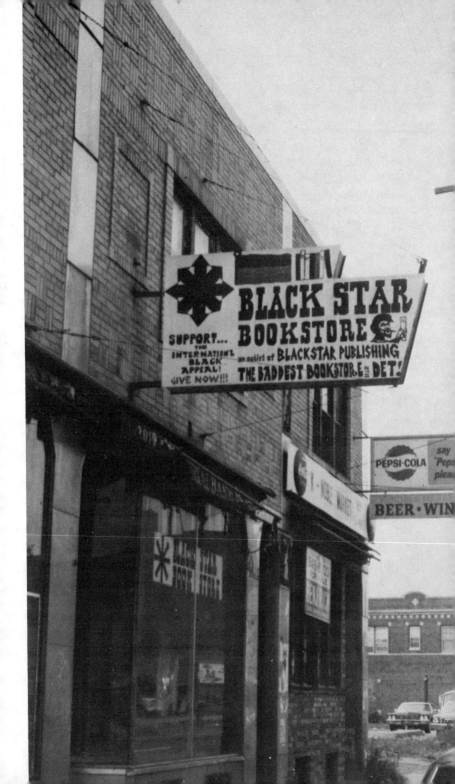

Chapter Four

The League
of Revolutionary
Black Workers

1

*A union of workers is power. They can, if they so decide,
control the economy of a country as large and powerful
as the USA simply by calling a general strike.*

League of Revolutionary Black Workers, in a special
UAW convention issue of *Inner City Voice,* November
1969

The success of DRUM bred a score of RUMs in other factories, as
well as an UPRUM (among United Parcel Service workers), an
HRUM (among health workers), and a NEWRUM (among *Detroit
News* workers). The elections at Dodge Main had demonstrated
that a whole range of media, legal, and neighborhood support
mechanisms would be necessary if DRUM and its offspring were
to survive even the first counterattacks of company and union.
Almost from the first wildcat, there were discussions on how to

*Opposite page: The bookstore of the League of Revolutionary Black Workers on
Linwood Avenue.*

weave an umbrella organization to unite the local RUMs and their support groups and allies. The final result was an organization named the League of Revolutionary Black Workers, which was legally incorporated in June 1969 and opened its headquarters at 179 Cortland Street four months later.

The League published numerous documents and position papers and had a finely drawn organizational chart, but it never functioned with the precision of a capitalist corporation or a Marxist-Leninist party. Rather than having a strict hierarchy, the League was organized into several components which had specific areas of work. Each component had a semiautonomous character which often reflected the particular personalities of the individuals in charge. There was a central staff which grew to 80 members, but the organization was tightly controlled by a seven-man Executive Committee made up of General Baker, Kenneth Cockrel, Mike Hamlin, Luke Tripp, John Watson, John Williams, and Chuck Wooten.

The relatively loose structure of the League did not prevent the organization from developing a clear sense of strategy. The League viewed company, union, and government as an interconnected system of power that gave an appearance of intransigence but actually did not regard any one battle as critical. The stakes were much higher than those involved in any single confrontation, and the system was flexible enough to allow ample room for error, limited failures, some accommodation of worker demands, and grudging change. The League also appeared intransigent; but it, too, viewed no single election, strike, or activity as more than one operation in a broader campaign. One reason the League was able to flourish was that its opponents, who were so precise in describing their own actions and motivations, habitually abstracted the League's actions from their historical and organizational context. They saw local League actions centering on limited demands as the sole concern of the organization. They never imagined that a leaflet at Jefferson Assembly and a poster at Northern High School and a door-to-door petition on Dexter Avenue were all part of a system of interlocked centers of power and influence. They did not understand that the League sought to create a multilevel power apparatus parallel to the power apparatus of the system it sought to destroy.

The most publicized League activity was the in-plant organizing led by General Baker and Chuck Wooten. The approach, following the pattern of DRUM, was to move plant by plant, building small core groups and perfecting models of organization, discipline, and ideology. DRUM led to the birth of ELRUM (Eldon Avenue Revolutionary Union Movement) in November 1968, and soon ELRUM had an even larger membership than DRUM. There was also a FRUM at Ford's River Rouge complex, a JARUM at Chrysler's Jefferson Avenue Assembly plant, a MARUM at the Mack Avenue plant, a CADRUM at Cadillac's Fleetwood factory, a DRUM II at Dodge Truck, and a MERUM at the Mound Road Engine plant as well as units at Chevrolet's Livonia factory, at Ford's Wixom plant, at the Huber foundry, at the Winfield foundry, at Chrysler's Forge plant, and at the Plymouth Assembly plant. Had each of these new RUMs been as broadly based and popular as DRUM and ELRUM, the League would have had the strength of a fledgling political party or an alternate union. The reality, however, was that many of the RUMs reflected potential rather than solid organizations. Sometimes only a handful of workers were involved. A few bulletins or a single action might be the extent of their activities. The situation at each factory was unique. At Paragon Steel in Detroit, there was no RUM organization as such, but people in contact with the League carried out a small strike. In CADRUM, at the Fleetwood Cadillac plant, there were many older workers who had a long and militant history of shop-floor activism, including struggles with Ku Klux Klan elements in the local union. Often the new RUM units contained company, union, and police spies. The ranks also contained many confused sympathizers, vacillators, and strident black nationalists. Careful work was required on the part of the top leadership to filter out these elements and to make a reliable unit. One of the ever-present dilemmas during the first year of League operations was whether to answer a new inquiry or to devote extra time to an existing RUM. The League leadership's time and energy were spread thin and the organization's structure was as fragile as a pyramid of playing cards. Funds were limited and the task enormous, but requests for aid and information kept coming in, not only from the Detroit area but from all parts of the United States. There seemed to be no limit on how far the RUM idea might reach. The League Constitution itself declared, ''We must act swiftly to help organize DRUM type organizations wherever there are black workers, be it in Lynn Townsend's kitchen, the White House, White Castle, Ford Rouge, the Mississippi Delta, the plains of Wyoming, the mines of Bolivia, the rubber plantations of Indonesia, the oil fields of Biafra, or the Chrysler plant in South Africa.''

The Baker group heavily emphasized the need to galvanize the new RUMs into tough and dependable units. They wanted all out-of-plant activities subordinated to this primary task. A number of other League leaders believed that it was just as essential to organize people outside the factories—in the neighborhoods, schools, and places of recreation. These leaders stressed the interrelationship and interdependence of all League activities. Mike Hamlin, in particular, was concerned about the possibility of the individual RUMs becoming isolated. Perhaps the most patient and low-keyed personality in the leadership, Hamlin spun a web of alliances and relations for the purposes of creating a good public image for the League and strengthening the links between the various League components. Hamlin emphasized the need for student and community groups which could carry on public demonstrations when court injunctions and other considerations barred workers from public activity. Hamlin also was anxious to see the white radicals in the city form some organization which could act in concert with the League, and he wanted to find a device to link up Detroit activities with those of the similar groups emerging in other locations. Hamlin recalled some of the early League days in an interview given to the authors in 1972:

We came to believe that the working class had to make

the revolution, had to lead the revolution, and that we had to concentrate our energies on workers. We didn't really understand what making a revolution entailed, what a proletarian revolution was, how it took shape, and how it developed. . . . I began to feel we must broaden our contacts within the community. We needed support to continue the struggle. I also felt we should build several kinds of resources to serve the struggle. We needed a printing operation, a legal apparatus, and stepped-up political education. . . . The League began to recruit large numbers of students and professionals. I think that our understanding of proletarian consciousness at that time was very low, and we did not do a good job of transforming the understanding of our new members. We were held together by personal loyalties rather than ideology. People were coming to us for the same reason we had started. They wanted to find ways to struggle. They would come in and we would do work, but our ideology remained unclear. Word of what was happening in Detroit got to workers in other cities. They began to wage similar struggles and they began to communicate with us. We started to discuss ideas about coalitions, affiliations, national caucuses, black worker organizations, and so forth. . . . Community organizing and industrial organizing are linked up. They go together. The working class should lead the community effort.

Watson shared Hamlin's views and added his own ideas on the use of media to build a secondary leadership and to combat the ideological underdevelopment of many rank-and-file League members. Watson considered it impractical and wasteful to have a few individuals scurrying from one plant to another in what amounted to a permanent state of frenzy. He had already demonstrated, with *ICV* and the *South End,* that a revolutionary newspaper could be an organ of mass political education. He wanted to extend that education by moving into films, radio, printing, and television. Watson felt that if the League could acquire its own media facilities, it could conduct mass political education on a scale unprecedented in Detroit or elsewhere. In a speech delivered on June 8, 1971, at a public meeting held in Detroit's Central Methodist Church, Watson gave his views of the need for political education:

> I want to emphasize that education and knowledge are the most powerful tools that we have available in engaging in the struggle to make a better world. It is through the control of knowledge that the ruling class maintains its power. The struggle over the control of knowledge itself is a political struggle. The ruling classes have for many centuries understood this very clearly. Back to the days when the typical statement that you might hear from a slaveowner was, "Hell no, I don't want my slaves to learn how to read and write because educated niggers become uppity." That's exactly correct, and the man understands it very clearly today.

Ken Cockrel, who was admitted to the Michigan Bar in 1968, was closely associated with Watson and Hamlin. Outsiders tended to view Cockrel as the League's "intellectual in residence," but his biography was similar to that of the other League leaders. His parents had come from the Deep South during World War II, and his first home was in one of the army barracks thrown up around 8 Mile Road, the northern city limit, to house blacks brought to work in the factories. Cockrel's father had a job at Ford, and his mother was the first black woman to graduate from Lincoln High School in Ferndale. Both parents died when Cockrel was twelve, and he was brought up by an aunt who worked as a supermarket cashier and an uncle who worked in various industrial plants around the city. Cockrel quit high school in the eleventh grade and hung around the streets for a while. His state of mind at that time was like that of many Detroit blacks; he was quoted in an October 14, 1973, article in the *Detroit News* as saying: ''I just knew I wasn't going to bang metal in some factory all my life. But I was in a general course in school and wasn't aimed at anything particular. So I joined the Air Force, like my brother Sye had done.''

In the Air Force, Cockrel got top security clearance and trained as a nuclear-weapons technician. When he got out, he thought he might try college. Turned down by Highland Park Junior College because he was a high school dropout, he was admitted to Wayne in 1959 as a conditional adult student in a special program for those who had not completed high school. Cockrel got a B.A. in 1964 and a law degree in 1967, just one month before the Great Rebellion. He soon joined a racially integrated law firm headed by Harry Philo. Cockrel and some of his law partners acted as the League's de facto legal component. In spite of the numerous criminal and civil actions involving League members, it was Cockrel's boast that no one, including himself, was ever convicted. Much of this remarkable record was a result of the brilliant courtroom performance of Cockrel himself, but various League policies were also helpful. The League discouraged inflammatory statements that could not be backed up, and it made a practice of investigating the past personal history of anyone wanting to join the League, especially anyone expressing extreme political views. Cockrel understood better than anyone else in the League the gamut of legal ploys that could be used against the organization. He was convinced that to survive and prosper it was essential to have a powerful presence within the media and within the community. In a retrospective interview given to the authors of this book in 1972, Cockrel said:

> If you are only dealing inside [the] trade-union context, then you are not able to have the kind of pressure from the people who are affected by working-class struggle who are not workers. You don't have any criteria that are developed.
>
> . . . The situation at the point of production itself is such that the kind of controls, the kind of political

discipline that is necessary for struggle to advance doesn't seem to me to be susceptible of being developed at the point of production independently of some interaction with other struggles inside the community and broader, more class-conscious, more programmatic input.

. . . We had to develop a concept of what to do when workers are fired for doing organizational activity, and you are not in a position to feed them, and you are not in a position to force the management to take them back, and you are not in a position to relate concretely to any of their needs. We had to confront incredible tactical questions. You are confronted with the questions of whether to try to force the union to get their jobs back, and if the union succeeds then the union is assisted and your influence diminished. On the other hand, if you make no response, you are in a position of having led workers out of the plant on the basis of an anti-racist, anti-imperialist, and anti-capitalist line, and having the man respond, and you can't do anything.

. . . When Chrysler is attacked in America, it pushes a buzzer and gets the Hamtramck Police Department. The whole city structure goes into action. At Ford, you are dealing with Dearborn. The fact that we closed down Dodge Main, the basic assembly plant for Chrysler operations in this entire country, means we got a response. We got police. We got injunctions from the courts. They tried to destroy our organization. They tried to kill leaders like General Baker and Chuck Wooten. Most all of the members of our central staff had to go to trial some time in the year of 1969.

Luke Tripp and John Williams held a middle position between those emphasizing in-plant organizing and those who saw the different League activities as equally important. Tripp and Williams were concerned about the political level of the average

League supporter, but they were hesitant about moving too rapidly in too many different directions. They thought that political education might be best served by a more intense contact with individual workers in small social and study groups, rather than by the ambitious plans Watson, Hamlin, and Cockrel began to advance. Tripp and Williams were the initial leaders of the Detroit Black Panther Party and did not want to see the mistakes of the BPP repeated. They were not pleased by talk of spreading the league to other cities, and they did not always approve of the interviews given by Watson, Cockrel, and Hamlin in which DRUM and the League were projected in glowing terms. As members of the Detroit BPP, one of their quarrels with the California headquarters was over the issue of working with John Sinclair, a white local counterculture poet with a flair for publicity on the issues of marijuana, psychedelic drugs, and the new music. They feared that the growing involvement of the League with white radicals might give rise to similar mismatches of interest and commitment. Tripp kept saying that the local organizational model must be perfected before it was ballyhooed around the nation. He summed up his view by saying, in the January 23, 1969, issue of the *South End,* that political education should "cultivate a firm and correct political orientation, an industrious and pure style of work, and flexible strategy and tactics."

A concrete example of what the out-of-plant organizers had in mind occurred during the period of 1969-1970 when the Detroit Board of Education announced a plan to decentralize control. The West Central Organization (WCO), a coalition of neighborhood groups based at first on the ideas of Saul Alinsky, had appointed John Watson as its director. WCO was concerned about whether the decentralization plan would be an improvement or a backward step for blacks. Watson organized a conference attended by 300 representatives from seventy organizations. Some of these were black groups and some were white or integrated groups willing to work under black leadership. They formed another coalition called Parents and Students for Community Control (PASCC). The immediate issue was community control of schools, a matter which involved community groups in almost every major American city; but under League urging PASCC began to be more than a community-control group. PASCC came to see itself as the beginning of a permanent citywide network of communications and action. Hundreds of rallies and meetings took place, and PASCC representatives made regular appearances on radio, on television, and in schools. PASCC soon found itself in strong opposition to the Detroit Police Officers Association, Donald Lobsinger's Breakthrough, the home-owners' associations, and citizens' councils.

A Black Student United Front came into being, with Mike Hamlin as its adviser. The organization soon developed branches in twenty-two high schools and published a citywide newspaper. The same ideological mixture of socialism and black nationalism which was found in RUM publications characterized the work of the students. One example of the organization's activity was a campaign launched to revoke the suspension of students who had taken part in a revolt at Northern High School in September 1969. Some of the demands were purely nationalist, such as the one that a black, red, and green liberation flag be substituted for the stars and stripes at the daily flag raising. Other demands dealing with curriculum, police in the schools, and selection of faculty amounted to calling for full student and community control of the schools, which was an educational counterpart of workers' controlling the factory. More important than any specific struggle, Black Student United Front was a municipal student organization which served as a youth section for the League of Revolutionary Black Workers. It extended downward to junior high schools and had connections with college groups. Students sometimes did leafleting and picketing chores at plants, and some were in training at the print shop and other League facilities. The publications of Black Student United Front stressed self-reliance. One original comic book which was given wide circulation contained a strong attack on substituting the heroism of a few individuals for action by masses of people. The student organization had a role independent of PASCC, but, at the same time, it was an integral part of the plan to gain control of the public school system.

PASCC struggled continuously with the Detroit Board of Education, which was controlled by white liberals and was presided over by Abe Zwerdling, who had close ties to the UAW. Unable to reach a satisfactory compromise with the board, PASCC was forced to organize for the local school board elections. Summer programs were set up in black history, photography, printing, and journalism to build skills. Three PASCC offices operated in Detroit and one in Highland Park, a suburb adjacent to Hamtramck. The PASCC plan was to have production-line workers as candidates for the community boards and to have students do most of the actual campaigning. Although 70,000 votes were recorded for PASCC slates, the effort ended in failure. In addition to the chronic problems of insufficient cadre, insufficient funds, and insufficient experience, PASCC faced the opposition of UAW and Democratic Party officials, who understood that if PASCC succeeded it would create a political machine comparable to their own. Some members of the League's central staff argued that the PASCC bid for control of the schools was premature and only drained off resources. Others, like Watson and Hamlin, were disturbed that not all of the executive board responded with sufficient enthusiasm to a plan that would have given them a foothold on local political power. Even in failure, PASCC illustrated the depth and vision of the League's approach.

PASCC activity had counterparts in other areas with greater and lesser success. John Williams headed a Catholic school complex in the North End for a time, Ken Cockrel was Research Director for a religious foundation, and Larry Nevels, a League stalwart, headed UNICOM, a neighborhood group which dealt with youth and various areas of social service. Edna Watson, John Watson's wife, initiated a hospital organizing drive which involved her with the predominantly white Medical Committee on Human Rights. Solid relations were built with the Guardians, a black policemen's association. Bridges were built to white radical organizations such as the local branch of the National Lawyers Guild and indigenous Detroit groups such as Ad Hoc, People Against Racism, and the Detroit Organizing Committee. Meetings were held continuously with other black militant organizations and with sympathetic black trade-union leaders who were willing to cooperate with the League on one level or another. The rudiments of an overall revolutionary strategy were present in the League's policies from the outset, but it was not always clear how the embryo was to develop to the point of contending for power.

2

We demand $500,000,000 in reparations.

Black Manifesto, issued in Detroit, Michigan, May 1, 1969

A specific instance of how the League dealt with strategic and tactical problems was its role in the Black Economic Development Conference (BEDC) held in Detroit, April 26-29, 1969. Financing for the conference was obtained through a grant from the Interreligious Foundation for Community Organizations (IFCO), a nonprofit foundation begun in 1966 by one civic foundation and nine Protestant, Catholic, and Jewish agencies. BEDC (pronounced ''bed-c'') was to explore various economic strategies for black people in America. League personnel had major roles in inviting guests, arranging panels, and influencing the ideological direction of informal discussions. The Interreligious Foundation for Community Organizations may have hoped for a kind of black capitalism or black welfare state approach from the conference; and Michigan Congressman John Conyers and Georgia State Representative Julian Bond got most of the official media limelight. But the real tenor of the meetings was articulated by speakers such as James Boggs, who talked on ''The Myth and Irrationality of Black Capitalism.'' What finally emerged from the conference was a call for black socialism. BEDC was to become a permanent independent national organization guided by a 24-member steering committee. Ken Cockrel, Mike Hamlin, Luke Tripp, John Watson, John Williams, and Chuck Wooten were named to that committee. Most of the others on the committee were people associated with James Forman, who had been a major leader in SNCC for six years and had recently resigned from a brief membership in the Black Panther Party. Forman had been instrumental in bringing the BEDC proposal to the attention of the League, and he was given the task of reading a *Black Manifesto* on May 1, 1969.

The *Black Manifesto* called for $500 million in reparations to be paid by white religious institutions to BEDC to provide blacks with economic self-sufficiency. The sum was considered an atonement by the moral guardians of white America for the way ''white America has exploited our resources, our minds, our bodies, our labor.'' The *Manifesto* pointed out that the mammoth sum came to only $15 per black person based on the official government figure of a black population of 30 million, a count which most blacks considered a low estimate. The churches and synagogues were expected to pay up at once or black militants would enter places of worship all over the country to disrupt services by reading the *Manifesto* directly to the congregation.

The economic proposals of the *Manifesto* itself were divided into ten specific projects whose radical political purposes were left unstated. Of the $500 million in reparations, $200 million was to be used to set up a Southern Land Bank which would establish cooperative farms throughout the South. $80 million was to be divided between four new publishing ventures to be located in Detroit, Los Angeles, Atlanta, and New York and four audio-visual centers to be located in Detroit, Chicago, Cleveland, and Washington, D.C. $30 million would be spent to create a research-skills center and $10 million for a training center in communication-industry skills. $130 million would be spent to establish a black university in the South. $10 million would be granted outright to the National Welfare Rights Organization to further its work with welfare recipients. $20 million would be used to establish a National Black Labor Strike Fund, and $20 million more would go to the United Black Appeal (soon to be called International Black Appeal) which would be charged with developing additional funds for BEDC. A final demand of the *Manifesto* was that whatever sums were left over from the conference budget should be used to get the permanent BEDC organization started.

Shortly after the first reading of the *Manifesto*, James Forman entered New York's Riverside Church to make the first disruption of a religious service. Although there was all but universal disapproval of the tone of the *Manifesto* and the tactic of disruption, many of the churches affiliated with the Interreligious Foundation for Community Organizations promised to make some payments to BEDC to avoid such pressure and to satisfy insurgents within their own ranks. The American Jewish Committee was the sole exception. That organization refused to be intimidated into contributing toward an enterprise it did not approve of and it withdrew from IFCO altogether, citing the *Manifesto* and BEDC as the causes of its departure. The monies that eventually went to BEDC did not begin to approach the multimillions demanded, but they were considerably more than most radical groups had to work with. BEDC itself was awarded $80,000 by IFCO, and its allied research group got an additional $79,000. Local organizations in every part of the United States received IFCO grants following BEDC approval. Many of these organizations were worker caucuses or groups with former SNCC activists personally associated with Forman. DRUM got an $8000 grant for its work at Dodge Main, and several other Detroit groups got similar aid. The West Central Organization received close to $30,000 to organize block clubs and neighborhood councils and to provide a citywide police-community relations program, food co-ops, employment services, and related programs. Eventually, IFCO earmarked an additional $200,000 for BEDC use in 1969.

In spite of the funds generated by the *Manifesto*, many of the in-plant League organizers considered BEDC a lot of pie in the sky. General Baker was suspicious of the political line of those who tried to con the system through a spectacular media campaign rather than sticking to the arduous task of organizing workers; and he refused to be on the BEDC steering committee. Baker was also wary of famous "outside" individuals who did not love DRUM the way Detroiters did and who had no permanent stake in the city. Cockrel, Hamlin, and Watson dismissed the objections of Baker as short-sighted and provincial. For them, BEDC was a way of acquiring the funds needed to orchestrate the full range of League possibilities. Others in the leadership shared some of Baker's misgivings but were willing to go along with BEDC for the same reasons as Cockrel, Hamlin, and Watson.

All the League leaders did agree that the proposal for an International Black Appeal (IBA) was one of BEDC's most important contributions. IBA was to become a national tax-exempt charity on the scale of Detroit's annual Torch Drive or the United Jewish Appeal. Factory workers and other hourly employees could allocate tax-deductible donations for IBA directly from their paychecks. Cockrel began a successful effort to get Internal Revenue approval for IBA's tax-exempt status at once, and John Williams was named its director. The UAW was approached about the possibility of taking contributions directly from paychecks and proved less hostile than expected. The UAW may not have realized that IBA would put potentially enormous financial resources into the hands of black revolutionaries, or the UAW may have been gambling that IBA was the first step toward the incorporation of League militants into the established system. IBA meant something quite different to the League. If each of the 250,000 black members of the UAW gave only $1 a month, the League would have a monthly budget of a quarter of a million dollars. This money could be used as a strike fund if it was funneled to friendly charitable agencies that could hire fired workers and support strikers. The possibilities were as broad as imagination could make them, and imagination was one ingredient the League had never lacked.

The *Black Manifesto* and IBA actually represented two contradictory approaches to financing. The *Manifesto* was an attempt at an outright "rip-off," depending upon white guilt for its success, and essentially it meant going back to the master's table for a handout. IBA was a self-financing approach dependent only upon the goodwill of black working people. The League considered BEDC and the *Manifesto* useful primarily because they started other projects capable of self-sufficiency. The ultimate peril of BEDC was that it had no organized mass base either to keep pressure on the churches or to control its leadership. The possibility that black clergy, "professional organizers," and others might usurp control of local or national BEDC operations was a clear and present danger. IBA, on the other hand, would be dependent on and responsible to a mass base.

One of the immediate concrete benefits of BEDC was the establishment in Detroit of Black Star Publishing under the leadership of Mike Hamlin. Black Star bought a building, purchased some equipment of its own, and shared in purchasing other equipment which was housed at a white printers' cooperative run by Fredy Perlman. Helen Jones, a League member, was in charge of the day-to-day operations at Black Star and had considerable decision-making authority, although she was ultimately responsible to Mike Hamlin. Black Star's major duties were to publish the newsletters and periodicals of the League's various components. Helen Jones also initiated a program to train League members in printing skills. She and Hamlin hoped to develop Black Star to the point where it could do commercial work well enough to become financially self-supporting. Black Star would then be able not only to carry on the League printing chores, but also to provide paid employment for League activists.

The printing and folding equipment shared with Perlman was another indication of the good and honest relations the League was able to maintain with many Detroit whites. Perlman had been greatly affected by his experiences in the French uprising of May 1968 and had set up the Detroit cooperative printing center to advocate libertarian principles. One of his goals was to make the print shop more than a service and convenience for radicals. Like

Helen Jones, he wanted to train people in the various skills associated with printing in order to make them independent of commercial printers. Upstairs from the print shop were the offices of the Radical Education Project, a spin-off from SDS which distributed low-cost radical literature locally and nationally. Perlman also printed *Radical America,* a journal edited first in Madison, Wisconsin, then in Boston, that began as an SDS publication and came to advocate a nonauthoritarian, worker-controlled communism. Other individuals in the cooperative were associated with the Detroit Organizing Committee, another SDS spin-off, which was trying to organize white workers into RUM-type groups. The haphazard connections between the various radical forces in the city puzzled government and police agencies. In August 1970, a Senate subcommittee headed by Senator James Eastland and Senator Thomas Dodd investigated the Detroit radicals and tried to tie in BEDC, the League of Revolutionary Black Workers, the Radical Education Project, and the Inter-religious Foundation for Community Organizations with the activities of the American Communist Party and an alleged Cuban plot to subvert the stability of the United States through terrorist bombings.

The fantasies and paranoia of the U.S. government aside, participation in BEDC was a significant step for the League. It was the first time the League had helped convene an important national gathering, and it was the first time it had reached out for substantial funding. IBA promised to become an instrument that could solve any number of financial problems on a permanent basis within a structure that would further develop the League base. BEDC had also given the League its first nationally famous ''convert'' in the person of James Forman. Following the April conference, Forman promised to move his personal residence to the Motor City, and he was named to the central staff of the League of Revolutionary Black Workers.

Chapter Five

Niggermation at Eldon

1

I work at a small shop in Troy. . . . Three weeks ago a woman on the day shift got her arm chopped off in a press. The week before this happened the press repeated and they said they'd fixed it and kept people working on it and then this lady got her arm chopped off. People were really freaked out; some of the people on days ended up quitting.

Denise Stevenson, in a statement to a People's Court convened by the Motor City Labor League, April 3, 1973

One of the major concerns of the League of Revolutionary Black Workers was the deteriorating working conditions at the point of production. In 1946 some 550,000 auto workers had produced a little over three million vehicles, but in 1970 some 750,000 auto workers had produced a little over eight million vehicles. Management credited this much higher productivity per worker to its improved managerial techniques and new machinery. Workers, on the other hand, claimed the higher productivity was primarily a result of their being forced to work harder and faster under

Opposite page: Section of a Diego Rivera mural, Detroit Institute of Arts. (Donor: Edsel B. Ford.)

increasingly unsafe and unhealthy conditions. The companies called their methods automation; black workers in Detroit called them niggermation.

Niggermation, not automation, was clearly the watchword at Chrysler Corporation's Eldon Avenue Gear and Axle plant. Clustered alongside four other Chrysler plants—Huber Foundry, Winfield Foundry, Chrysler Forge, and Plymouth—Eldon employed a workforce of over 4000, of which 70% was black. Eldon covered over a million square feet, was surrounded by another half-million square feet of storage and siding areas, and housed 2600 machine tools of 170 types. In a report to the National Labor Relations Board on November 30, 1971, Chrysler Corporation described Eldon as "engaged primarily in machining metal parts for rear axles of most Chrysler-built automobiles, for which it is the *sole* source, and assembling the parts into completed axles." Workers considered this key plant the most niggermated factory in Detroit.

Even though Chrysler acknowledged how vital Eldon was to its operations, working conditions at the plant continually deteriorated. These poor conditions reached such proportions that by 1970 harassment, industrial illnesses, injuries, and deaths on the job pushed Eldon workers to the breaking point. After James Johnson shot and killed two foremen and a job setter, his attorney, Ken Cockrel, said, "We'll have to put Chrysler on trial for damages to this man caused by his working conditions." The Johnson jury was taken to Eldon, the "scene of the crime," to observe for itself the conditions which Judge Philip Colista had called "abominable" and which UAW Safety Director Lloyd Utter termed "inexcusably dangerous" and evidence of "a complete neglect of stated maintenance procedures." The jury agreed and concluded that James Johnson was not responsible for his actions. That August, during the local contract negotiations, Chrysler admitted to 167 separate safety violations at Eldon; yet a year and a half later, in January of 1971, the Michigan Department of Labor found hundreds of violations of the Michigan safety code still uncorrected. In a separate case brought against Chrysler by

Johnson, he was awarded workman's compensation of $75 a week, beginning from the day of his "breakdown."

Eldon workers knew that James Johnson was not an isolated case. Serious provocations, injuries, illnesses, and deaths were the realities of their everyday work. On May 26, 1970, less than two months before Johnson fired his M-1 carbine, another death had occurred at Eldon. Gary Thompson, a black 22-year-old Vietnam veteran, had been killed when his defective jitney overturned and buried him under five tons of steel. UAW Safety Director Utter investigated the cause of the accident. On November 12, 1970, his written conclusions were sent as an official union inter-office communication to Art Hughes, the Assistant Director of the National Chrysler Department:

> I examined the equipment and found the emergency brake to be broken; as a matter of fact, it was never connected. The shifter lever to the transmission was loose and sloppy. The equipment generally was sadly in need of maintenance, having a lost steering wheel in addition to other general needs. I also visited the repair area and observed other industrial trucks in this area that were sadly in need of repair, noting: no lights, lack of brakes, horns, broken LP gas tank fasteners, loose steering wheels, leaky hydraulic equipment, etc. I was informed that there is supposed to be a regularly scheduled maintenance procedure for this equipment in this plant. I was also informed that operators are instructed to take trucks to the garage and tag them when they are in need of repairs. However, it seems to be the practice of foremen, when equipment is needed, to pull the tags off the equipment in the repair area that badly need corrective maintenance and put them back into service on the floor. . . . Finally, a general observation as we passed to and from the location of the fatal accident: there seemed to be little attempt to maintain proper housekeeping except on the main front aisle. Wa-

ter and grease were observed all along the way, as we proceeded. Every good safety program has its basic good-housekeeping procedures. Proper steps should be taken immediately to improve conditions within this plant.

Thirteen days before Gary Thompson's death, Eldon had claimed the life of Mamie Williams, a 51-year-old black woman who had worked for Chrysler for over twenty-six years. Mamie Williams had been ordered by her doctors to stay home because of a dangerous blood-pressure condition. Chrysler, however, had sent her a telegram telling her to return to work or be fired and lose all the benefits she had accumulated in almost three decades of employment. An intimidated Mamie Williams had returned to her job on the first shift in Department 80. One week later, she passed out on the line and died shortly after being taken home.

A year before the deaths of Gary Thompson and Mamie Williams, Eldon had taken the life of Rose Logan, a black janitor. Rose Logan had been struck in the plant by an improperly loaded jitney whose driver's vision was blocked. Her doctor told her to stay off her feet, but Chrysler's doctors ordered her back to work. She returned to Eldon from fear of losing her job, developed thrombophlebitis in her leg, and, like Mamie Williams, ended her service at Eldon in a coffin.

Higher production at Eldon had not been achieved with advanced technology and automated assembly-line procedures, but through the old-fashioned method of speed-up. The single goal of the company was to increase profit by getting more work out of each individual worker. Eldon conditions were typical of conditions in the industry. Even when there were technological changes, usually only one segment of the assembly line was automated, so that the workers on other segments had to labor more strenuously to keep up. Often, the automation eliminated interesting jobs, leaving the more menial and monotonous tasks for people. Many of the "new" machines were not technological advances at all, but simply updated models of tools introduced as early as the 1920s and 1930s.

Health and accident data on the auto industry were difficult to obtain. Only in the early seventies did the UAW and the Department of Health, Education and Welfare begin to make studies in this area. One important report did appear in 1973. Called the *Health Research Group Study of Disease among Workers in the Auto Industry,* it was based on figures compiled by the National Institute of Occupational Safety and Health and was written by two medical doctors, Jannette Sherman and Sidney Wolfe. The report estimated 65 on-the-job deaths per day among auto workers, for a total of some 16,000 annually. Approximately half of these deaths were from heart attacks. There were also some 63,000 cases of disabling diseases and about 1,700,000 cases of lost or impaired hearing. These statistics did not include many long-term illnesses endemic to foundry workers and others exposed to poisonous chemicals and gases, nor did they include deaths and injuries by accident. Even these limited figures made it clear that more auto workers were killed and injured each year on the job than soldiers were killed and injured during any year of the war in Vietnam.

The hazardous conditions were supposedly compensated for by high wages. Auto workers were among the highest-paid workers in the United States, yet wage rates were deceptive. In the 1920s, Henry Ford made headlines by promising $5 a day to every worker in his enterprises. Ford workers soon discovered that it was not quite $5 a day for not quite everyone. Fully a third of all Ford workers never got the $5 a day. Likewise, at Eldon, the 1969 $4-an-hour average Chrysler wage proved a fiction. Before any deductions and without the cost of-living factor, which did not cover all workers and was never more than 21¢ an hour, most job categories at Eldon paid around $3.60 an hour and none paid more than $3.94. Workers found it difficult to get figures on per-hour pay for their particular job, and they were often cheated out of increases by complex union and company clerical procedures. What the workers did know was that overtime had become compulsory and that most of them needed the time-and-a-half paid for overtime to keep pace with inflation. Census Bureau figures revealed that the value of the products shipped out of the plant, minus the cost of materials, supplies, fuel, and electricity, came to $22,500 a year per worker, as compared to an average wage of $8,000 for a worker putting in a 40-hour week. During the period 1946-1969, wages had increased by 25% while profits went up 77%, dividends 60%, personal corporate incomes 80%, and undistributed corporate profits 93%. The industry moaned about its cycle of booms and busts, but in 1970 General Motors remained the nation's (and the world's) largest manufacturing enterprise. Ford was the third largest. And Chrysler, "the weak sister," was fifth.

Niggermation at Eldon gave rise to three separate rank-and-file opposition groups. The one with the longest record in the factory was a militant trade union group led by Jordan Sims, the black chairman of the shop stewards' committee. A radical group called Wildcat began publishing a newsletter in February 1970, and ELRUM, the local unit of the League of Revolutionary Black Workers, made its official appearance in November 1968. The three groups, separately and in various combinations, produced a steady barrage of information for the workers and succeeded in closing down the plant in several successful wildcat strikes. Chrysler was more than a little concerned about this activity. If Eldon were closed for any lengthy period, all gear and axle production would stop; and with that stoppage, all of Chrysler would stop. Chrysler remembered how, in 1937, General Motors had been forced to recognize the UAW when it occupied Fisher Body #1 in Flint and Fisher Body in Cleveland, the only plants having GM's valuable dies. Eldon had the same sort of pivotal role in Chrysler production. At this point of maximum vulnerability, Chrysler faced one of the largest concentrations of black workers in the industry. Eldon was Chrysler's Achilles' heel. Chrysler knew this, and so did the League of Revolutionary Black Workers.

ELRUM's history was similar to that of DRUM. Meetings, rallies, and newsletters built up a hard core of supporters and a much larger number of sympathizers. Leaders of ELRUM such as Fred Holsey and James Edwards found themselves under continual pressure from company, police, and union. Physical assaults were frequent, but the ELRUM leadership did not crack under the pressure. On January 22, 1969, ELRUM led over 300 workers to confront the local union leadership with a grievance list in much the way DRUM had confronted the leaders of Local 3. Five days later, ELRUM called a strike to back up its demands. ELRUM kept out 66 percent of the workers the first day of the strike and 50 percent the second. The company's retaliation was to fire some two dozen workers and to discipline 86 others.

In retrospect, the League evaluated the January 1969 strike as premature. Too many ELRUM members were knocked out of the plant, and the remaining base of support was insufficient to maintain the struggle at the same level as in the previous six months. Despite these facts, ELRUM continued to fight, and it continued to have a cadre and sympathizers in the plant. During the early part of 1970, ELRUM once more took a leading role in plant struggles, and it arrived at a working coalition with other militants.

2

You don't read about them in Newsweek *or see them on television. They're too dangerous. They're too dangerous to the system to have information about the kind of work being done at Eldon to be disseminated widely. This is a war we're talking about. There is literally a war going on inside the American factories. This is a violent struggle. Sometimes it is organized and guided. Most times it is unorganized and spontaneous. But in the course of this struggle more American workers have died than in all the four major wars.*

John Watson, interview in *Quaderni Piacentini* (Italy), Winter 1970

One of the key figures in the new series of events at Eldon was a white worker named John Taylor. In August of 1972, he gave the authors of this book a retrospective account of the events at Eldon as he had experienced them. At the time of the interview, John Taylor was a member of the Motor City Labor League. His personal testimony regarding the period from 1968 to 1970 is a textbook of what was wrong with the company and the union. It also presents a candid view of the problems within the ranks of the insurgents themselves:

My name is John Taylor. I wasn't born in Detroit. I was born in West Virginia. My father was a coal miner who worked in the mines for seventeen years. My grandfathers on both sides were coal miners. My grandfather on my mother's side was the recording secretary for the first miner's local in that part of the country back in 1916. We moved to Detroit in 1949 as part of the migration of white Appalachians northward. My father started to work at Chevrolet gear and axle plant as a production-line worker in October 1949 and he retires in 1975. My mother works at the Federals Department Store putting price tags on clothes. She's worked there since 1952 and expects to retire soon. I went to the Detroit public schools and Wayne State University. I came out with a bachelor's degree in English and a law degree. Along the way, I worked eight years for the Better Business Bureau in Detroit, a capitalist front organization, and I worked for Chrysler Corporation on the management side as a workman's compensation representative. That job took me into almost every Chrysler plant in the Detroit area. It put me into contact with literally hundreds of injured workers per week. I worked there from June 1966 to September 1968. In November of 1968, I got a job as a production-line worker at Chrysler's Eldon Avenue Gear and Axle factory, the same factory where I had worked for management.

I was asked to resign my management job because of what they called a "bad attitude." The truth is that the company was fucking the workers on compensation. One of their devices was to refuse to discuss the cases with the union. They claimed workman's comp was covered by statute and therefore not part of the contract and therefore not negotiable. My feeling was that while the substance of the decisions was not negotiable, the administration was and was therefore grievable. I thought I should discuss these cases with the various shop stewards. I did what the union should have done. I gave the stewards an outline of the rights of workers—their constituents. I noticed that, during a period of nine days, about every steward in the place was in my office. I didn't find out until several years later that Jordan Sims had noticed what I was doing and had made it part of his program as Chairman of the Shop Stewards' Committee to send all of the stewards to see me. Finally, he came in himself and we had a long rap. I gave him a copy of the statutes. I used to have almost daily relations with the Labor Relations Committee. I remember on more than one day how they would say, "Oh, we're going to have a rough afternoon coming up because Sims is coming to bargain." That's the kind of reputation Sims had.

After I got kicked out of Chrysler management, I went back to Wayne State; but I didn't want to be a lawyer or a teacher. I wanted to organize, and the logical place seemed to be the plant. I had the reputation in the Eldon Personnel Department of being the best comp man they had ever had. I talked them into letting me work hourly, and they put me into Department 75, first as a conveyor loader and then I worked up to being a precision grinder. That's the best job I ever had in my life. I didn't have any organizing agenda at that time. The only politics I had came out of the *Fifth Estate,* Detroit's underground paper. I had never read Marx or Lenin. The first time I read the *Communist Manifesto* was late 1969. I thought, "This is far out. They are talking about this plant." That was an important event for me.

One funny coincidence from that time is that I entered the plant on November 8, 1968, and on November 10th some black workers in other departments founded ELRUM, the Eldon Avenue Revolutionary Union Movement. They had been turned on by the agitation at Dodge Main and became an affiliate of the League of Revolutionary Black Workers. I would like to relate these events in the sequence I lived them, rather than strict chronological order. I will come back later on and fill in the most important dates and events.

Our steward in Department 75 on the third shift was a man named Frank McKinnon. I got to know him when I was in workman's comp because McKinnon was a witness in a case involving a fight. Chrysler had a policy of firing the aggressor, so the question of who started the fight was important. McKinnon gave me a statement that the worker had started the fight. I found out later he lied to me. That was the kind of steward he was. When I got to be a worker, he refused to write up my safety grievances. A number of us also had grievances relating to pay raises due us because of promotions. We were supposed to get a 5¢-an-hour raise within a week, and it took me six weeks to get mine because the foreman wouldn't do the paperwork. He was trying to save on his own budget, and McKinnon wouldn't write up the grievance about it. That's how things worked at Eldon.

My safety grievance typifies the problems in that factory. I worked on what they call a modern grinder. We used to laugh about it because there was nothing modern about it at all. It was ancient. We had to burn off the rough edges of rangers which looked like donuts with metal teeth. This part went into the differential. There was a lot of fine dust generated by this grinding. The company put vents on the machines to hold this down, but every shift the filters would get clogged. The supervision would never give us the little time needed for someone to come and do some maintenance on them. I requested a mask. I got this thing that didn't look right and asked for the box it came in. It turned out to be for paint and gas fumes and was no help against dust. I ran all this down to McKinnon, but he refused to deal with it. So I called for a department meeting. I organized around him. The union President wouldn't schedule the meeting for more than two weeks because he said we had one word wrong in our petition. Richardson [the President] was just pissed because he had just taken office, and now, less than two months later, there was dissatisfaction with one of his stewards. Richardson told me straight off he wanted people to cool off because he didn't want angry people in the union hall. That's another indication of the union's attitude. They do not want to deal with angry workers.

I started seeing Sims in the cafeteria every morning. This was in early 1969, and he suggested I get on the union bylaws committee. I worked on that for a year with Sims and a guy named J. C. Thomas. We drew up some bylaws that would have made that union as honest and democratic as unions can be in this period. Needless to say, those bylaws were never presented to the membership.

By 1970, we had gotten to a situation where Chrysler was making most of its money off small cars, the Valiant and the Dart. One reason things got so bad at Dodge Main was that is where they made those cars. Behind the need for increased production and because they wanted to harass the union, Chrysler did a lot of firing, disciplinary actions, and all sorts of bullshit. There was attempted speed-up in my department at Eldon. One foreman arbitrarily raised the quota on the grinder machine, which was totally against the contract. What we did was lower to 400 instead of the usual 700 gears and that cooled his ass about a speed-up.

On April 16, 1970, things built up to what we call the Scott-Ashlock Incident. There was a black worker named John Scott who was a physically small man. His foreman was a fairly large guy from Mississippi named Irwin Ashlock. They got into an argument, and Ashlock picked up a pinion gear and said he was going to smash Scott's brains out. Scott complained to his steward, and the union took it up with the company. Well, Chrysler came up with the claim that Scott had taken a knife from his pocket—you know, like all blacks carry knives. They claimed Ashlock had a right to protect himself, and rather than discipline

Ashlock, they were going to fire Scott. This sparked a wildcat strike which shut the place down for the whole weekend. That was a beautifully successful strike. It had an old-fashioned unity—young and old, black and white, men and women. Everyone was militant. The skilled tradesmen went out too. At a union meeting a white worker named John Felicia, who had seen the whole thing, spoke from the stage at the hall. There were maybe a thousand people there. Felicia said there were white workers at Eldon and black workers at Eldon, but the main thing was that they were all workers and that he had seen the whole thing and that John Scott was telling the absolute truth and was totally in the right. The company needed our gears for those Valiants, so they backed down.

Everyone thought we had won, but then, after a couple of weeks, the company started acting up. They threatened to discipline the second-shift stewards who had led the walkout. They began to have foremen follow these guys around, and then, on May 1st, they were told toward the end of the shift that they were all going to be suspended for an unauthorized work stoppage in violation of the no-strike clause of the contract. They were shown the door leading to the street. What happened was that a guy named Clarence Thornton shoved the plant guards out of the way and led everyone back into the plant. This was shift time. I remember meeting a steward, and he said, ''We're shutting her down. Go home.'' By midnight, the factory was shut down. Chrysler went for an injunction and got it. The union lawyer from Solidarity House refused to defend Local 961 on the grounds it might bring legal action against the whole union. They sold out the strike. They advised us to go back to work without our stewards. We worked most of that summer without any stewards. Both Jordan Sims and Frank McKinnon were fired in this action.

In response to those firings, a grouping called the Eldon Safety Committee was formed which included myself, some members of ELRUM, and the fired stewards led by Jordan Sims. Our program was to research and document the issue of safety in the plant. We got advised by lawyers Ron Glotta and Mike Adleman that we had the right to refuse to work under abnormally dangerous conditions. That would not constitute a strike, and the company could not get an injunction. We saw that we had an umbrella for closing down Eldon. We were so naive we thought words meant what they said. When you look at our leaflets of that period, you will see that we quote the law and all that stuff. We put out a few leaflets, but events overtook us. The plant was indeed abnormally dangerous. On May 26, 1970, this was proven when a man named Gary Thompson was buried under five tons of steel when his faulty jitney tipped over. Thompson was a black Vietnam veteran about twenty-two years old. The jitney he was running was full of safety flaws.

On May 27th, we set up picket lines. By "we," I mean the Eldon Safety Committee and the League of Revolutionary Black Workers. This was not as successful as the first strike, but it cost them 2174 axles over two days. We're proud of each and every one of them. The three wildcats within a month and a half cost them 22,000 axles during a period when they desperately needed them for their Valiants. Chrysler immediately fired me and three members of the League: James Edwards, Alonzo Chandler, and Rob McKee.

I need to backtrack here to tell something about ELRUM. Like I said before, they had started on November 10, 1968. My first awareness of them was when they began to put out leaflets. There was an immediate response, about 50 percent positive and 50 percent negative. The negative response came from the older black workers and of course from white workers, mainly because the ELRUM language was harsh. They called people "Toms," "Molly-Toms," "hoinkie dogs," "pigs," etc. No one seemed to have trouble with calling the supervision those names, but this was something different. The older people definitely had a lot of trouble with their whole tone. In early 1970, there was an election for convention delegates. That was just before the Scott-Ashlock Incident. Given their numerical superiority in that plant, black workers could have elected an all-black slate. There were like thirty-three separate black candidates, and ELRUM put out a leaflet calling them Molly-Toms and all that. That divided the black vote.

ELRUM was already in bad shape by that time. In January of 1969, there was a lot of complaining about the coldness in the plant and about union discrimination against blacks. Chrysler disciplined some ELRUM people who had lost time from their jobs to do an action against the union. A wildcat followed, and after that twenty-two ELRUM people were fired. I think that broke the back of ELRUM right there. I think those actions were premature. There was no way to logistically support that strike. They had no outside mobilization. It was just premature. Still, everything we ever did at the plant was premature. Maybe it was vanguard activity, and they just didn't have any choice. Anyway, through 1969, the *Inner City Voice,* the League paper, was sold at the plant. I had no personal contact until early 1970, about the time of the convention.

At that time, I was still mainly involved in the bylaws struggle and troubles in my own department. Still, I used to see their leaflets and groups of us would discuss them, blacks and whites. I would say that we might not be able to relate to the rhetoric, but what they were saying was true. That was the position Jordan Sims took too. A lot of his enemies said he was the secret leader of ELRUM, in an attempt to erode his base among black and white workers. Sims said their language was crude but they were telling the truth. He would defend them as aggressively as he would any militant. That was a position of principle. I should say that I wasn't all that aware of all they were doing. I can say that the young white workers didn't like them. They could relate to what I said, but they had a hard time with ELRUM.

What really turned people off was this one leaflet they put out on the union secretaries. There was an old retiree named Butch and several white secretaries in the office. ELRUM put out a leaflet running that these white women were prostitutes for Elroy Richardson, the black President of the local. They ran all kinds of vicious stuff that people could not relate to. We knew these women and did not perceive them in that fashion. People were really put off by that issue. Another thing is that some of those young black workers who were enthusiastic about the leaflets never joined ELRUM, and some of them crossed the Safety Committee picket line. So there was this mixed response to ELRUM as we went into 1970.

Things were very complicated by 1970. Local 961 had its first black President. This was before the Scott-Ashlock Incident. ELRUM had supported the black slate in 1969, but now it had become critical and was calling Elroy a Tom, a fat-belly faggot, etc. When the wildcat came, ELRUM dropped that and supported him again. You can say that Richardson had a united plant behind him, but he was too incompetent and inept to be a leader. He had it all in his hands at the time of the wildcat following the Scott-Ashlock thing, but he blew it.

After the wildcat, the ELRUM cadre and myself worked on the Safety Committee. I did most of the research and writing because that was an area I had expertise in. They did most of the organizing for the strike. We met at League headquarters on Cortland Street. People ask if I felt any nationalism or reverse racism, and I can say I did not. I had a lot of basic respect for what they were trying to do. When they said, "Come on over; it's all right," I did and it was. I also had a nodding acquaintance with Ken Cockrel from law school. That may have helped, but our main contact with the League was General Baker. We had lots of contact with him and also with Chuck Wooten. They both came on the picket line with us, even though they didn't work at the plant. I would say the performance of the ELRUM people around the safety strike was exemplary.

I need to backtrack again. By early 1970, I had come to realize that I had to get beyond Departments 74 and 75. I knew you had to have an organ of some kind, a mimeoed sheet. I think that came from seeing the ELRUM example. I thought it was correct when they said whites should work with whites, which was what I was trying to do, even though I was doing it on my own from what I see now [in 1972] as correct instincts. A little earlier, a paper called *Wildcat* had been given out. People in my department had picked it up and read it. Then, early in 1970, they began to put out the *Eldon Wildcat,* a mimeoed plant newsletter. At that point, I was ready to leap out. I waited until they were at the gate, and I told them I worked in the factory and wanted to do some articles for them. We set up a meeting. Those people were experts at plant newsletters. I became identified with them immediately because people spotted my writing style.

The *Wildcat* people were Old Left. They were so secretive they had crossed over to paranoia. They used false names and all that stuff. They didn't want to expose their shit to open struggle. My opinion, then and now, is that that is an incorrect way to work. They strongly advised me not to distribute *Wildcat.* It was their policy that outsiders distributed. My opinion was that the paper had to get into the plant. We were only covering one gate. One morning I went out and took some papers and gave them out at another gate. It soon got around the plant that I was the publisher of *Wildcat,* which was a mistruth. I was only a junior member of that circle. They would edit the shit out of my articles. They would change the content and the style. Sometimes we did this together, but sometimes they said there wasn't time. I usually didn't mind, but they would put in bad stuff sometimes without consulting me, which put me into a trick as I was identified with the paper. Other workers held me responsible. I found out later that two people in the group took the position that I was only a contact and had brought my troubles upon myself by identifying with the paper in an overt way. You must remember that ELRUM was open with their thing. I thought that was correct, and I was open with mine. That made it easier to trust each other.

What we did during that period was have ELRUM put something out one day, *Wildcat* the next, and the Safety Committee the third. Then we would start the cycle going again so that there was a steady stream of information and agitation. It was like a united front. People knew I was associated with the Safety Committee, and stewards would take me off on the side to show me violations. Management tried to keep me from going out of my department on my break. They got a guy to pick a fight with me so we both could get fired. They tried all that shit.

ELRUM did not participate as fully as it could have in gathering information, and on the day of the strike they tried to stop distribution of the *Wildcat.* My brother was giving them out, and they said this was basically a black action and he should get out. Anyway, he didn't move. I don't think that was correct, but overall ELRUM was very good. The trouble was that after Rob, Alonzo, and James were fired, they had no one else to carry on. That was after the other twenty-two had been fired. Their thing was just ripped. Then they made a bad mistake, which may have been unavoidable given problems within the wider context of the League. That summer and fall they only put out one leaflet. They lost their visibility. They could have had workers from other plants distribute. They could have gone to union meetings, which was something I did. They went sometimes, but they were into a program of disruption. I didn't think that was correct, and I couldn't work with them on that. I thought it was insulting to those workers who had come to the hall in good faith to take care of whatever business they thought important. I thought it was disrespectful.

I think it would be fair to say that they were not good at dealing with people within the class who did not agree with them but who were not enemies either. I don't know what internal education the League was giving them on this. I don't know what kind of instructions they were getting. If there is no structure by which people's actions can be criticized and reviewed, you get into this kind of situation.

ELRUM still had a few people inside, but they were essentially not doing much. Now, in 1971, union officials came up for election. ELRUM ran a candidate named Eric Edwards, a guy who I have a lot of respect for. He ran a strong third as a straight ELRUM candidate, getting 342 out of about 1000 votes. That indicated a residue of support. The company and the union were running a heavy organized barrage against Jordan Sims, who was running against Frank McKinnon for President. Sims could have won with the solid help of older workers, but they were turned off by his association with ELRUM. Jordan and I went over to the Cortland offices and talked with Baker, Wooten, and a whole bunch of them. They had always seen Sims as a sellout and right-wing opportunist. I don't think that was correct. Anyway, he told them he didn't want their endorsement, which would be a kiss of death. The first day of the election, ELRUM did not come out in favor of Sims, and Jordan was ahead. The second day they endorsed him, and the vote turned away. I believe that was an indication of how negative the older folks had become to ELRUM. That was one factor in his defeat. It would be interesting to know who made the decision to endorse him.

The union ran its usual shit on us. They challenged 284 ballots because of dues default which is strange because you have check-offs at Chrysler, so if someone is behind, it is not their fault but the union's and the company's. I analyzed those ballots, and 90 percent of them were in black production units, and I think they would have gone to Sims. They would have put him over as President of the local.

The administration, the international, and the company had sold this program that we were all violent individuals. They even said I was a member of ELRUM! They said I was a violent motherfucker. We got into a situation in the hall the night we were tabulating. We were there as challengers, and they brought in armed guards with shotguns, carbines, and pistols. They were provocative as hell, trying to get us into a fight. I'm convinced they wanted to gun us down. We took our time real easy. I even took my shirt off so people couldn't claim I was strapped [carrying a gun]. There was one argument which was really hot where James Edwards raised his voice, and the whole table got surrounded by those guards. These black guards were hired under the instructions of George Merrelli, the Regional Director. I got into a hot dispute with Russell Thompson, who was solid with the administration. Some ELRUM people came over, and Thompson reached into his shirt for a piece. I saw the guards starting over, so we just split, me and the guys from ELRUM. We were not prepared to handle that shit. What is interesting is that most of the people counting the ballots were older black women, and they were physically afraid of ELRUM people. They thought ELRUM people had guns and were going to go berserk. I knew right then that there had been a tremendous failure of ELRUM. You can't have people in the plant afraid of you in that way. Also, the same women who were afraid of ELRUM were not afraid of me. Several of them went out of their way to say this.

A similar incident occurred around the safety strike. It happened at the East Gate, which is a principal gate for the second shift coming in. The second shift is basically black and young, with little seniority. This is the 2:30-10:30 shift. James Edwards was on the gate, and at one point, James grabbed a white worker and slapped him around. Now, we had agreed there would be no violence, on advice of our attorneys, so that we could preserve the strike's legality. James violated our organizational decision. That hurt us. When people heard about that, they turned against us. They even cut a hole in the parking-lot fence so they could get in easier.

I almost did a similar thing myself. I grabbed this one dude I had a thing on. He had caught me outside on the street one day and slugged me on my blind side. I had this plan for getting him that day, but I didn't. Maybe a policy of violence would have been better. Slapping some of those fuckers around might have made a difference. I don't know; but we had decided not to, and I stuck to that decision. We sure as hell moved too fast. We hadn't organized our base correctly. We weren't ready for that strike hit. We should have agitated more around the issue of Gary Thompson and on safety in general. We could really have made it hot, but as a result we had a not totally successful strike for which we got fired. You must understand we were genuinely angry at the death of Thompson. It verified everything we had been saying. We got self-righteous. In our arrogance, we failed to note that Memorial Day was on Friday. The people were getting triple pay for working. We couldn't have picked a worse day for a strike. It's just incredible that we didn't consider that factor. We were wrong and stupid.

These events took place in May 1970. On July 15th, James Johnson entered the factory and blew away two foremen and a job setter. He was looking for his shop steward, Clarence Thornton. That was the same guy who had led the fired stewards back into the plant by shoving the guards aside. That was exemplary because Clarence was an older dude, about 46 years old with 23 years' seniority. He was considered a good steward. Clarence was one of those sold out by the union. They left the stewards in the street for a time, and when Clarence came back, he had to sign a statement that if there was any further trouble he would get permanently fired. When Johnson first approached Clarence about his grievances, Clarence told him, "I can't do much for you because I just got back myself." Clarence had been intimidated and sold out to the point where it was no longer safe for him to fight for his membership. Johnson saw his union could not function for him and decided to deal with it himself. Those connections are important. The whole preceding set of events was to break down the stewards so they wouldn't defend their people. The company refused to deal with safety and other legitimate grievances. That's why we say Chrysler pulled the trigger. Chrysler caused those deaths. Yes, indeed, James Johnson was just an instrumentality.

It's important to note how ELRUM related to white people. The first thing is around the distribution of their leaflets. They would always refuse to give those leaflets to white workers. It wasn't until around March of 1970 that they could respect my practice enough to give them to me. Then James Edwards would go through changes about that. He would wad them up in his hand and sort of pass them to me surreptitiously so none of the black workers could see him giving a leaflet to a white. When ELRUM had its wildcat in January 1969, there was no attempt to relate to white workers about their demands. Consequently, many white workers crossed their lines, and many black workers who had close friends in the white force took the same position. They could not relate to the strike because they perceived ELRUM as having taken a racist position. One of the interesting aspects of the safety strike was that the Eldon Safety Committee was a coalition of trade unionists, ELRUM black revolutionaries, and white revolutionaries, mainly myself.

What happened to the Safety Committee is instructive. There was a steady process of attrition among the trade unionists, one of whom was a white named George Bauer, another of whom was Frank McKinnon. Some dropped out early. Some stuck right up to the strike. At the end, we had only Jordan Sims, J. C. Thomas, and a couple of others. During the strike, the trade unionists stayed for the first-shift picketing and then, except for Jordan Sims, were never seen again. The revolutionaries stayed with it to the bitter end because they had more than trade-union reform to fight about. That may be a clumsy formation, but the point is they were going to fight as long as they could. George Bauer, a skilled trades steward whom I have a lot of respect for, was fired with the other second-shift stewards. He participated actively in giving us safety information, but he never took part in picketing or in various confrontations with the union. George Bauer was not and is not a racist, and he has encountered a lot of opposition with his own skilled tradesmen. They call him a nigger-lover. George has a quick temper. He used to be a professional boxer. He got into an argument outside the plant with an individual who had scabbed during the wildcat, and George decked him. This was outside the plant. Management moved to fire him, and the union wouldn't write a discharge grievance for weeks. Eventually, George got back in there, but he understood that he had better be careful.

Our first confrontations with the union brought a reduction in the ranks of the Safety Committee. Reuther had been killed, and the international was using that as an excuse to keep the hall closed. We insisted on the right to use our own hall. We were using the conference room to get information, write leaflets, discuss strategy, etc. Elroy Richardson came in and told us to leave. We stood up and confronted him, saying he would have to throw us out. He said he'd call the police. We said, "Fine, Elroy, you want to call the police, call the police." He went away and left us alone. The next day, when we came back, the conference room was locked. Some of the unionists felt uneasy and talked about going to lunch. James Edwards and I went over to the door. I tried to pick the door with my knife, and we put our shoulders to it. Then we went outside and found a window. We got screwdrivers and got the conference-room window open. We had to actually break into our own hall. We got in and opened the conference-room door. As soon as they saw this, some of them went to lunch and never came back. We started having the meeting, and another of the stewards got more and more agitated. He got on the verge of physically attacking me because I had broken into the hall. He had a very heavy thing on how Walter Reuther had been the black man's friend and ally. He was very insulted that I, a white man, had desecrated the memory of Reuther's death. He went into this thing with me and left and never came back. That was another contradiction in our ranks.

The reaction of the people in my own department to the strike bothered me. I was on the West Gate, where most of my department comes in. I'll never forget this. Almost unanimously, the people in my department and people I knew did not go in when they saw me picketing. They talked to me, and some of them even gave out leaflets. What a lot did, though, was go to another gate. I couldn't understand that for a long time. What it meant was that they could relate to me as a person, but not to the politics of the situation. There was the additional problem of how they related to the ELRUM people who were on the gate with me. This reinforced my assessment that we moved too fast. We had to do more agitation. We cost Chrysler 2174 axles, but we could have done more. We also succeeded in exposing the Chrysler-union cooperation to the workers in the plant. That is, we produced the documentation on all the safety violations the union wouldn't deal with. This was dramaticized by the death of Gary Thompson. Even the UAW couldn't ignore that. Our strike lifted the consciousness of everybody. It used to be that workers wouldn't take the leaflets or would throw them away. Now, people at the plant almost always take the leaflet, put it in their pocket, and read it inside. That is very positive and indicates a level of consciousness higher than in most plants and higher than it had been in their plant.

How workers relate to material given at the gate isn't understood by most people in the movement. When *Wildcat* first appeared, ELRUM tried to front them off by physical threats. The *Wildcat* people came back, and ELRUM backed off. ELRUM remained extremely hostile to the *Wildcat,* even after it became known I was associated with it. ELRUM had the opinion that the *Wildcat* was from the Communist Party, and they had minimal respect for the CP. They thought the *Wildcat* was racist and an outsider sheet.

I would like to say something about other radical groups which made interventions from 1970 onwards. Up front, let me say that I am presently a member of the Motor City Labor League, a Marxist-Leninist revolutionary group. Now, Progressive Labor came out to the plant in the summer of 1970 and started selling their paper, *Challenge.* I approached them at the gate one day. This was after I was fired. I looked like an ordinary worker. I was working at Budd Wheel at that time. They assumed I worked at Eldon, and I was shocked at how they related to a person whom they perceived as a typical worker. They were condescending. I ran a little bit about my involvement in the safety strike, and they were very critical of that. They said their policy was to ignore the unions. They assured me that they would be there every week and were not fly-by-night leftists. What happened was that they managed to antagonize a lot of folks, as is their fashion. This was done to the extent that one day some white workers came out and beat the shit out of them.

That indicated a failure of sorts. They told me the same thing had happened at Cadillac. That physical assault was the end of their presence, and they haven't been seen since.

The reaction of the Socialist Workers Party is interesting because I'm not aware they had any reaction at all to what was going on at Eldon. They never contacted Sims, myself, or anyone in ELRUM to speak at a forum or do any internal education for them. I want to say something about their Detroit activities in the late sixties. At that time I was working for the Better Business Bureau, and I used to go to their Friday-night socialist forums at the Debs Hall. I went pretty regularly for almost a year. Not once did anyone ever approach me politically or be even minimally friendly. I was like a fixture for a year, but they just ignored me. Maybe they thought I was an agent or something, but that has always struck me as a totally ripped practice. You have to be blind or myopic to ignore what was happening at Eldon, and I have never seen them relate in any way out there. If they have worker cadre, they sure as hell aren't at Eldon, Budd Wheel, or Dodge Main.

The only other groups to do any work are the Motor City Labor League, Revolutionary Union, and International Socialists. Revolutionary Union has mainly tried to get on with some stewards at Eldon, but they haven't distributed leaflets or done any public work. International Socialists have been extremely interested in Jordan Sims. They wanted to do a national campaign around his discharge in pretty much the way the Angela Davis thing worked for the CP. The Motor City Labor League has had a public presence in the form of leaflets, and we have been working with the various people and with Jordan Sims.

It's a truism that struggle creates strength. It is also true that you have to find issues that affect people's lives and that you agitate and organize around those issues with the point of view of making some gains and of exposing the concrete contradictions. The aftermath of our strike was that Jordan Sims ran for President of that local [Local 961]. He maintained his membership and was narrowly defeated by Frank McKinnon, the white steward. The election was literally stolen from Jordan. Now, there is a scandal about the embezzlement of funds by McKinnon and other officials. Very large sums have disappeared for over ten years, and apparently George Merrelli, the Regional Director, knew about it. That would make it reach right into Solidarity House. People in the plant have gotten a pretty high consciousness about this whole set-up. We managed to get the Department of Labor into the process. We showed we were correct on the statutes and the contract. They had to expose their hand in a situation affecting the health and lives of those workers. We have developed a hard core of people at Eldon who go to union meetings.

There's 60-70 people who know how to function. The company and union could just give up, but they can't do that because of the key nature of Eldon. The stakes are too high. But the company, union, and Labor Department continue to shit on people, which just creates more strength for us. Eventually, they'll have to move the factory out of Detroit or let us have it.

3

In the stamping plant, which we know is a hazardous area anyway, I got my fingertip severed off in a press. They sewed it back on. . . . But that isn't as serious as some of the other things that have happened in the Rouge area in the past. Six men in a basic-oxygen plant were killed, and there wasn't enough left of those men to put in a decent shopping bag.

Wesley Johns, in a statement to a People's Court convened by the Motor City Labor League, April 3, 1973

John Taylor's recounting of the struggle at Eldon points up some of the problems facing the militants who wanted to carry out the RUM strategy. Many nationalist-minded blacks were attracted to the RUMs. Although very militant and vocal, the RUMs often held back the development of class consciousness among other workers attracted to the wider League program. This gap between secondary and primary leadership grew wider after the strike of January 1969. All the members of the League executive would have curbed some of the more counterproductive language in ELRUM leaflets, but there were occasions when Baker and Wooten sanctioned approaches some of the other League leaders would not have approved of. Excessive emphasis on the contradictions between workers not only alienated whites who might have been neutral or sympathetic, it turned away many blacks. Older workers, who had a large stake in improving working conditions, especially disliked the wholesale attacks on "hoinkies" and "Toms," considering them incorrect ways to get sustained and positive action. ELRUM's attitude toward individuals such as Jordan Sims and supporters of *Wildcat* posed another kind of problem. ELRUM was somewhat sectarian toward them and judged that Sims, at best, was an honest reformist stuck in trade-union attitudes, and at worst could turn out to be another of those "traitors from within" the League warned about. The consequence of ELRUM's attitude was that the organization drew too rigid a line of demarcation between itself and other forces in the plant. Ken Cockrel voiced the additional criticism that the ELRUM workers fired in January had failed to build a defense committee in the plant and in the neighborhoods. He believed that the hostile ELRUM attitude toward white participation and working with nonrevolutionary blacks was retarding rather than building their struggle.

ELRUM clearly failed to rally women to its ranks. Two of the workers killed at the plant during this period were women, and their deaths were an indication of the harassment and poor working conditions women faced. It was an open secret that dating foremen had its rewards, just as refusing them had its punishments. One young black woman who suffered from drowsiness caused by excessive noise got a job classification which would take her away from moving machinery, but she could not get it acted upon because of union indifference and the hostility of her foremen. Several other women in well-known incidents on the shop floor, were forced to tell off supervisors and union representatives after they became tired of fending off constant sexual advances. ELRUM bulletins spoke of the special problems facing the "sisters" in the plant, but ELRUM never developed a concrete program for dealing with such problems.

ELRUM activists generally bypassed the UAW altogether once they were out of the plant. This caused a gradual breakdown of ties with some of the more militant workers in the factory. Jordan

Sims, even after being fired in 1970, went to union meetings regularly and organized his forces as he might have had he been still working inside the plant. Sims continued to contend for power in the union, and on May 23, 1973, after several highly questionable elections, he defeated Frank McKinnon 1599 to 735 and became President of Local 961. As an elected union official and still co-chairman of the United National Caucus, Sims was now able to carry on his fight from within the UAW hierarchy. He demonstrated an honest and aggressive unionist stance during his first year in office.

Citing shortcomings in the ELRUM performance in no way diminishes the importance of the work carried out over a two-year period. A handful of revolutionary-minded production-line workers had set themselves against the company and the union, and against the timidity and weariness of many workers. Taylor, a white Appalachian, called them exemplary; and their nationalism notwithstanding, he considered them the best leadership to have emerged in the plant. Many who criticized ELRUM for making mistakes retained their jobs and continued to keep their mouths shut while the ELRUM men were fired and often blacklisted from the industry. Students and teachers at universities who didn't put in eight to ten hours a day at Eldon did not always comprehend that the clumsiness of some phrasing or tactical action was as much a product of fatigue as of poorly developed political skills. The League leadership itself was concerned with arriving at a proper evaluation of the Eldon experience. From the summer of 1970 onward, the League began a serious rethinking of its tactics, strategies, and personnel.

4

I don't own anything. I'm about $1000 in debt. I work at Dodge Truck. . . . I started on the afternoon shift,

*working ten hours a day, six days a week. I punched in at
4:30 and punched out at 3:00 in the morning. I slept the
rest of the day and then got up and went back to work. I
work in the paint department, which is on the second
floor, and during the summer the temperature is about
130 to 150 degrees.*

Richard Wieske, in a statement to a People's Court convened by the Motor City Labor League, April 3, 1973

No plant seemed more different from Eldon than General Motor's
much-vaunted Lordstown Vega factory in Ohio. Constructed in a
farming area adjacent to steel-mill towns, Lordstown was tech-
nologically the most ambitious factory in the auto industry.
Lordstown was operated by the GM Assembly Division (GMAD),
which engineered jobs to a fraction of a second and weighed paint
wasted in the dye vats by the ounce. Lordstown bragged of the
fastest assembly line in the world! It produced 103 cars per hour.
Dodge Main officially turned out only 64 cars an hour, although
workers said production often went up to 76. At Ford's Mahwah
plant, the official speed was 52 cars an hour. The Lordstown
"miracle," according to GMAD, was due to mechanization of
jobs, robots, and sophisticated computer controls: in short, automation. Twenty-six Unimate robots did most of the welding.
The Assembly Line Production and Control Activity (ALPACA)
was the main computer control while Product Assurance Control
(PAC) supervised actual production. Best of all, most of the 8000
workers at Lordstown were young and so anxious to work that a
trailer-camp city opened right across the turnpike from the factory.
There were no large minority groups in the factory, and the
workforce had no known old-time radicals or hard-core unionists.
The only problem with Lordstown was that it didn't work. The
Vega turned out to be one of the worst-built cars in America, and
two years after GMAD took over, 97 percent of the workers voted
to strike over working conditions. The three-week Lordstown

strike of 1972 destroyed the automation myth. Unable to explain the strike in realistic terms, the media called it an "industrial Woodstock." The simple truth was that the list of Lordstown complaints could have been written by any worker at Eldon or Dodge Main. If the streamlined production of a highly automated plant at Lordstown was in any way significantly different from what transpired at older plants, the difference was not evident either to the average worker on the line or in the quality of the final product.

Emma Rothschild devoted a chapter to Lordstown in her perceptive book, *Paradise Lost: The Decline of the Auto-Industrial Age*. Her conclusion was: "The major principle of Lordstown production is the speedup, as developed in the 1910's." The line moved so rapidly that workers could not keep up with it and often did their jobs improperly. The quality-control supervisors, not wanting to increase costs in their departments, let the defective parts pass, hoping they would be caught somewhere down the line. Some 23,000 Vegas had to be recalled for defective parts in 1970, vindicating anew Ralph Nader's evaluation of Detroit cars as "unsafe at any speed." The workers at Lordstown complained of the dreadful monotony of the work, as well as the speed. They complained of capricious layoffs and disciplinary crackdowns. Many of them voiced hatred of the assembly line itself and questioned the necessity of capitalist division of work. Almost all the workers stated that they were not going to put in thirty or forty years in the plants the way their parents had. They wanted more from life and were willing to do more than just talk about it. Absenteeism, especially on Mondays and Fridays, soared. Management complained of chronic and wholesale tardiness, sabotage on the line, and "unreasonable" worker attitudes.

GM complained about its workers; but like Chrysler, it refused to improve the conditions of work or real wages. True to their hard-headed, tough traditions, GM executives said that whenever there was a reorganization and consolidation in the plants there would be strikes. Ten reorganizations by GMAD had produced eight strikes. That was how it was in the auto industry. The quality problem was overblown, according to the executives, and would be corrected through managerial adjustments. Joseph Godfrey, the head of GMAD, told *Automotive News* in October 1971, ''The workers may complain about monotony, but years spent in the factories leads me to believe that they like to do their jobs semi-automatically. If you interject new things, you spoil the rhythm of the job, and work gets fouled up.''

As workers were killed and maimed in the plants, and as they challenged the necessity of the assembly-line system itself, top executives painted pastels of happy and affluent workers. In early 1972 George B. Morris, Jr., Vice-President of General Motors and Director of Labor Relations, gave this impression of how a $10,000-a-year worker lived to Haynes Johnson and Nick Kotz of the *Washington Post,* who included it in their book, *The Unions*:

> . . . he lives in Flint, or one of the communities around Flint, he's got a hell of a nice home, two-car garage. He has two cars.
>
> He's got a trailer that he hooks on the back of one of those cars and he hauls his boat up north and he's got a hell of a big outboard motor on the back of that and does that on the weekend in the summer. And he probably has a summer place up north, too, on one of the fine lakes in northern Michigan.
>
> In the wintertime, he puts a couple of snowmobiles on that trailer and hauls them up there. He leaves Friday night while you and I work.
>
> I guess I'm not affluent by my definitions here. But this fellow has everything you could aspire to. You come to our plants and look in our parking lots on Friday and see how many of them—even second shift people—will be there with their trailers and their campers and have them all loaded.
>
> . . . Do you think all the people that are driving up I-75 are corporation presidents and bankers and stock brokers

and lawyers? The hell they are. They're hourly rated people that work in those plants. What more do you want? If affluence is too strong a word, this is certainly not a pauper society we're talking about. This is a fellow who has aspired to material things and has them.

Chapter Six

Finally Got the News

1

*Many music lovers don't know that nearly a whole
generation of original and highly talented musicians in
Detroit were either snuffed out or forced to flee Detroit
to keep their music careers alive. You'd come into a
studio, cut a record, and they'd pay you maybe $20 and
a bottle of whiskey. It didn't matter if the records sold
ten copies or if they sold ten thousand.*

Eddie "Guitar" Burns, interview in *Fifth Estate*,
September 5, 1973

In Detroit, more than anywhere else in America, popular culture
and the political rebellions of the sixties were interwoven. An early
sequence in *Finally Got the News,* a film the League of Revolutionary Black Workers made about its activities in 1969-1970,
shows one auto worker picking up another in front of his house.
They are first-shift workers, and as they drive down one of the
expressways named after an auto industrialist, the only commentary is an urban blues song.

*Opposite page: Mural at St. Bernard's Church depicting black leaders and
supporters. The portrait of Elijah Muhammad has been defaced.*

Please, Mr. Foreman, slow down your assembly line.
Please, Mr. Foreman, slow down your assembly line.
No, I don't mind workin', but I do mind dyin'.
Workin' twelve hours a day,
Seven long days a week,
I lie down and try to rest, but Lord knows I'm too tired to sleep.
Lord knows, I'm too tired to sleep.
Please, Mr. Foreman, slow down your assembly line.
I said, Lord, why don't you slow down that assembly line?
No, I don't mind workin', but I do mind dyin'.

The song was written and recorded by Joe L. Carter in 1965 when he was a production-line worker at Ford Rouge. Like most of the Detroit blues singers, Joe L., as he billed himself, had been born in the South, worked regular jobs during the day, and played mostly on weekends. The Detroit blues sound had never had much of a mass audience. Other than brief spots on some black radio stations, its exposure was mainly limited to the red-light district around Hastings Street which began to be torn down in the late fifties in the name of urban renewal. The blues singers often had colorful names and played unusual instruments. The only one to achieve national fame was John Lee Hooker, but there were many others, including Washboard Willie, One-String Sam, Doc Ross, Faye Thompson, Eddie Kirkland, and Bobo Jenkins. They played a down-and-dirty urban blues that spoke of the agony of everyday industrial life. John Lee Hooker worked in a steel mill. Doc Ross worked for GM. Bobo Jenkins pumped gas at a filling station, and he worked for twenty-four years for Chrysler. Roselyn, a folk singer who made her appearance in the seventies, told *Fifth Estate* reporter Pat Halley in September 1973: "Anybody who plays music in Detroit plays the blues sometimes." Halley commented, "Anybody who lives in Detroit lives the blues sometimes, if not all the time."

During the sixties, groups began substituting vocals for in-strumental lines and mixing in gospel elements. Berry Gordy, an autoworker, founded Motown Records, and soon the entire

country was listening to a new "soul" sound. The most famous
Motown group was Diana Ross and the Supremes, a group of
women who began as a teenage trio trying to sing their way free
from the poverty of one of the city's most dangerous housing
projects. Most of the other Motown singers had similar back-
grounds. Small groups all over the city practiced faithfully and
performed whenever possible in hopes of making it to the super big
time, which, for Diana Ross, the girl next door, meant million-
plus album sales, appearances on network television, and a starring role in Hollywood's *Lady Sings the Blues.* For every Marvin
Gaye and Mary Wells, for every Aretha Franklin (Reverend
Franklin's daughter) and Della Reese, there were hundreds of
unknowns singing, writing, and performing all over the city.

The music of the white population of the city had not fared
nearly so well. The fifties and sixties all but wiped out public
performances. The gypsy violins of Del Ray were ignored to
death. The music of Eastern Europe was forgotten, or transformed
into the champagne froth of a Lawrence Welk, or reduced to the
polkas played at Polish weddings. The Greek music which had
thrived around Monroe Street for decades underwent flagrant
commercialization following the success of the films *Never on
Sunday* and *Zorba the Greek.* The old-timers who played
mountain tunes on folk instruments disappeared as electric
bouzoukis took over with tunes bearing little relationship to the
bouzouki music of Greece, which had clearly political lyrics and a
waterfront origin. Most Arabic music degenerated into mere
accompaniment for belly dancers, who sometimes were the same
gyrators who used to perform at the Empress Burlesk. Aside from
the music of groups building on black musical traditions, the only
white music that prospered was the country-western style transported north by migrating Appalachians. On Detroit bandstands
such as those along Jefferson Avenue, Third Avenue, and around
the ballpark, small groups mixed traditional country favorites with
new and original compositions. Eventually the style broke out of
its characterization as "Nashville" sound in much the same way
black music had broken out of the "race" music category.

The inclusion of Detroit music in the League film was not accidental. The League people had always been supportive of the popular and fine arts, and their ranks included painters and poets. *ICV* gave lavish space to original artwork, poetry, cartoons, and photography. The *South End* carried on this policy to such a degree that Sam Cohen, an anarcho-Reichian playwright who made Wayne one of his foci, stated that the Watson regime at the *South End* was more friendly to him than any other regime in the decade. RUM leaflets and newsletters featured original drawings and poetry. One anonymous mock-heroic poem which came out of the Dodge Main struggles became an organizational trademark, with the words FRUM, CADRUM, JARUM, and so on substituted for DRUM.

> Deep in the gloom
> of the oil-filled pit
> where the engine rolls down the line,
> we challenge the doom
> of dying in shit
> while strangled by a swine. . . . . .
> . . . . . . For hours and years
> we've sweated tears
> trying to break our chain. . . . . .
> But we broke our backs
> and died in packs
> to find our manhood slain. . . . . .
> But now we stand
> for DRUM's at hand
> to lead our Freedom fight,
> and now 'til then
> we'll unite like men. . . . . .
> For now we know our might,
> and damn the plantation
> and the whole Chrysler nation
> for DRUM has dried our tears,
> and now as we die
> we've a different cry

> for now we hold our spears!
> U.A.W. is scum
> OUR THING IS DRUM! ! ! !

Other popular and fine arts were part of the Detroit scene of the sixties. At one time, there were six independent theatre groups performing on proscenium stages, in coffee houses, and in church basements. All of them had substantial black participation, and the Concept East was founded to stage plays written by blacks and performed mainly by blacks. The most ambitious of the theatre groups was the Unstable Coffeehouse, an enterprise run by Edith Carroll Cantor, a socialist. The Unstabled featured poetry, chess, and dance some weeknights; and on weekends, plays early in the evening, folksinging later on, and jazz after hours. The Unstabled produced works by Detroiter Ron Milner and Reverend Malcolm Boyd, who was then based in Detroit, as well as a rich selection of plays by Jean Genet, Le Roi Jones (Imamu Baraka), William Saroyan, Tennessee Williams, Edward Albee, Jack Gelber, and Samuel Beckett. One original play called *Sitdown '37* was created for the UAW and was presented in Flint on the 25th anniversary of the Flint sitdown strikes which unionized GM. The play was well received by the workers, the majority of whom had participated in the struggle. Many wept openly, and there was wild cheering at the closing scenes of triumph.

Two quite different publishing experiments aimed at mass audiences appeared at the same time as the theatre groups. One was a magazine called *On the Town* that was black-owned but interracially staffed. It was published from 1963 to 1964 and tried to combine bar listings and humor with serious commentary on music, the new Detroit theatre, and politics. It circulated approximately 10,000 copies of each issue, almost entirely within the center city. A more aesthetically oriented venture that continued to thrive in the seventies was Broadside Press, founded by librarian and poet Dudley Randall. Begun with private savings, Broadside became one of the most important black-poetry publishers in the United States. Randall introduced poets such as

Sonia Sanchez, Don Lee, Nikki Giovanni, and Etheridge Knight. Broadside published a book which honored Malcolm X with poetry by black and white writers, and it published many established writers such as Gwendolyn Brooks and Le Roi Jones.

Detroiters have always complained about the neglect of the arts in their city, but virtually every schoolchild in the city has been taken to see the Diego Rivera murals in the Detroit Institute of Arts. Covering four immense walls, the frescoes depict automaking at Ford's River Rouge plant. The main panels are montages in which machines hover like robot monsters, spewing forth flames and poisonous gases as workers with glaring eyes, and curses under their breath, labor before hostile foremen and plant visitors. Sharp, almost cartoonlike insets ridicule Henry Ford, while small details such as red stars on a glove and a handwritten WE WANT on a workman's paper cap emphasize Rivera's revolutionary perspective. The murals are capped by a homage to the four races of mankind and the natural abundance of the earth. The renowned Mexican muralist completed his nine months' work in 1933, and many city leaders wanted the walls whitewashed as soon as the scaffolding came down. The *Detroit News* and the Catholic Archdiocese were particularly incensed, but the work was spared the destruction accorded the Rivera murals done for New York's Rockefeller Center, which were demolished by the same people who had commissioned them. The Rivera frescoes became familiar to the people of the Motor City through the years, and radicals were especially fond of using them in their literature. Sections of the murals appear in *Finally Got the News* and on the cover of a 1973 publication of the Motor City Labor League.

The Rivera murals at the Detroit Institute were matched by street developments in 1968. On a building on Mack Avenue, under the supervision of artists who had done similar work in Chicago, black Detroiters painted a Wall of Dignity. Some of the scenes depicted the glories of ancient Africa, but most were a litany of black struggles in America. The figures of Marcus Garvey and Malcolm X were prominent, yet most of the work focused on anonymous and angry blacks smouldering with rebellion. Across the street from the Wall, the facade of St. Bernard's Church was decorated with similar work. The huge center facade depicted a black Pharoah, while side panels emphasized mass struggle and contemporary leaders such as Martin Luther King, Elijah Muhammad, Adam Clayton Powell, and Malcolm X. Most of the work was done by Eugene Eda and Bill Walker, the artists who also did much of the work on the Wall of Dignity.

Diego Rivera himself could not have wished for a more popular or public art. Bill Walker was quoted in a September 1971 *Liberation* article written by John Weber as saying, "In questioning myself as to how I could best give my art to Black people, I came to the realization that art must belong to ALL people. That is when I first began to think of public art." John Weber, a white associate of Walker's, wrote that over thirty such projects had been done in Chicago, and that by 1969 they had begun to involve white and Latin artists as well as blacks. Like most revolutionary and mass art, the muralist movement was little discussed in aesthetic journals. Needless to say, no funds were available for keeping Detroit's Wall of Dignity in a state of good repair.

As always in the Motor City, traces of the history of the working class, of racial conflict, and of the popular arts mingled on the same neglected corners. One block west of the Wall of Dignity was an Arab community center where authentic Middle Eastern music was sometimes performed, and several blocks beyond the Arab center were blues bars. On nearby Garland Street, there was the now forgotten house which had been the scene of a race riot in 1924 when it was purchased by Dr. Ossian Sweet, the area's first black home-owner. Several blocks to the east of the Wall were the Mack stamping plant and the former Briggs plant, two Chrysler factories with long histories of radical worker organizations. A mile to the south, in another decaying neighborhood, a string of hillbilly music bars was adjacent to more factories owned by Chrysler. In the midst of all this stood the building on which the murals were painted. It had been burnt out during the Great Rebellion. Formerly, it had been called Fairview Gardens and had been used as a roller-skating rink and a wrestling emporium. On the bricks upon which the Wall of Dignity was painted, there had been wrestling posters advertising various ethnic heroes and villians such as Killer Kowalski, The Sheik, Chief Don Eagle, Mr. Togo, Man Mountain Dean, and Lou Klein.

2

I think Finally Got the News *represents both a breaking of new ground and simultaneously an endpost of some kind. At the same time it signals the end of white film-makers making films about other people's struggles, it re-opens a whole area and direction long ignored by the New Left—that of the lives and importance of ordinary working people in this country.*

Peter Gessner, film-maker, in a letter to Dan Georgakas, July 1, 1972

Finally Got the News, the League's most ambitious art project, began in the spring of 1969. A group of whites working in New York Newsreel, a radical film-makers' collective, had the idea of making a film about DRUM in much the same style as the ones they had done on the Black Panthers. Although most of the Newsreel group of that period favored the Black Panther-Weatherman thesis that the revolution would be led by a relatively small group of elite professionals with a mass following based in the lumpen proletariat, the group that wanted to do the Detroit film had a worker orientation. In June of 1969, Jim Morrison headed a small Newsreel delegation to Detroit, where they collected over twenty hours of taped conversations and gathered various League documents. Most of the help given to them was from Cockrel, Hamlin, and Watson.

The raw material gathered by the Morrison group was favorably received by New York Newsreel, but there was some hesitation about providing funds for an actual film. An exasperated Morrison took fund-raising into his own hands by undertaking an ill-fated hashish-smuggling scheme that netted him a ten-year prison sentence when he was caught at the Canadian border. Morrison served over three years before escaping from an honor farm when he realized he was not going to be paroled. He remained at large as of 1974 and was given a screen credit on the final film, although he did not do much work on the actual production.

Shortly after Morrison's venture, the main body of Newsreel came up with funds, and a Newsreel unit was sent to Detroit. From the beginning, the group had two factions. Stewart Bird, René Lichtman, and Peter Gessner saw their task as one of making a film which accurately presented the strategy and activities of the League. The others had a grander objective. They felt that both the white and the black movements in Detroit needed to be updated by an injection of Weatherman and Panther thinking. Rather than making films, this faction headed by George DePugh set about making an ideological intervention into the local political structure.

One of the first problems confronted by Newsreel was the attitude of the League itself. A majority of the leadership believed in a low public profile. Many of them did not want any film-makers, much less white film-makers, covering meetings, demonstrations, and factory agitation. They thought workers who were moving toward them might be frightened off. They also feared that the film would ultimately be useful to the companies, police, and union for gathering intelligence about League activities. John Watson had a much different vision of what the film could be. He saw the tremendous outreach a movie would provide both in educating and in organizing. Watson took personal responsibility for the film and secured League approval for the project.

The division of opinion over the film was a precursor of the issues that would cause a split within the League ranks in 1971. Those who were most dubious about the film were the people most concerned about the dangers of premature national exposure, of coalitions with whites, and of the use of mass media. They expressed their uneasiness in many ways. During the early stages of shooting, they did not stop nationalistically oriented workers from running off white camera crews, and they often failed to inform the film-makers about key public events. Many of the League units under their personal supervision never appeared in the film. Their hostile attitude eased as the film-making proceeded, but it was never totally erased.

The reluctance of these League members to have a film made about them was in marked contrast to the attitude of many radicals in the sixties, who often seemed to measure their success by the number of times they appeared on television. The League rejected such a publicity-conscious approach and was very concerned with the image the Newsreel film might project. The League definitely wanted the usual "by any means necessary" rhetoric omitted or curtailed. Watson insisted that the film be conceived within a teaching rather than a reporting framework. He knew that Newsreel's audiences were primarily the white college students who made up the bulk of the "movement," but he wanted this film's explicit Marxist message to be directed toward an audience of black workers. Although the typical Newsreel audience would benefit from the film, their needs would be secondary to those of black workers. Bird, Lichtman, and Gessner were more pleased than upset by his orientation, but many difficult meetings were required to hammer out specific methods.

Watson's first notion was to use a lot of heavy Marxist terminology and quotations. He was soon persuaded that it would be more effective to have different League leaders speak informally in the same way they would speak to a group of workers. The title of the film, *Finally Got the News,* was taken from the words chanted by General Baker to workers during the 1970 elections at Dodge Main:

> Finally got the news
> How your dues are being used.
> Be bad, be bad, be bad, be bad, be bad!
> Can't do nothing if you ain't bad!

The approach ultimately adopted was to give a theoretical view of how the working class, led by black workers, could make a revolution, with most of the actual footage showing how the League handled concrete problems arising from its revolutionary perspective. The effective montage history of American labor which opens the film was primarily the idea of Stewart Bird, who saw it as a way of covering a complex subject with images rather than words. The ultimate decisions about this and other sequences were worked out in joint meetings. Watson generally indicated the overall direction, while the Newsreel team solved the technical problems. Both groups agreed that League people should be trained in technical skills. This training did not work out as well as it could have, but toward the end of the collaboration League members were doing some of the camera work and other technical tasks.

The first half of *Finally Got the News* presents a clear exposition of the idea that black people in the United States have been and continue to be exploited primarily because they are workers. In an opening sequence, Watson says:

> You get a lot of arguments that black people are not numerous enough in America to revolt, that they will be wiped out. This neglects our economic position. . . . There are groups that can make the whole system cease functioning. These are auto workers, bus drivers, postal workers, steel workers, and others who play a crucial role in the money flow, the flow of materials, the creation of production. By and large, black people are overwhelmingly in those kinds of jobs.

Scenes within the Detroit factories and interviews with local leaders such as Ron March and Chuck Wooten supplement the more general approach of Watson with specific details. These sequences emphasize the deteriorating work and safety conditions within the factories. They reach an artistic peak when the off-camera voice of Ken Cockrel denounces capitalism in a long tirade that can only be described as a prose poem. Against placid scenes

of executives ''working'' at their desks, a ''voice from the ghetto''
says:

> They give you little bullshit amounts of money—wages
> and so forth—and then they steal all that shit back from
> you in terms of the way they have their other thing set
> up, that old credit-stick-'em-up gimmick society —con-
> sumer credit—buy shit, buy shit—on credit. He gives
> you a little bit of money to cool your ass and then steals it
> all back with shit called interest, which is the price of
> money. They are mother-fucking, non-producing, non-
> existing bastards dealing with paper. . . .
>
> He is in mining! He went to Exeter. He went to
> Harvard. He went to Yale. He went to the Wharton
> School of Business. And he is in ''mining!'' It is these
> mother-fuckers who deal with intangibles who are
> rewarded by this society. The more abstract and in-
> tangible your service, the bigger the reward.
>
> What are stocks? A stock certificate is evidence of
> something which is real. A stock is evidence of *owner-
> ship*. He who owns and controls receives—profit!
>
> This man is fucking with shit in Bolivia. He is fucking
> with shit in Chile. He is Kennicott. He is Anaconda. He
> is United Fruit. He is in mining! He's in what? He ain't
> never produced anything his whole life. Investment
> banker. Stockbroker. Insurance man. He don't do
> nothing.
>
> We see that this whole society exists and rests upon
> workers and this whole mother-fucking society is con-
> trolled by this little clique which is parasitic, vulturistic,
> cannibalistic, and is sucking and destroying the life of
> workers everywhere; and we must stop it because it
> is—evil!

Another telling sequence in this part of the film deals with two
Ford executives, one black and one white. Only the black

executive speaks; but like some two-bit actor from a vulgar Marxist playlet, his white superior chews on a cigar and leers approvingly at every word. The black explains how company and union come together to work for the benefit of the ''greater society.'' This ventriloquist act would have been farcical in a fiction film, but it succeeds admirably as a real-life interview.

The first section of the film concludes with the 1970 plant election at Dodge Main. Rather than lock-stepped, black-bereted, leather-jacketed Panther units, the film shows rather ordinary people becoming very angry with the system. Workers by the busloads arrive waving clenched fists and shouting, ''DRUM-DRUM-DRUM-DRUM.'' General Baker is heard over the megaphone directing the chanting as the workers, young and old, men and women, enter the union hall. They have to pass other workers, many of whom are black. These men wear union caps and stare at the DRUM forces in the way police stare at peace marchers. The class line is drawn very sharply in terms of psychological identification as well as economics. Some workers have identified with the master, and some with the revolution.

What is most striking in these emotionally charged scenes is that the struggle transcends a simple plant election. The people who are politically in motion are people who work on the line every day, people who drive their own cars, people who own homes, people who have families, people who may even own the proverbial color television set. These same people are very obviously and very enthusiastically supporting an anti-capitalist revolutionary organization. Workers viewing such footage can identify with the kind of people participating and with the kind of action being taken. They can see that being a radical does not require becoming an incredible, gun-slinging hero who defies the police with every breath. An election is one of the lowest levels of mass action, but it is mass action nonetheless, and not elite action, just as the strike and the boycott are mass actions in which the people serve themselves rather than relying upon a group of elite warriors.

The second half of the film never regains the sharp ideological and artistic focus of the part which ends with the Dodge election.

There is a valiant attempt to deal with the relationship of white workers to revolutionary black workers that might have been the subject of an entire second film. Retired Appalachian-born white workers are shown sitting on the porches of their frame houses. They drink beer and play guitars as they put forth a very heavy anti-company line that comes near to matching the RUM positions until an old man concludes, ''Everyone in this country is almost in revolt. We want to get more money. Everyone else is getting their share. Certain groups are doing good—the colored and the mothers on welfare.'' Watson's voice cuts in to explain the paradox created by racism: ''The white workers face the same contradictions in production and life as blacks do. If they work harder, they think the enemy is 'the nigger.' If life is worse, the problem is 'crime in the streets.' . . . [George] Wallace raps the money barons and the niggers; and these white workers love to hear it. . . . Many white workers end up being counter-revolutionary in the face of a daily oppression which should make them the staunchest of revolutionaries. . . . We are calling for the uplifting of the working class as a whole.''

Watson's analysis is sound, but he offers no solutions, not even a transition strategy. His lack of program in this area reflects the League's indecision on the matter. Filmed interviews with white working-class students pick up the problem from another angle. The students speak poignantly of the alienation felt by their fathers and mothers. They argue for an alliance with the League, but it is clear that they speak as individuals. The scenes are a kind of brave hope in the future that only succeeds in revealing the enormous problem racism presents to those who would unite the working class.

Similar problems surround the treatment of black working women and the role of community organizing. Hurried sequences do little more than register the film-makers' awareness that such topics need further investigation. Again, the film reflects the League's poorly thought-out positions on these vital questions. Some footage showing the funeral of a ten-year-old boy accidentally shot by the police is decidedly out of rhythm with the rest of the film in spite of its attempt to link the life of the factory with the violence of everyday life. Ken Cockrel's summation interview is less effective than it might have been because it follows these disconnected and only partially thought-out sections.

The erratic second half of the film is partly the result of problems that nearly destroyed the film completely. While the three Newsreel film-makers already mentioned were working on making a film, the rest of the Newsreel group in Detroit was involved in politics. As part of their program of intervention, the Newsreel people organized an anti-repression conference to which they invited Robert Williams, recently returned from exile in China, Emory Douglas of the Black Panthers, and Ken Cockrel. The ideological tensions between the Panthers and the League had become public knowledge. Cockrel emphasized that as of that time (January 1970) no one in the League's orbit had been killed by police or had been sentenced to a jail term. His tone made it clear that he thought the League's tactics were the major reason for this fact, and that Panther tactics were not needed or wanted in the city of Detroit.

In spite of its lack of a single black member, the Detroit Newsreel group continued to push the Panther line as well as maintain pressure for a Weatherman approach among whites. The radical forces within the city became increasingly annoyed that a small outside group with no local membership base and no local work continued to advocate projects contrary to the wishes and detrimental to the safety of local activists. The League, for its part, became indignant when it learned fees and expense money were paid to the Panthers by a group that always claimed poverty when approached for funds needed by local people. The mounting pressure on Newsreel caused an internal collapse, and the group decided to give its equipment to a cultural group in Ann Arbor and to leave the city. The League responded by seizing the Newsreel equipment on the revolutionary ground that the group had raised money for the purpose of making radical films, which was what the League proposed to continue doing, and on the legal ground that the seizure was in lieu of unpaid speakers' fees. Bird, Gessner, and Lichtman did not approve of the manner in which the League took the equipment, but they agreed to continue working on the film as individuals even though the Detroit Newsreel group had ceased to exist.

3

Near the freeway
you stop and wonder what came off,
recall the snowstorm where you lost it all,
the wolverine, the northern bear, the wolf
caught out, ice and steel raining
from the foundries in a shower
of human breath. . . .

Philip Levine, ''Coming Home,
Detroit, 1968''

Shortly after the seizure of the Newsreel equipment, John Watson founded Black Star Productions. A fund-raising letter of late 1970, addressed to the general public and signed by Rachel Bishop, described Black Star's objective as ''to produce and distribute films dealing with the most crucial social and political issues of our times.'' John Watson, in a similar fund-raising letter dated May 5, 1971, said Black Star films would serve ''as a means of political education and as a real alternative to the current lack of such films.'' Black Star was organized as a component of the League, yet its haphazard staff, at one time or another, included the three former Newsreel people, Nick Medvecky, and an Italian with experience in making revolutionary films. The immediate goal of Black Star was to arrange for the widest possible distribution of

Finally Got the News and to use that film as a basis for soliciting funds for future films.

Watson made a trip to Europe in the spring of 1970 to promote Black Star. He was interested in selling copies of *Finally Got the News* to European distributors, and he wanted to secure additional film-making equipment, which was cheaper to purchase in Europe. He visited Scandinavia, England, Germany, France, and Italy. His greatest success came in Italy, where a segment of the film was sold to Italian television and copies were acquired by extraparliamentary groups and the Italian Communist Party for distribution to their members and supporters. The film was also shown as one of the supplementary films at the 1970 Pesaro Film Festival.

Watson's efforts in England, France, and Germany were not as successful, although he did make some minor sales. Many Europeans found it hard to relate to a film dealing with blacks as workers, especially a film without the flamboyance the films about the Panthers had made them accustomed to. They *were* impressed that the League itself had made the film, rather than being merely the subject of someone else's production. Although distribution of *Finally Got the News* was generally limited to a few politically motivated fringe groups, many contacts expressed an interest in seeing whatever future films Black Star made.

Watson's first stop in Europe was Sweden, where he visited Glanton Dowdell, a League exile with an unusual personal history. Dowdell was forty-seven at the time of Watson's visit and had fled the United States after being charged with forging $65,000 worth of government bonds. One of his co-defendants had been murdered in Detroit, others had pleaded guilty, and there had been attempts on Dowdell's life. Like Malcolm X, Martin Sostre, and Eldridge Cleaver, Dowdell had a criminal background. His specialty had been armed robbery, and much of his political career involved being in charge of security. Dowdell was also a gifted artist and an articulate politician. In the mid-sixties he had taken part in a variety of united front activities which had generated funds for radical organizations. He had operated a small art gallery, helped organize the Detroit Black Art Conference, and painted a famous *Black Madonna* portrait in a short-lived alliance with Reverend Albert Cleage, with whom other League people had worked in the Freedom Now Party. Dowdell had been active in physically removing drug pushers from around some black high schools, and he was rumored to have been an inspiration for the armed robbers who preyed on after-hours clubs owned by the Mafia and black racketeers. In 1966, he, General Baker, and Rufus Griffin were charged with trying to start a riot on Detroit's east side, and he received a suspended sentence. During the Great Rebellion, the police destroyed his art gallery, and he was shot at several times. Dowdell established a Solidarity Committee for the League when he settled in Sweden, and after receiving official status as a political refugee he brought his wife and five children to live with him in exile.

The film was important in establishing Dowdell as a genuine political figure, and it aided him in his struggle with the Panther committee in Sweden. The tensions which had been growing between the Panthers and the League in the U.S. had spilled over to Europe. Dowdell had been treated by the Panthers as an interloper and a dangerous rival. The resourceful Dowdell eventually made significant contacts with prominent politicians in Sweden, and he organized a conference for the League in which major Swedish and Finnish labor organizations participated. Ken Cockrel and Luke Tripp also visited Dowdell during 1970 to bring him up to date on the defense work being done in his behalf and to elaborate on new League plans.

The potential represented by Dowdell, the Italians, and the various European contacts never materialized into the kind of network Watson had in mind, but his partial success indicated that his international plans for Black Star Productions were not without substance. Upon his return to the U.S., Watson explored other possibilities. One of the most promising of these was a projected film about drug addiction. Carolyn Ramsey, who had met Watson through the West Central Organization, worked on a script and did some work with Wayne's television station to pick up technical

skills. Other activities included agreements with various Arab
sources to circulate Palestinian films in the U.S. One about Al
Fatah was secured and distributed. The activity of Black Star
Productions and the existence of *Finally Got the News* brought
Watson into contact with film stars Jane Fonda and Don Sutherland. In early 1971 he advanced the idea to them of doing a
feature-length film about the life of Rosa Luxemburg, a leader of
the German Communist Party who was arrested and murdered in
1919. Paula Hankins, who had been working with Watson since
the first issues of *ICV*, got together a first draft of a script.

The more time Watson devoted to Black Star Productions, the
more criticism he accumulated from the factory-oriented leadership. Luke Tripp approved of *Finally Got the News,* but thought
the Rosa Luxemburg film was pure escapism. People like Baker
and Wooten felt that Watson was retreating from the League's
work in the factories and becoming dazzled with the notion of film
success. They noted that he often got carried away by specific
projects and they joked about the rare breed of Belgian dogs
Watson had long raised and sold for side income. They said
Watson was getting his priorities mixed up. Hamlin and Cockrel
generally backed Watson because they saw *Finally Got the News*
and future productions within the BEDC context. Watson's own
view was that films could be a tremendous source of revenue,
while giving the League ideological clout the mimeograph-minded
activists had never conceived of. Jane Fonda wanted to help Black
Star and offered to use her influence at Warner's to get apprentice
training for League people; but in a letter to Watson written on
April 16, 1971, she touched on doubts similar to those advanced
by the in-plant organizers:

> The main questions asked are why do a film that would
> require so much money to portray a revolutionary
> heroine that the masses of Americans would have diffi-
> culty relating to when the time, energies, and resources
> could be spent to make several movies about our own
> rich history of struggle? Why, if one is intending to
> make a revolutionary film that will move people in

America, go outside of America when we have our own
culture, heroines, and heroes that need to be portrayed
for us to develop a sense of our past so we can have a
vision of our own, unique future?

Eventually the various projects of Black Star Productions fell
victim to the general collapse of the League, but the film *Finally
Got the News* remained as a solid contribution to radical film-
making, able to survive the organization it was made to promote.
Some film critics considered it a radical classic comparable to the
memorable *Salt of the Earth,* made in the 1950s. *Finally Got the
News* had spoken of a specific time and a specific experience in
cinematic and ideological terms that would remain relevant as long
as working people were not able to control their own lives.

4

"It seems to me," said Booker T.,
"That all you folks have missed the boat
Who shout about the right to vote
And spend vain days and fruitless nights
In uproar over civil rights. . . ."

"I don't agree," said W.E.B.
"For what can property avail
If dignity and justice fail? . . ."

"It seems to me," said Booker T.—

"I don't agree,"
Said W.E.B.

Dudley Randall, "Booker T. and W.E.B."

While Watson was busy developing Black Star Productions, Mike Hamlin was opening another cultural front. Hamlin had become concerned about the relationship between progressive whites and the League, as well as the general lack of a League public education program. Meeting with several white and black activists, Hamlin developed the concept of a book club-discussion forum. Perhaps a hundred people might be persuaded to attend monthly sessions to hear a radical speaker analyze a book dealing with problems the League considered relevant. The device was aimed openly at whites and middle-class blacks. Hamlin hoped to develop their revolutionary consciousness and to provide a middle-class cushion against possible media and police attacks upon the League. The speeches at the book club could be mimeographed and made available for those unable to attend the actual discussions.

An initial sample mailing to gauge interest brought an astounding 400 positive responses, and membership in the club grew to over 800 during the first year of operation. The very success of the idea soon proved to be another point of contention within the League leadership. The in-plant leadership perceived the book club as one more diversion of funds, personnel, and interest from the problems of black workers. They believed that the black middle class was virtually useless and that if the League was going to spend any energy on whites it should be with white workers. Hamlin's response was that the League needed a working relationship with the black middle class, progressive whites, and various community organizations to avoid isolation and defeat. If anything, he thought the in-plant leaders should encourage the rank and file to take part in the book club to deepen their comprehension of complex social and economic issues.

The book club also advanced another Hamlin project. White individuals and white organizations such as Ad Hoc, People Against Racism, and the Detroit Organizing Committee had worked with the League on different projects. Hamlin wanted to see these forces forged into a white umbrella group that could be some kind of rough counterpart to the League. Jim Jacobs, one of the most effective Detroit Organizing Committee members and a frequent writer on working-class struggle in Detroit, believed that Hamlin had what amounted to an infatuation with the idea of getting groups together and consequently minimized important ideological differences. Generally, however, Hamlin's effort was greeted enthusiastically as a direct attempt by the League to link up white and black militants in a structured rather than a personal system of contacts.

The fruit of Hamlin's initiative was the creation of the Motor City Labor Coalition, which soon became the Motor City Labor League (MCLL), a group which at one time or another in its development contained almost all the active indigenous white radicals in the city. The two key organizations in putting MCLL together were Ad Hoc and People Against Racism. Ad Hoc was led by Sheila Murphy, a young woman with a reputation as one of the most militant, committed, and diligent Detroit activists. Her Irish-American father had been the distributor of the anarchist-oriented *Catholic Worker* in Detroit. He believed in voluntary poverty, pacifism, and a fundamental reordering of church priorities. Sheila Murphy had grown up in tough neighborhoods and had developed the kind of personality stereotyped by the image of a scrappy Irish redhead. She had worked as a secretary for the West Central Organization. According to her own account, WCO had the only stencil-maker available to radicals in the city, and she got to know almost everyone engaged in mass agitation. These people included John Watson, Ken Cockrel, and Justin Ravitz. In time, Murphy began to take a leadership role in different groups which used church financing for radical projects. Her groups usually had loosely defined memberships organized around specific issues.

People Against Racism was primarily the creation of Frank Joyce, a radical with a substantial history of trying to organize white people to fight racism within their own communities. Joyce's groups tended to be tightly knit operations with broad programs and demands. He was born in Royal Oak, a Detroit suburb, and he had been a boyhood friend of Tom Hayden, one of the founders of SDS and an anti-Vietnam War organizer. Joyce's personal style was very much in the mode of SDS-type radicals of the sixties. He participated in many national conferences, traveled to North Vietnam, and worked in Chicago as a staff member of the defense committee of the Chicago 7 (Tom Hayden, Dave Dellinger, Rennie Davis, Abbie Hoffman, Jerry Rubin, John Froines, and Lee Weiner), who were accused of conspiring to disrupt the 1968 Democratic convention. Joyce was frequently consulted by forces outside Detroit regarding national mobilizations around one issue or another. He was the major Detroit link to the national white movement and was acquainted with almost everyone who was politically active in the Detroit area.

MCLL had many women in leadership roles and tried drawing in individuals with long-time radical experience in the city as well as recruiting new activists. One of the major MCLL thrusts was the book club; and even after the League split in 1971, the book club sessions continued. The format for the sessions was for the audience to be grouped at tables, each with a discussion leader. After the featured presentation, there was discussion at the tables in which everyone was urged to participate; and later, there were questions from the tables to the speakers.

MCLL had a split of its own in 1972, but the concept of the book club forum had taken root. The group which continued with the MCLL name began to focus its book club topics more sharply on problems related to local radical history, mass culture, and the use of media. A separate series of programs for women dealt with cultural as well as purely political questions. The MCLL newspaper, the *Journey*, published poetry and fiction and devoted half a page of each issue to the writing of children. One of the more ambitious MCLL cultural projects was a plan to stage a play based on Harriet Arnow's novel *The Dollmaker*, which had a Detroit setting.

The group which broke away from MCLL took the name From The Ground Up, and it too developed book club forums involving hundreds of people. Aside from their inherent intellectual value, the book club forums of both organizations served as devices for bringing guest speakers to Detroit from all parts of the country. These speakers included prominent attorneys, labor organizers, poets, historians, and activists who related their own experiences of struggle to the local scene. From The Ground Up also set up a complete printing center to back up its activities. This center was designed to do commercial work so that it might become self-sustaining as well as to prepare leaflets, booklets, posters, and other agitational material. The organization also established a From The Ground Up Bookstore.

The bookstore was yet another expression of the Detroit movement's intense seriousness about mass education. The League had set up a Black Star Bookstore in 1970 in a stretch of Linwood Avenue which included Muslim Mosque #1, the Shrine of the Black Madonna, and Central High School. Ernie Kalimoto, an able militant who had met Baker and Tripp on the Cuba journey of 1964, had come from New York to run the bookstore. Originally thought to have an almost unlimited funding base in the Black Economic Development Conference, the operation eventually fell apart from lack of the capital needed to provide a wide selection of books. In 1972, a China-Albania bookstore was opened across the street from the old Black Star Bookstore, but it sold only Peking publications and served more as an organizational headquarters for the Baker forces than as a real bookshop. MCLL had a similar set-up, with a small bookstore in the front of its offices. The From The Ground Up Bookstore had a different character. Under the management of Jack Russell, the husband of League activist Michelle Russell, the store was considered a prime financial and ideological resource. Instead of restricting itself to a narrow range of "approved" material, the bookstore stocked an assortment of diverse radical literature which might be of interest to the city's militants.

5

And you the audience of indifference
in the bleachers of your set up judgeship
will have no choice.
The war will be brought into the stands.

C. G. Johnson, untitled poem

The underground press and counterculture of the 1960s sought to destroy the straight, materialistic, unfulfilling world of Middle America through a nonviolent and beautiful revolution shorn of the ugliness of politics and ideology. First by winning over America's youth, then by taking over all cultural and social institutions, the counterculture hoped to accomplish even more than the political revolutionaries of the 1930s had advocated. Those who pursued this course in a sincere effort to bring change to America were soon crushed by capitalist realities. Stripped of the political sensibilities it consciously rejected, the counterculture, like the Motown sound, was easy prey for the money boys of Broadway, the ad agencies, organized crime, Hollywood, and the recording industry. Its music, health foods, drugs, hairstyles, mysticism, and colorful clothing were transformed into new commodities to be sold in the American marketplace.

Exactly where the counterculture left off and hard-core revolutionary culture began was not always clear in the sixties. Mammoth anti-war events reflected both. The counterculturalist of one summer might be the political activist of the next, and vice versa. Those who regarded themselves as primarily political activists, especially those in SDS, were often enthusiastic about the spirit of the counterculture and the beauty of its artistic efforts while remaining uneasy about drugs, nonviolence, and the notion that youth could be regarded as a revolutionary social class or category. They realized that the counterculture challenged the authority of the state, the nuclear family, and the traditional political party by raising searching questions about the quality and purpose of everyday life in much the same manner as what they called the New Left. Despite these similarities, the frivolous and self-destructive nature of many counterculture activities repelled many political activists and the working people they were trying to reach. The huge outdoor concert at Woodstock, New York, was followed by another at Altamont, California, where all the ugliest aspects of the counterculture asserted themselves before film cameras, which even recorded "live" a murder by the Hell's Angels motorcycle gang hired to protect the Rolling Stones rock group. Advocacy of the drug culture ultimately posed an irresolvable contradiction to the political necessity of cleansing the cities, especially the ghettos, of the heroin, cocaine, and pill traffic which bred street violence and indirectly paralyzed social movements.

The counterculture succeeded in generating a new feeling of liberation which came to characterize much of the sixties. To develop and sustain the proposed cultural revolution, it was necessary to integrate that revolution into the everyday lives and politics of ordinary people and to keep it beyond the grasp of capitalist co-optation and commoditization. Political focus and organizational structure were crucial to maintaining the momentum and integrity of the counterculture, and only the political revolutionaries sought to provide that focus and structure. For them, a successful cultural revolution could only come upward from the people within the context of an overall social, economic, and political revolution.

In Detroit, the relations between the counterculture and the political revolutionaries became especially strained and guarded. The erratic poet John Sinclair, with his Artists' Workshop just off the Wayne campus, was the most visible example of the counterculture. Sinclair wrote a regular column for the *Fifth Estate* in which he espoused music and drugs as viable revolutionary weapons of a youth insurgency. Originally hostile to talk of violent revolution, Sinclair had a change of heart in the midst of the Great Rebellion and hoisted a huge "Burn Baby Burn" sign on top of his home overlooking the Lodge Expressway. The police promptly shot up the sign and the house. Some time later, Sinclair formed a White Panther Party whose first programmatic demand was "Full endorsement and support of the Black Panther Party's 10 point program and platform." Many of Detroit's revolutionaries regarded that idea as dubious in itself; the second demand was simply ridiculous: "Total assault on the culture by any means necessary, including rock and roll, dope, and fucking in the streets." In the next years, Sinclair's closest associates would be convicted on bombing charges and Sinclair himself would be sentenced to ten years in prison in a celebrated marijuana case. In his 360-page memoir of the period, published in 1972 and titled *Guitar Army,* Sinclair exposed the gap between himself and the Detroit revolutionaries by simply avoiding all mention of the politics and views of the League of Revolutionary Black Workers or those of the people who flowed into and out of groups such as the Motor City Labor League. His omissions included Justin Ravitz, the attorney who did the legal work leading to Sinclair's own release from prison. Sinclair's path after getting out of prison in 1971 took him out of Detroit to the nearby university town of Ann Arbor, home of the University of Michigan, where his major activity was organizing musical concerts.

Rather than depending on the outside ranks of the counter-culture, the political revolutionaries in Detroit drew on their own ranks for artistic and cultural work. Besides the film-making and the book club forums and the bookstores, the revolutionaries encouraged the use of original artwork and writing in all their publications. One of the most original and distinctive artists to emerge from the revolutionary cauldron was b. p. Flanigan (who capitalized only his last name in order to draw attention to the importance of the collective clan name and to minimize the importance of the individual personal name). Flanigan came from a working-class background. He had served in Vietnam, had been addicted to heroin, and had been seriously injured while working at Ford Rouge. Flanigan had a vision of a cultural renaissance in which murals, poetry, and other art forms would be a major revolutionary tool for expressing anti-capitalist and anti-elitist views. Stylistically more complex than most writers in political circles, Flanigan employed the latest literary and artistic techniques in work that focused on his personal experiences. He encouraged others to talk about their lives in the same way, shunning current artistic or movement fads in favor of a personal style. He hoped that, one day, there would be no more artists, only humans with their individual and communal songs to sing. He published a wall-poster poem called "The Ceremony" in 1972 that had the power of an ideological manifesto while sticking close to the particulars of the Detroit experience:

"dearly beloved,
we are gathered
here today in . . .

. . . detroit, michigan: home of the "motown sound"/gm/ford/
chrysler/rats in the kitchen and roaches in the bathroom/no heat
in winter & nothing cool when the summer comes/pistons pounding
out a DRUM beat . . . "do you take" . . . "to love and cherish"
. . . woodward avenue/junkies, whores & little kids on the way up
to take their places/a dime bag to get the day over with
. . . "and do you take" . . . "to have and to hold" . . . the day shift,
afternoons, midnights—at least 8 hrs. with the devil in hell/
rouge, chevy, fisherbody (makes dead bodies), budd, eldon gear
& axle, dodge main, jefferson, iron foundries & specialty forge
foundries/monsters that eat alive & spit out bloody hands/feet
pieces of skin and bone/& with regularity—A DEAD BODY!!!
. . . friday nite . . . get that check/carry it on home to the crib
(with wife and kids), then get out on the street: get fucked up/
(reefer, jones, coke, ups & downs, johnnie walker black & red)
try to freeze your head/can't think about the shit starting
all over a gain on monday./. . . "and now a message from our sponsor"
watch tv/listen to the radio/read papers/they all say: "buy this,
get that & YOU TWO can be a success."/damn, brother, sister,

a success in this motorized, computerized, iron & steel jungle is
just staying alive!!!

"in sickness and in health"   detroit, michigan/any city
"for better or for worse"   my/our home

"until DEATH

do us part."

Chapter Seven

Black Workers Congress

1

Our objectives: 1. Workers' control of their places of work—the factories, mines, fields, offices, transportation services and communication facilities—so that the exploitation of labor will cease and no person or corporation will get rich off the labor of another person, but all people will work for the collective benefit of humanity.

Black Workers Congress manifesto, 1971

From the first days of DRUM, workers and activists from every part of the United States had communicated with the Detroit group to learn how to set up similar organizations. The League of Revolutionary Black Workers had been developed to weld the Detroit RUMs into a single political unit, and many League members were interested in finding the best method of expanding the League and the RUM idea into every major city in the nation. Some of the people in the League believed it was sufficient to set an outstanding example in Detroit and let others imitate that model independently. Others thought such an approach was too haphazard and that the League should create a national organization

Opposite page: James Forman reading a statement outside New York's Riverside Church, May 11, 1969.

just as DRUM had created the League. The name ''Black Workers Congress'' was adopted for the projected organization, and at one time the BWC concept had the support of the League's entire Executive Committee.

The decision to form a separate organization with a new name rather than franchise League chapters in other cities reflected a close reading of the history of other black organizations which had recently tried to organize nationally. Police infiltration, financial stresses, and the problems of limited personnel had crippled RAM, Malcolm X's organization, and the Black Panther Party. The Detroiters did not want to find themselves in a position where one or more of their key leaders became indicted for something done in the name of the League in places where the League could not exercise daily supervision over activities.

The Black Economic Development Conference of April 1969 gave the League its first major national podium and deepened some of its contacts with groups in other parts of the country. The League soon drew up a manifesto and a call for a Black Workers Congress founding convention. The thirty-two objectives of the manifesto mostly concerned workers' demands, the elimination of racism, the liberation of women, and foreign-policy questions. The workers' demands were for what amounted to workers' control of production, leading to the formation of a socialist state. The question of racism was dealt with by calling for the granting of strong cultural autonomy to all minorities who wished it, for dismantling of the police apparatus, and for specific programs to combat racism wherever and in whatever form it existed. The demands regarding women dealt both with sexism on a strictly sexual level and with its manifestation in the workplace. The foreign policy items supported various national-liberation movements, called for an immediate end to the war in Vietnam, and advocated diplomatic recognition of China and Cuba. The principal vehicle for bringing BWC into existence was to be a series of black united fronts and third-world alliances backed by a complex network of printing shops, neighborhood service centers, student organizations, and economic cooperatives. The manifesto's final demand was for the eventual creation of a black revolutionary political party, although little was said about its specific nature or precise ideological orientation.

The manifesto received an excellent response, yet the in-plant League leadership began to cool toward the whole idea. They felt that continued success in the factories had a higher priority than organizational ties with like-minded people in other cities. They were concerned that many of the Detroit RUM units were beginning to run out of steam. In February 1969, Chuck Wooten had been fired from Dodge Main after striking a supervisor, and Sidney Lewis, an incorporator of the League, had been fired in August for striking a foreman. Other organizers and sympathizers were being eliminated from the plants as a result of similar incidents or disciplinary actions by the company with the collusion of the union. By the summer of 1970, ELRUM had nearly ceased to exist as an open organization, and in other plants the local RUMs had to remain semi-clandestine to preserve themselves. The in-plant leadership argued that the League was in no position to launch a national drive because it must tend to its withering base. These leaders wanted the resources, energy, and personnel being expended on book clubs, film-making, printing, BWC matters, and community work to go into direct plant operations. They asked Ken Cockrel, Mike Hamlin, and John Watson to spend more time with workers and their immediate problems.

The BWC advocates replied that the League could not advance secretively, worker by worker, plant by plant, but must leap forward, making massive and simultaneous gains in various sectors of public work. The operations being criticized as diversionary were, they argued, essential to maintaining organizational momentum. Dismissed workers would never be rehired unless there were strong defense committees with popular bases able to apply mass pressure. The same kind of mass pressure was crucial to discouraging, exposing, and defeating the provocations of company, union, and police. Films and publications were central to educating the worker base and spreading the League program to the general public. One film like *Finally Got the News* was more valuable in teaching and inspiring workers than many hours of discussion and study.

The political disagreements between the League leaders began to feed personal antagonisms. The in-plant people charged that the BWC wing liked to be with ''bourgeois'' people and with white folks more than they liked to be with black workers. Cockrel was cited for having what was termed an arrogant and authoritarian attitude toward comrades. Watson was charged with having become a dreamer who let transoceanic trips and film-making fantasies replace his former vision of a worker-led American revolution. Hamlin was said to be so enamored of the idea of a national organization that he had lost his common sense. As for James Forman, who had entered the League through BEDC and was one of the strongest advocates of BWC, he was the wrecker and splitter Baker had suspected him of being all along.

The BWC supporters had countercharges. They said that the Cortland office, Baker's personal headquarters, had become a disgrace to the League. Visitors and members alike complained of its inhospitable atmosphere and its generally cluttered, dirty, and rag-tag appearance. Women said they were afraid to go there for fear of verbal and even physical assault. The BWC wing charged that some of the so-called plant organizers were just hangers-on who lived in League facilities and took League salaries but who did more drinking than organizing. Many of them were simple-minded black nationalists or had a street-gang mentality, and this outlook had pervaded the workers' ranks to such a degree that only a stiff internal-education program could rectify the situation. Baker and Wooten were said to be paternalistic to workers, accepting and sometimes lauding their low level of ideology simply because they were ''basic brothers off the street.'' John Williams and Luke Tripp were criticized for lacking the imagination to see that the BWC approach would revitalize the organization and that the media materials being prepared would do quickly the educational work they thought must be done on a laborious one-to-one basis. Cockrel complained that some of the League ''organizers'' were involved in petty crimes that had nothing to do with the organization and constituted an unwarranted drain on its legal resources. The BWC people underscored their arguments by saying that they had been largely responsible for gathering most of the resources which made the League possible and that every time they proposed a new step forward the others invariably resisted them.

The internal quarrels continued for more than a year. There was a purge of some members in late 1970, including Ernie Kalimoto and others who might have become the core of a competent secondary leadership. Cockrel, Hamlin, and Watson seemed harder and harder to get hold of and were often absent from the city on one project or another. In the early part of 1971, pursuing leads for Black Star Productions, Watson took a trip to the Middle East, where he received a commendation from the Arab guerrilla organizations for his work in publicizing their views in the United States. Cockrel traveled to the West Coast several times. While there, he tried to convince Angela Davis to entrust her defense to an all-black united front instead of relying exclusively upon the Communist Party, of which she was a member. (Davis had been accused of abetting an escape attempt by black prisoners, a charge she was later acquitted of.) Hamlin spent more and more time in the company of Forman. Personal ill feeling intensified, and much of the organizing work within the city continued to wind down.

The situation reached a decisive phase when Cockrel, Hamlin, and Watson issued what amounted to an ultimatum to the rest of the Executive Committee. They demanded an internal-education program frankly aimed at thinning out the ranks. All cadres and members of the organization must agree to support fully all the published objectives of the League. There would be no more backroom mutterings from nationalists about "white journalism" or that "Marx was a hoinkie." Certain members of the central staff would be purged, and there would be a reshuffling of responsibilities based on the outcome of the internal education.

The BWC advocates were not interested in just winning a vote of confidence in the Executive Committee by a 4-3 or 5-2 margin. They wanted to convince the others that their policies were the only ones that would lead to growth and that, without unity of purpose within the executive, votes and programs were relatively meaningless. When their views were rejected, Ken Cockrel, Mike Hamlin, and John Watson formally resigned from the organization, ending political and personal friendships that in some cases had involved their entire adult lives. They stated that they would devote their full time to building a BWC that was totally independent of the League. Although many activists involved in the League components under their personal direction went with them into the new organization, most of the League's members and sympathizers were unprepared for a split among the top leadership. Through their inaction, they supported neither side. The resignations became public on June 12, 1971. By the first of the year, those who remained in the League were making plans to affiliate what was left of the organization with a group called the Communist League. The League of Revolutionary Black Workers had become history.

2

Above all, I will wage the ideological struggle—the drive for political education. I will continue this work that I have tried to do most of my adult life with vigor. For it is my duty to help make black revolutionaries.

James Forman, *The Making of Black Revolutionaries,* 1972

James Forman was a key figure in the split between the League and BWC. He had been instrumental in organizing BEDC and would play a similar role in setting up the machinery for BWC outside of Detroit. The funds generated by Forman and BEDC had allowed Cockrel, Hamlin, and Watson to put some of their out-of-plant projects into practice. Forman viewed the League as subordinate to BWC, a position in sharp contrast to the League belief that BWC would be a creature of the League. Willingly or not, by intensifying frictions caused by the internal weaknesses of the League strategies, organizational structure, and personnel, Forman served as a major catalyst in dividing the League against itself.

Forman's background was impressive. A good ten years older than most of the League leaders, he had been raised in a working-class section of Chicago's South Side and, like Mike Hamlin, had served in the Korean War. He had gone to the South in 1958 as a reporter for the *Chicago Defender* and soon found himself drawn to activism. He became part of the newly formed SNCC in 1960, and from 1961 to 1966 was the organization's Executive Secretary. Stokely Carmichael and H. Rap Brown gained more fame than Forman, but many people in the movement regarded him as the "brains" of SNCC. In 1967, designated the International Affairs Director of SNCC, he traveled throughout Africa and represented SNCC at an important UN meeting in Zambia. Following this trip, Forman played a central role in winning 50 percent participation for blacks in the National Conference for New Politics' founding convention in Chicago. He scared a lot of whites into voting for this arrangement, but this victory in what was billed as a new party and a new politics proved to be short-lived since the conference never got off the ground. In February of 1968, Forman took the post of Minister of Foreign Affairs of the Black Panther Party, but fierce personal and political disagreements led to his resignation in July of the same year. He then began developing BEDC and by the spring of 1969 had joined the central staff of the League. In addition to his political work, Forman had written a book, attended most national black conferences of importance, and lectured extensively, building up a reputation as one of the leading black revolutionary organizers and theorists.

When Forman arrived on the Detroit scene, he brought along his national prestige, large-scale financial resources, and solid contacts throughout the country. Forman considered Detroit to be a launching pad for a new national organization. BEDC would be used to attract initial funding and publicity for an organization that would be larger and more effective than even SNCC had been. The League would serve as the model for many leagues in urban, rural, and academic settings. Forman's approach was tied to his own personal style. He was the perpetual traveler, wheeler-dealer, organizer, and thinker who supposedly knew what was happening at the base. He was the revolutionary connection bringing local groups the latest news and plans of the ''brothers and sisters'' in other places. BEDC was a typical Forman production in that it brought together hundreds of people who spoke in the name of America's black population, yet who were not themselves unified in any significant manner and who often represented only themselves or paper organizations. Forman meant BWC to be something quite different.

BWC would complete a personal and historical transformation in the black movement by linking the Southern and rural experience of struggle to the Northern and urban experience. It would link the vital poor people's movement of one region to the new working-class movement of the other, using some of the personnel of SNCC and the League, the highest expressions of each of those struggles, to begin its work. This vision reflected important insights into the developments of the late sixties; yet BWC eventually failed in its goal of reproducing DRUM and League organizations on a national scale. From the start, BWC suffered from excessive personalism, theoretical simplification, and lack of a solid center of organized mass support.

BWC was built from the top down, and the top of the pyramid was occupied by James Forman, the titular national leader. He traveled almost continually, linking up former SNCC contacts, new workers' groups, and local black militants. Forman spoke with the authority of his own long experience and with the authority of his connection with the League. The forces which had come with him into BWC were soon getting directives on how to proceed with national, regional, and local projects. When they asked Forman to take on the editorship of the BWC paper, however, he refused on the grounds that to do so would mean becoming stationary in the city of Detroit, a condition he could not accept. What Forman did want to do was make sixteen educational films of one to two hours duration. They would feature himself as the speaker and his writings as the subject matter. Letters to John Watson gave instructions on how the films could be made in a single whirlwind week. Forman's projected films were not to be real cinema in the way *Finally Got the News* had been, but simply filmed lectures. These films would be used in the Frantz Fanon Institutes Forman planned to create in every large city. The institutes were conceived as revolutionary training centers which would teach the thought of Fanon as interpreted by Forman and grafted on to the organizational approach of Forman. This organizational approach, in turn, was outlined in a series of pamphlet essays which were collected under the title *The Political Thought of James Forman.* The 200-page paperback was printed for BWC use by Black Star Publishing, mainly through the efforts of Helen Jones and Fredy Perlman.

Forman's political thought was less a system of ideas than a series of demands sprinkled with organizing suggestions. It was primarily an attack on existing oppression rather than a proposal for a new system. Forman's organizational speeches and public writings were often at variance. While speaking, he hailed the League as the most advanced black organization to appear in the United States and the first black organization to try seriously to apply Marxism to American conditions; yet in his 550-page book *The Making of Black Revolutionaries,* he devoted less than a page to it. The League was stuck into a chapter titled "The Black Manifesto"; and in a chronologically incorrect sequence, only Mike Hamlin and John Watson were mentioned by name. Hamlin wrote a preface to *The Political Thought of James Forman* in which he pledged Black Star Publishing to publicizing ideas that would help the formation of a political party capable of leading the American revolution. Forman's own introduction was far less precise and used loose nationalistic phrasing to make its points:

> I am extremely elated that Black Star Publishing is printing as its first book this collection of speeches and writings that are all geared to helping to make revolutionaries of black people in the United States. There is a great deal of—but not enough—descriptive literature on African people wherever they exist. Much of this literature does not address itself to capitalism and im-

perialism as being integral to the cause of racism, and certainly does not hold high the banner of armed struggle by All-African People as the only ultimate solution to ending these destroyers of humanity, to the establishment of a new and just society capable of ending all forms of human exploitation.

The Forman idea of revolutionary theory and practice, "Formanism," reflected a precise, if restricted, sense of organization and an amalgam of popularized theoretical tendencies of the sixties. The major organizational form was the umbrella group operating with a popular front strategy. The organizations had plans for becoming mass-membership groups; but more important than gaining members were the immediate goals of organizing conferences, workshops, and lectures and producing documents. This procedure would attract outside funding and prepare the ground for political-education classes. The end product of this program was supposed to be the creation of Frantz Fanon Institutes. In effect, Formanism substituted ideological struggle for struggle over material conditions. The focus had to remain ideological because people were recruited into study groups and organizing commissions rather than action groups prepared to deal with immediate issues. Reduced to study groups and organizing commissions, politics was effectively separated from the problems of work and daily life. The education itself was anti-colonial, anti-racist, and anti-imperialist, but ideas were not presented in the context of a serious class analysis of the roles blacks play in America or of the state of mid-twentieth-century capitalism. Unlike the economically grounded and disciplined organizational approach of Marxism-Leninism, the approach of Fanon-Formanism was exemplified by loosely structured groups stressing psychological interpretations of social reality and the accumulation of technical skills. Formanism was less a program for moving toward power than a defensive tactic for dealing with oppression.

3

I don't have skills like a secretary or something. I went into the factory because it was the only place where I could get a job making decent money, but if you stay a lady, you don't make it out there. They all put the pressure on you.

Carla Cook, a production-line worker at the Eldon Avenue Gear and Axle plant, in an interview with the authors on August 19, 1972

The founding convention for BWC was more than a year in the making. It took place in Gary, Indiana, in September 1971, shortly after James Forman, Muhammad Kenyatta (a Philadelphia-based black activist), and Helen Jones returned from a trip to China and Vietnam. Over 400 delegates from all parts of the country participated. Many of them were disheartened to hear of the Detroit schism, for Detroit was to be the headquarters of BWC and the League membership was to have been its first mass base. The ultimate consequence of the split was that the League would be one of the few black worker groups specifically excluded from possible membership. In spite of this situation, the convention sessions were lively and the atmosphere optimistic.

At least one-third of the delegates to the founding convention were women, and there was significant participation by third-world groups that were not of African heritage. Both of these facts were related to a conscious attempt of BWC to have a wider active base than the League had enjoyed. BWC membership was open to all third-world people: Asian Americans, Native Americans, Arabs, and Latin Americans. The BWC manifesto included many specific items important to women, such as a commitment to day-care centers, equal pay for equal work, and paid vacations for housewives. The keynote speech was given by John Watson, who reiterated the importance of seeing third-world people as workers:

> Since slavery, Black labor has continued to assume particular importance in the development of both domestic capital and international imperialism, primarily because the Black female and male workers are the final prop, the ultimate mainstay, onto which capitalism shifts its weight in order to survive.
>
> Black workers have remained a source of the cheapest, most productive labor. First as agriculture labor, then as miners, merchant seamen, government transport and service workers, dock and warehouse workers, etc., and finally as the most exploited section of the proletariat in light and heavy industry. Today, Black and other Third World workers are still solidly entrenched at the base of the proletariat.

The delegates to the Gary convention had gathered to discuss plans of action. Some of the representatives from the South had already begun RUM groups in Atlanta and Birmingham, but their hopes for a national workers' organization were never to be fulfilled. Most of the convention's time was spent in setting up a national newspaper and an elaborate commission structure to investigate and advance various areas of work. The manifesto spoke boldly of people learning many skills and of those with skills sharing them. Like most BWC ideas, these remained real only on paper. From the convention onward, the organization bogged down in endless discussions on how to proceed, whom to charter, whom to place in positions of authority, and a multitude of bureaucratic questions. The printing apparatus of BWC churned out more materials for internal organizational affairs than for agitation at the factory gates or in the streets.

BWC proved to be a particular disappointment for the women who had belonged to the League. Even though many women had worked hard for the League and had positions of secondary responsibility, the League had never allowed a strong woman leader to emerge, and few women had been on the central staff. Its materials gave little emphasis to the strategic role of women in making the American revolution. Early in the League's history, Edna Watson, Paula Hankins, and Rachel Bishop had initiated an organizing drive among hospital workers, partly to give female leadership to one area of work. They were not supported by the rest of the organization in the manner they expected, and the work had to be abandoned. DRUM had only one woman, Betty Griffen, on its election slates and ELRUM had none. Most women in the League had strong personalities and were hard workers; but they invariably found themselves under male supervision, whether they were involved in printing, organizing, or writing.

The League's Executive Committee was openly hostile to the women's liberation movement, which it generally referred to as the "white woman's liberation movement." Most of the male cadre proudly expressed chauvinistic attitudes, and some members of the workers' components were charged with physically abusing women. The League considered women's liberation as it was then being discussed a divisive issue; and although at times there were women's committees, the League never drew up a program for women. For all their gruffness, the League males were not nearly so reactionary as some of their enemies liked to paint them. Some of the roughest talkers were the men most likely to help out with babysitting, cleaning, shopping, or cooking. Helen Jones and Mabel Turner were key personnel at Black Star Publishing, and women were also central to the operations at Black Star Productions. The Executive Committee, in the person of Mike Hamlin, also went out of its way to contact Michelle Russell, a board member of Resist, an anti-war organization, and a member of the executive committee of New University Conference, an organization of radical college teachers. Russell was persuaded to move to Detroit, where she became a member of the League on the eve of the split. She served as an important member of BWC and local Detroit groups working against police repression.

More than anyone else associated with the League, James Forman had been an open advocate of the women's liberation

movement. Some of the women considered this position an indication of Forman's great sophistication and genuine understanding of the revolutionary process, while others became suspicious
that it was a device to increase his narrow power base in the
League. When BWC was formed, many women had hopes that
Forman's leadership would result in women having more
responsibility than they had enjoyed in the League. These hopes
went unfulfilled.

The tensions over women's liberation were complicated by
what Detroiters called ''the white wife question.'' Both Mike
Hamlin and Ken Cockrel began living with white women after the
League was formed. Some of the black women in the organization
took that as a kind of rebuff to black women, and some workers
cited it as another aspect of Hamlin and Cockrel's growing alienation from the black base. The people who formed BWC felt that
the matter had been dealt with many times in the past and did not
need a new airing. Watson reminded his old associates of the
internal havoc the white wife question had caused in UHURU;
Charles ''Mao'' Johnson had withdrawn from activism partly
because he refused to defend himself constantly for having a white
wife. James Forman, whose wife was also white, figured in the
controversy as well. Despite Watson's warning, the issue disturbed BWC as it had disturbed the League. The tragedy of the
whole discussion of white wives was that, justified or not, it often
divided many of the black women in the League and in BWC from
the most flexible and innovative leaders while reinforcing vague
nationalist feelings in others.

BWC's position on women, like its positions on most questions,
was more or less irrelevant in the long run, since the organization
never really came to life. An early BWC announcement spoke of
the two main pillars of the organization as being the League in
Detroit and the black workers' group at Ford's Mahwah plant in
New Jersey; but the Mahwah group, like the League, never
became part of BWC. As much as Forman and others traveled
from city to city, the BWC skeleton could not put on flesh. BWC
remained a scheme for possible unification, a promise without
fulfillment. The problems in each region were different, but one

constant was that too few people were attempting an immense work with too limited resources. With no strong base to build on, BWC could establish no centers to which people could be brought for training and inspiration. There were no real-life models to be studied. Government, unions, companies, and rival political groups chewed at the edges of each local. BWC produced reams of proposals and organizational manuals, but no real organization—lots of ideology but limited political practice. By its own estimates, BWC never had a formal membership above 500—little more than the number that attended the founding convention.

The organization was top-heavy, and the only real links between the units were the thought and person of James Forman. This personalism proved catastrophic, for in spite of his vast experience, his organizational skills, his ideas, and his pronouncements, Forman could not get BWC moving. Detroit was the national center of BWC; Mike Hamlin was its official chairman and John Watson its major thinker, aside from Forman. Even so, as late as January 1972, or almost three years after BEDC, Forman had not yet sunk any roots in the city. He wrote the central committee of BWC, stating, "For more than two weeks I have been in Detroit, Michigan, trying to arrange my life so I could work out of Detroit as a home base. . . . I have never spent much time in Detroit in the technical study of our work here and sharing experiences. My trips have usually been of short duration and my conversations limited to a few people."

These tenuous ties between Forman and the ostensible center of the organization were indicative of the quality of his BWC contacts throughout the nation; and, as Forman himself stated in his report of January 17, 1972, "I was in closer contact with the realities of the national situation than probably anyone else in the organization." BWC developed major problems of credibility when people discovered that things often moved because of a show, a bluff, or white guilt, rather than because of a solid organizational push. Forman was constantly moving himself around and urging others to do the same, but the BWC "work" he was engaged in invariably turned out to be just another meeting. The numerous directives and reports written by Forman were indicative of the organization's style. Unlike the vivid, well-thought-out language of Cockrel and Watson or the spirited language of the RUM writers and General Baker, Forman's writing was dull, bureaucratic prose, complete with points and subpoints occasionally spiced with a slogan or revolutionary jargon. Elaborate agendas, tedious meetings, and internal debate were the hallmarks of life in BWC. In this sense, Formanism came more and more to represent the antithesis of the League, which had always been more concerned with worker action and power than with ideological talk. BWC was increasingly caught in the trap of Formanism. People became weary of attending one conference after another only to discover that it was still the next city which had the mass base or was about to launch the organizing drive that would put BWC on the map. Demoralization led to attacks on the leadership of James Forman. People began to comment openly that he did all of his writing in the first person.

4

Point of information: What is the Executive Secretary's practice in terms of organizing industrial workers?

Bill Thomas, speaking at a February 1972 meeting of BWC's Detroit branch

The first substantial attack on Forman's hegemony came from Ken Cockrel, who charged him with incompetence and egotism. Cockrel described Forman's reports as vague, programless, and individualistic. Cockrel wanted to know why the central committee had never received a full report on what was accomplished in China and North Vietnam or on how people were being selected for subsequent trips. Cockrel called Forman "an American

Airlines revolutionary'' who junketed around the country trying to build organizations through deception and intrigue, a person more interested in personal power than in the organization's welfare.

A BWC commission met in Detroit in February 1972 to investigate Cockrel's charges. After two days of almost continuous meetings, the commission voted against Cockrel. Few of its members supported Forman outright, but the majority felt that Cockrel had not proved his charges and that the organization's problems could not be blamed on one individual. Cockrel, Michelle Russell, Ted Spearman (one of Cockrel's law partners), and Gregory Hicks, who had been active in *Black Student Voice,* left BWC. Over the next year the Detroit chapter all but melted away. John Watson took a ''leave of absence'' to return to Wayne State University and finally get a degree. Fred Holsey, who had been a leader in ELRUM, Chuck Wilson, who had represented the League at an international conference in Italy, Paula Hankins, who had been active since the founding of *ICV,* Carolyn Ramsey, who had worked at Black Star Productions, and Larry Nevels, who had headed UNICOM, were among those who resigned, decimating the Detroit chapter to the point of not even having a staff around which to build a base. The same process occurred in BWC chapters all over the country.

Throughout this difficult time, Mike Hamlin retained his position as national chairman, but by April 1973 he and the other central-committee members had had enough of Forman and Formanism. In a 43-page paper, the surviving BWC headed by Hamlin expelled Forman for his role in the League split and the failure of BWC. The paper was extraordinarily candid and was virulently anti-Forman. It stated that the early critiques of Forman voiced by John Williams, speaking for the League, and later repeated by Cockrel were essentially correct. Neither Williams nor Cockrel was spared personal attack, but the dispersed former League executive was united, two years after its fatal split, regarding the role of Forman in its disintegration.

The BWC paper stated that ''James Forman was in search of a base and the League represented the future.'' It described Forman as ''secretive, paranoid, furtive, and individualistic to the bone.

Commanding large sums of money, sections of the (League) leadership drew closer [to him] and sections of the leadership pulled away.'' Briefly, the paper stated how Forman had failed to win leadership posts in the League. John Williams had replaced Forman as head of International Black Appeal, and Ernie Kalimoto had been voted an educational position Forman had specifically asked for. As plans for BWC began to develop, Forman had made it a practice to bring his supporters into Detroit, where they came into verbal and physical conflict with many League members working in the factories. Forman had held meetings all over the country tacking together students and ''movement'' activists. At those meetings he had told people that, with some bright exceptions, in Detroit there was a ''cancer'' of reactionary nationalism, male chauvinism, and lack of political education. The in-plant leadership of the League had correctly perceived, the paper went on, that BWC leadership was being transferred out of Detroit hands. As one of many components, the League would be ruled by BWC policy decisions, which would, by and large, be James Forman's decisions. The BWC paper stated in capital letters: ''OUR CONCLUSION IS OBVIOUS. JAMES FORMAN OPPORTUNISTICALLY DESTROYED THE LEAGUE, DOING THE WORK OF THE BOURGEOISIE.''

Forman's response was that he was being made the scapegoat for the failure of first the League, then BWC. People did not understand that his ''getting acquainted'' sessions and his ''sharing of experiences'' approach was as political as more programmatic aspects of work. He felt that the personal attacks on him were evidence of how much educational work had *not* been done and that his ability to raise money was an indication of how much better he understood political processes than his facile critics did. He defended his style of work as necessary because of the personal dangers inherent in his vanguard role and the vanguard role projected for BWC. Lacking any home base in BWC, however, he could not muster the votes to prevent his expulsion.

Even before the move against Forman, BWC had begun looking for a new strategy. By the autumn of 1972, BWC was a public participant in a movement to create a new American communist party. The organizations involved in this movement included Puerto Rican groups, Chicano groups, Asian-American groups, and primarily white groups which had origins in the old SDS. The New York-based *Guardian,* a newspaper with a posted circulation of more than 25,000, was involved in the unity effort and sponsored a series of forums to air theoretical differences. These forums had an average attendance of 500 persons, and one which included Mike Hamlin among its four speakers drew an audience of 1200. All of the participating groups emphasized work among the industrial working class. Their Marxism tended to rigid orthodoxy which had more in common with the ideological theories of the thirties than with the evolution of Marxist thinking in the postwar decades. The groups demonstrated nearly uncritical acceptance of the theories of Joseph Stalin and Mao Tse-tung. The Communist Party U.S.A. was seen as a major enemy of the American working class, and people who challenged Stalinism or Maoism were denounced as Trotskyists, anarchists, and petty-bourgeois intellectuals. The single major difference from the thirties was that the genuine participation of blacks and other third-world people in leadership roles was central to the strategy of the proposed new party.

5

General Baker had good rapport with the gut-bucket element in the plants, but he wasn't sure he trusted those intellectuals. Gen would run his thing on you, but you could deal with Gen. I never had any trouble with Gen.

Jordan Sims, in an interview with the authors, August 19, 1972

By late 1971 the League of Revolutionary Black Workers had begun a transformation of its own. Originally the League wanted to continue its struggle with Formanism from within BWC. John Williams and other representatives attended a Baltimore conference and other meetings, but they soon concluded that the exclusion of the League was final and irrevocable. They continued with their plan for International Black Appeal; but it began to flounder and like BWC remained more of a plan than a reality. Within a short time, the League ceased public activity and began a startling change in style and theory. Chuck Wooten had come into contact with members of the California-based Communist League, a small organization which espoused a rigid Marxist approach emphasizing heavy reading and memorization of the works of Mao and Stalin. Robert Williams (no relation to the Robert Williams who had been in exile in Cuba and China) moved from California to Detroit, where he became the theoretical leader of the individuals remaining in the League. Intense self-criticism sessions and study groups became the prerequisites for continuing membership. Most of the students dropped away, and many individuals, including Luke Tripp, became inactive. The worker components which had been physically the most sloppy and ideologically the most casual sections of the old League became highly structured, disciplined, immaculately clean, and ideologically dogmatic.

The secretiveness which had characterized the Baker approach became more pronounced than ever. The China-Albania Bookstore was opened, but there were few public meetings and almost no publications. Some members of the League holding professional jobs were ordered to give them up to work in the factories or to serve the organization. This proletarianization of the ranks was the most rigid and crudest possible application of Lenin's dictim of "fewer but better" revolutionaries. When the organization resurfaced, it had become the Detroit branch of the Communist League. Baker remained one of its principal leaders.

Knowledge of precisely what the Communist League was doing remained sparse until the spring of 1973. Most of the former League sympathizers were put off by the heavy Marxist terminology, the Maoist paraphernalia, and the whole sectarian environment of the Communist League. That spring, however, members of the Communist League began to attend social functions given by other groups, called on former League members, and showed visible work in the factories. Their personal attitudes had undergone an astonishing shift. They were extremely polite to whites and seemed anxious to form alliances with similarly oriented groups. The line of the Communist League was very much like that of the groups with which BWC was working. The Communist League advocated a new multinational (interracial) communist party based on Marxism-Leninism. The organization accepted whites and all third-world people as members. Just how much of the old RUM membership the Communist League had managed to keep in contact with and how many new recruits it had gained was a matter known only to the organization, but obviously some kind of continuity existed. At least fifty members of the Communist League were visible in the summer of 1973 during a series of wildcat strikes which swept the Detroit auto plants. Perhaps it was only coincidence, but each of the three Chrysler factories to suffer major wildcats in that summer had had an active RUM unit.

The Communist League's strict organization, self-discipline, and stress on Marxist ideology represented a specific set of solutions to some of the problems which had plagued the earlier League. Baker's RUM strategy had often seemed more dependent on spontaneous mass action than on the work of preexisting organizations. At other times his groups seemed like industrial guerrillas whose unrelenting attacks would eventually spark a general uprising. The freewheeling style of the old League had been compared by some Detroiters to that of the Industrial Workers of the World or "Wobblies," an anarcho-syndicalist formation that had a mass following in the first decades of the twentieth century. The League idea that one vast general strike could end wars and abolish capitalism itself suggested even programmatic parallels with the IWW. For the League activist, like the convinced Wobbly, each battle over wages, hours, or conditions was only so much preparation for the final struggle to abolish the master class. The daily fights with the boss were the furnaces in which revolutionary fighters were forged. The *Industrial Worker* of June 3, 1909, had stated: "The very fights themselves, like the drill of an army, prepare the worker for even greater tasks and

victories.'' In summing up the contradictions faced by the IWW in
his *We Shall Be All,* published in 1969, historian Melvin
Dubofsky could almost have been writing about the contradictions
which faced the League of Revolutionary Black Workers:

> The organization's refusal to sign contracts raised prob-
> lems that the IWW never resolved. American employers
> were never particularly happy dealing with labor unions,
> and certainly under no circumstances would negotiate
> with a labor organization that refused to sign contracts
> and insisted that capitalists had no rights worthy of
> respect. Hence, employers constantly used the IWW's
> no-contract principle to rationalize their own resistance
> to any form of collective bargaining. If the IWW could
> not negotiate with employers, how could it raise wages
> and improve working conditions? If it could offer the
> members nothing but perpetual industrial warfare, how
> could it maintain its membership, let alone increase its
> ranks? On the other hand, if the IWW did sanction
> contracts, win recognition, and improve its members'
> lives, what would keep them from forsaking rev-
> olutionary goals and adhering to the well-established
> AFL pattern? If the IWW began to declare truces in the
> class war, how could it bring about the ultimate revolu-
> tion? In the end, IWW leaders usually subordinated
> reform opportunities to revolutionary necessities, while
> the rank-and-file, when it could, took the reforms and
> neglected the revolution.

The Black Workers Congress and the Communist League rejected both the reformist ideas associated with traditional trade
unionism and the freewheeling, libertarian ideas associated with
the IWW. Like many white radicals who had belonged to the
organizations collectively called the New Left in the sixties, the
black revolutionaries of BWC and CL were seeking organizational
and ideological theories that emphasized the role of industrial

workers and professional revolutionaries. The disappointments, frustrations, and failures of the sixties when the movement had been infused with an anti-authoritarian and egalitarian spirit often led to sectarianism and to rigid notions of hierarchy and centralism in the seventies. One of the distinctions of the League of Revolutionary Black Workers had been that it had tried to combine its developing Marxist perspective with a structure that allowed considerable independence to its various units and individual members.

Ken Cockrel and his associates in Detroit considered the politics of the Black Workers Congress and the Communist League to be "playing in the sandbox." They felt that both BWC and the Communist League were organizational retreats to old forms which had failed in the past and would fail in the future. Cockrel believed that rigid cadre groups dealing with ideological subtleties were not essential to making a bid for power either within the factories or outside. He advocated building mass movements around immediate and pressing social issues. As an attorney, Cockrel had immediate familiarity with the manner in which judges and city officials won elections. He thought a radical thrust in that area would be profitable. Partly through accident and partly through a deliberate selection of cases, Cockrel had become a major adversary of the Detroit Police Department. From the time of New Bethel onward, Cockrel had risen steadily to become Detroit's most well-known and influential radical. More than any other single individual, he was identified in the popular mind and in the mass media as the personification of a serious black revolutionary. By the autumn of 1972, one of his white law partners had won an important judgeship in the local criminal court system, and Cockrel himself began to speak seriously of making a bid to become the Mayor of America's fifth-largest city.

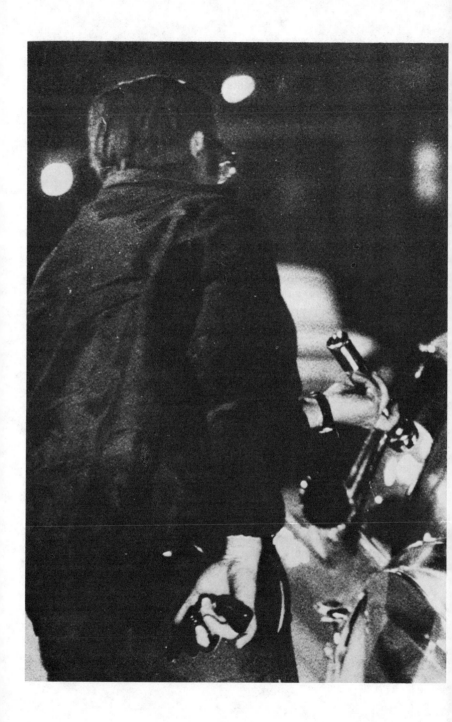

Chapter Eight

Stop the Robberies, Enjoy Safe Streets: STRESS

1

I am not saying that the white people of Detroit are different from the white people of any other city. I know what has been done in Chicago, I know what prejudice growing out of race and religion has done the world over, and all through time. I am not blaming Detroit. I am stating what has happened, that is all.

Clarence Darrow, in a speech to the Ossian Sweet jury in 1925

In 1967, during the height of the Great Rebellion, three white police officers killed three unarmed blacks at the Algiers Motel located on Detroit's main street. The shots were fired by David Senak, Robert Paille, and Ronald August. The victims were Auburey Pollard, Fred Temple, and Carl Cooper.

Senak's grandparents on both sides were Czechoslovakian

Opposite page: An ununiformed STRESS officer investigating a suspicious car, with his revolver behind his hip.

183

immigrants. His father worked for Holley Carburetor and his mother was a keypunch operator for Chrysler. Before joining the Detroit Police Department, Senak did a four-month hitch with the Air National Guard. At the time of the Great Rebellion he was 23.

Auburey Pollard's parents had come from the South in 1943, the year of the race riot. His mother was a laundress and housekeeper for white families; and his father, who had spent some years in the Navy, worked in Chrysler plants. Pollard had gotten work as an arc welder at Ford in October 1966, but he was soon demoted to laborer and left his job in March 1967. The 18-year-old Pollard had done fifteen days in the Detroit House of Correction for striking one of his high-school teachers. One of his brothers, Chaney Pollard, 21, was in the U.S. Marine Corps at the time of the Great Rebellion; the other, Robert Pollard, 17, was in the Michigan Reformatory at Ionia doing a three-to-ten-year sentence for having robbed a newsboy of seven dollars.

Ronald August, 28, had enlisted in the Navy and had been proud to be on the ship that had picked up astronaut Scott Carpenter. His father was a tool grinder. August had joined the police department in 1963, when he found all skilled job opportunities closed to him.

Fred Temple, 17, had quit school in the eleventh grade and had gone to work at Ford. His father had worked as a machine operator at Thompson Products for twenty-four years.

Robert Paille, 31, was of French Canadian background and had served in the Air Force. His father had been a lumberjack.

Carl Cooper, 17, had been in trouble with the police since he was 13. His mother worked as a power sewer at Walker Crouse Enterprises, and Cooper began hanging around the motel after he was laid off from his job at Chrysler.

The events which brought these six Detroiters into a deadly confrontation have been exhaustively and sensitively recorded in John Hersey's *Algiers Motel Incident.* Shorn of its particulars, the story is typical of police-black confrontations in the city. People of the same class origins, people sharing many similar problems, came face to face at gunpoint as problems of race negated their commonality. Those who held power in American cities had historically manipulated racial differences and violence to divide their opposition, to limit criticism, and to maintain control, even though things sometimes got out of hand. The Great Rebellion was only the most destructive among hundreds of rebellions during the period, and it fit into a historic pattern as old as the United States.

Slavery had never existed in Michigan because the state was part of the slave-free Northwest Territory, and blacks had worked and lived as free people since the days of the earliest settlements. Detroit, the last station on the underground railroad, had been a frequent meeting place for militant abolitionists. A plaque just off the Fisher Expressway a few blocks from the city's courthouses marks the site where John Brown, Frederick Douglass, and a group of Detroit abolitionists had a historic meeting some eight months before the raid on Harpers Ferry. Fifty miles north of Detroit, the Republican Party had been formed by people with strong anti-slavery sentiments.

Racism also had a long history in the city of Detroit. A serious race riot had taken place in 1833 and another in 1863, in the midst of the Civil War. In the second instance, white workers had burnt out the black section of town after the newspapers fed their fears that freed black slaves would flock northward and take away all their jobs. A few years later, the first national organization of American workers, the National Labor Union, established its headquarters in Detroit. One of its two major leaders, Welsh-born Richard Trevellick, argued unsuccessfully that the union should accept blacks as members. As a compromise, he urged the National Labor Union to take the position that blacks and convicts should receive equal wages for doing the same work as free whites. He was again defeated. Trevellick and other labor spokesmen continued the unsuccessful fight against racism in the Greenback-Labor Party and the Knights of Labor. Lily-white unionism became entrenched with the rise of the American Federation of Labor, and immigrant workers coming into cities like Detroit were taught that if they were white, no matter how difficult circumstances were for them, life for their children would be "all right."

Racism grew so virulent that, by 1924, the Ku Klux Klan's influence in Detroit enabled its write-in candidate for Mayor to win the election with 123,679 votes. He was prevented from taking office only when 17,000 of his votes were taken away on technicalities, allowing the otherwise runner-up to become Mayor on the basis of 116,807 votes. A state proposal to outlaw parochial schools during the same period was defeated 2-1, but it garnered 353,817 votes. Fiery crosses and men in white hoods were no novelty in the Detroit streets of the twenties. On July 11, 1925, ten thousand people cheered KKK delegates as they flayed at "Catholics, Jews, and niggers." On September 9 of the same year, hundreds of whites, led by the KKK, attacked the home of Ossian Sweet, a black doctor who had recently moved into an all-white neighborhood. The Sweet family was armed and fired upon the mob in self-defense, killing one white. Dr. Sweet, rather than the rioters, was put on trial, and it took all the legal and oratorical skills of Clarence Darrow to gain an acquittal. Mob attacks on black families daring to move into previously all-white neighborhoods have remained a constant problem through the 1970s.

The KKK remained 200,000 strong during most of the twenties and thirties, and it bred an even more extreme organization called the Black Legion. From 1933 to 1936, the Black Legion was involved in some fifty murders in the state of Michigan. The Legion's enemies were not only blacks, Jews, and Catholics, but communists and union organizers. During the same decade, Father Charles E. Coughlin, a Catholic priest advocating a mixture of racism and populism, won an enthusiastic mass following in the region through his radio programs and publications. Coughlin's anti-Semitism became so outrageous that he openly defended the Nazi regime in Germany and had to be silenced by the Catholic hierarchy when the United States entered World War II.

All these forms of bigotry were cleverly manipulated by Detroit corporations. Each new white immigrant group had to fight its way into the good jobs and better neighborhoods. The corporations consciously pitted the groups against one another, being most blatant with regard to blacks, who at one time were used exclusively as strike-breakers. Henry Ford elevated the divide-and-rule principle to a full-blown racial strategy, and one of his payoffs came when 800 black workers at the Rouge plant were the only rank-and-file group to put up a physical fight against the UAW during its final organizing drive in April 1941. The vigilante and lynch tradition had corporate counterparts too. All the major firms hired private detectives and did surveillance on employees as a matter of routine. Again, it was Henry Ford who led the way. He hired ex-prizefighter Harry Bennett to organize a private Ford army of 3000 men who were primarily ex-cons, prizefighters, wrestlers, football players, and other "tough guys."

The race riot of 1943 was one of the consequences of institutionalized racism in the city and the auto industry. The labor shortage caused by World War II brought black workers into the city by the tens of thousands, but they remained locked in narrowly defined ghettos and found social and economic progress virtually nil. Tens of thousands of white Appalachians came into the city at about the same time. The old generation of mainly immigrant workers looked upon both newcomer groups with distaste, but found it easier to accept a white hillbilly accent next door than a black skin. The violence which ensued, fed by the tensions of the war years, was strictly racial: whites against blacks with the whites led by a nearly all-white Detroit Police Department. Thirty-four people died, hundreds were injured, and millions of dollars were lost through property damage and lost work hours. The riot was the most violent in American civil history, though it was to pale before the Watts uprising of 1964, just as Watts would be only a prelude to Newark and then to the most violent rebellion of all—the Great Rebellion of 1967.

The violence of 1967 was significantly different from that of the earlier Detroit explosions. The riots of 1833, 1863, and 1943 had been conflicts between the races. The 1967 Rebellion was a conflict between blacks and state power. In 1943, whites were on the offensive and rode around town in cars looking for easy black targets. In 1967, blacks were on the offensive and their major target was property. In some neighborhoods, Appalachians, students, and other whites took part in the action alongside blacks as their partners. Numerous photos show systematic and integrated looting, which the rebels called "shopping for free." Even so, the Rebellion was entirely a product of the black movement of the sixties, and that in turn had been a direct consequence of the frustrations and unkept promises of the postwar era.

However people defined it, the Great Rebellion struck fear into the white population of the city of Detroit. The National Guard and police used to quell the fighting were nearly all white. Many of these men undoubtedly had fathers and mothers who had been in the plants during the thirties when blacks were used as scabs and when the police and the National Guard were used against the unions. Now, they had become the guardians of legitimacy. Their gut fear of black liberation, combined with the long tradition of racism, was to increase in the following years. Instead of a private army like Henry Ford's or a clandestine Black Legion, white Detroiters put their faith in these men, the armed power of the state. The Detroit Police Department in particular became the front-line force against black liberation.

2

I wanted to start in an apprenticeship in electrical work, or plumbing, or carpentry. Any apprenticeship. But the doors were closed then, it seemed to be, because every place I went they just weren't hiring. . . . the Police Department had always had a recruitment drive, so to speak. . . . I went down there and put in the application, and within a few weeks I had heard that I was accepted. I learned about it a month before we were married.

Ronald August, Detroit police officer, quoted in John Hersey's *Algiers Motel Incident,* 1968

The Detroit Police Department of 1967 in no way represented the estimated 35 percent of the population which was black. First, there were only 217 black officers in a force of 4709. These blacks held only nine of the 560 posts of sergeant or higher, only three of the 220 posts of lieutenant or higher, and only one of the 65 posts of inspector or higher. During this same period, 35 percent of the city's civil service employees were black, as were 35 percent of the public-school teachers.

Following the Great Rebellion, the police department received a $15,000 grant to bring up the number of black officers. Despite 1700 written inquiries and 375 formal applications, only several dozen blacks were hired in the course of a year. The slowness in hiring blacks was matched by an intense interest in not losing any whites. The city's total population had declined by 100,000 in the decade of the sixties while the surrounding metropolitan area was zooming from 2.4 million to 4.2 million. Ninety percent of the increase in the metropolitan area was accounted for by whites while the city's white population declined by 20 percent. The median age for the whites who remained within the city limits was 36, compared to a national median age for urban dwellers of 28. The *Washington Post* of February 20, 1973, summarized the population shifts by calling Detroit a city which was getting "blacker, older, and poorer." The white exodus had involved the working class as fully as the middle class. Policemen wanted to move their families out of the city too, but the city had a rule that its police must live within the city. False addresses and other ways of evading this provision became common and were winked at when they involved whites. The department also allowed an officer a one-year period of grace to find a Detroit address after being hired, and in a key ruling the department permanently exempted 400 officers from having to comply with the rule at all. A Police Community Relations Sub-Committee staff memo of March 25, 1968, described the situation as intolerable. "The people in the black community see this move as one allowing an occupation army to occupy the city during the day and return safely to their homes in the white suburbs at night."

The *Detroit Free Press* undertook a survey in 1968 of attitudes within the police department. The gap between the black and white officers shown by the survey reflected the polarization within the city. Over 50 percent of the white police thought that housing opportunities were equal for both races, that job opportunities were equal, and that blacks were *favored* in the schools. Among blacks, 8 percent thought that job opportunities were equal and only 3 percent thought that housing opportunities were equal or that blacks were favored in school. Seventy-two percent of the detectives and 50 percent of all the white police believed that the police treated blacks fairly. Eighty-seven percent of the blacks thought otherwise, 56 percent saying that blacks were treated very unfairly and 31 percent saying that blacks were treated slightly unfairly. Forty-seven percent of the white police thought the Great Rebellion had had obvious long-term negative effects, while almost the same percentage of blacks believed the opposite. Sixty-four percent of the white patrolmen thought that the Great Rebellion had been planned in advance, while 72 percent of the blacks in all ranks thought it had been spontaneous.

The Detroit of 1968 was deceptive. Liberal Mayor Cavanagh, the candidate of TULC, was still in city hall. The highest officers of the largest corporations in the city had rallied behind the New Detroit Committee, which had pledged multimillions of dollars to rebuild the city in a fresh outburst of racial cooperation. The UAW, the most liberal of all the major trade unions, stood ready to do its share, just as reliable Wayne State University, under the leadership of liberal President Keast, was prepared to hold its doors open round the clock, twelve months a year. In spite of these good intentions of the liberals, conditions of life, work, and education were so harsh for black people that *ICV, DRUM,* Watson's *South End,* and the League of Revolutionary Black Workers found a ready audience for their revolutionary ideas. The city was growing physically and spiritually uglier all the time. Its violence was so intense that it became the national leader in murders. Detroit had called itself "the Arsenal of Democracy" during World War II. Jerry Cavanagh had referred to it as "the All-American City." Now, the newspapers dubbed Detroit

"Murder City, U.S.A." Again and again, as the policies of liberalism failed in the schools, in the factories, and in the streets, the guns and nightsticks of the Detroit Police Department were the reality Detroit blacks and their allies had to face.

3

The DPOA believes . . . the charges of police brutality are part of a nefarious plot by those who would like our form of government overthrown. The blueprint for anarchy calls for the destruction of the effectiveness of the police. Certainly, it must be obvious that every incident is magnified and exploited with only one purpose. A lot of well-meaning people, without realizing their real role, are doing the job for the anarchists.

Carl Parsell, President of the Detroit Police Officers Association, in *Tuebor,* December 1968

During 1968, the Detroit Police Department became involved in a series of incidents in which the racism of its officers was the major factor. The first incident occurred on May 3, 1968, during the Poor People's Campaign led by Reverend Ralph Abernathy. A rally had been scheduled to be held at Cobo Hall, Detroit's convention center near the City-County Building, the Ford Auditorium, the Veterans Memorial Building, and other structures of the attempted waterfront resurrection begun in the fifties. The demonstration, which was being telecast over a local channel, was peaceful and orderly until a car stalled. At that point, the police suddenly became extremely agitated and, almost without warning, mounted a cavalry-style charge upon the demonstrators. Nineteen people were seriously injured in the action.

Phillip Mason and Sam Dennis, officials of the U.S. Department of Justice, observed the melee and were quoted in an article about the incident published in the November 13 edition of the *Detroit Free Press.* Mason stated, "I saw old ladies being pushed and manhandled, grabbed by the collar and pushed out doors. I saw young men being beaten with billy clubs." Dennis added, "I saw officers ride horses into a crowd which I judged to be under control. In addition, I saw officers strike individuals in that crowd for no apparent reason. . . . I asked several command officers to pull other officers back. They attempted to but were unsuccessful. In fact, one command officer was knocked down by a patrolman. . . . All of this was over a stalled car well out of any traffic. Police were insensitive."

Black and liberal spokesmen denounced the actions of the police. State Senator Coleman Young told the *Michigan Chronicle,* on June 1, "If the mayor is afraid to take on the DPOA [Detroit Police Officers Association] then we will do it for him. Otherwise this city is headed for a bloodbath." This and other protests led to some face-saving gestures from the mayor's office, but little else. The furor over what came to be called Cobo Hall I had barely quieted down when a new incident occurred in the same area on the occasion of a rally for George Wallace's presidential campaign.

Cobo Hall II involved over one thousand black and white demonstrators who gathered on October 29 to express their displeasure with Wallace's candidacy. Some Wallace backers came to Cobo Hall carrying aerosol spray cans with incapacitating chemicals similar to the Mace used by police. When one of these cans was used on a black demonstrator, fistfights broke out and the police flew into action. Their pro-Wallace sympathies were obvious. They made virtually no attacks on Wallace people and seemed to single out white anti-Wallace demonstrators for the roughest treatment. The idea of containing the violence seemed to have no priority at all. The police violence was more flagrant than during Cobo Hall I. Bystanders, reporters, and photographers were beaten. Even James Herman, a field investigator for Mayor Cavanagh's Community Relations Commission who was specifically assigned to observe the event, was injured by the police. In a typical incident, a busload of Wallace supporters threw hunks of scrap iron at a group struggling with a Wallace-ite. The people hit by the iron were attacked by the police, while no action was directed toward the bus. Numerous individuals complained of being beaten at the rally and at police headquarters afterwards. Sheila Murphy, then 20 and a staff organizer for Ad Hoc, which had raised money to assist Detroiters involved in earlier conflicts with the police, told news reporters shortly afterwards that the police warned her that they would kill her if they got her alone.

An even uglier incident followed a few days later at the nearby Veterans Memorial. On the night of November 1, an organization of police officers' wives was giving a dance in the first-floor ballroom. Over a hundred couples were in attendance, enjoying some ten barrels of beer and the quiet sounds of the Ron Ross Quartet. On the sixth floor of the same building, the black Ebenezer A.M.E. Church was holding a teen dance featuring the hard-driving contemporary rhythms of the Seven Sounds. The two parties had no reason to interact and might not even have known about each other's presence except for inadequate facilities. The Veterans Memorial was so poorly planned that people had to take elevators to free floors because the ballroom floors didn't have a sufficient number of toilets.

As the evening progressed, word began to circulate among the policemen that black hooligans were causing trouble in the elevators. Women, in particular, complained of obscene gestures and sexual threats. In a sequence of events that was not entirely clear, several Detroit police stopped two separate groups of black teenagers outside the building. The teenagers were beaten and kicked, and at least one shot was fired.

The incident was like many a Detroit catch-you-in-the-parking-lot brawl, except for the participants. On one side were armed white police officers, and on the other, some of the sons and daughters of Detroit's black elite. James Evans, 17, who was hospitalized overnight because of the beating given to him, was the son of the Director of the Fisher YMCA. Another hospitalized teenager, Derrick Tabor, 17, was the son of a minister, and he managed to get a call through to his father, who got to the scene while the beatings were still in progress. The 15-year-old son of Reverend Nicholas Hood, Detroit's only black councilman at the time, was not personally injured but was an eyewitness to the whole affair.

Black pressure for a full investigation soon ran into what was termed a "blue curtain of silence." DPOA President Carl Parsell said that his men had been taunted and harassed to the breaking point by "Negroes," but he admitted he wasn't sure if they were the same "Negroes" who were at the church dance. A security guard reported that three black teenage stragglers in the elevators who were not connected with the dance left after he confronted them. James Heaney, 60, an attorney and realtor who had run for Mayor in 1965 as a candidate from the ultraconservative Greater Detroit Home-Owners Council, backed up the police and security guard. He said that he had been in the building late that evening and had been threatened by some black teenagers.

Whatever substance there was to the allegation that some anonymous black youths had threatened people in the elevator, it soon became clear that the two separate groups of teenagers attacked by the off-duty police had not done any taunting. In addition to the beatings, kickings, and shooting, a car had been hauled away, and when it was returned its owner found it plastered with George Wallace stickers. Many officers who had not taken part in the actual violence had not taken any steps to stop the beatings, a sworn duty they were required to carry out by the same laws which required them to carry their guns. Eventually nine men were suspended because of the incident. James H. Brickley, a white Assistant Wayne County Prosecutor, made a public statement on November 16 in which he declared that the attacks had been unprovoked and that there was no evidence that the police or their wives had been abused or insulted by the youths who were attacked. Brickley added that, even if they had been, the action taken was totally illegal: "The policemen, with varying degrees of participation, threatened and assaulted the Negro youths without

provocation or justification. At no time, did any of the police
officers identify themselves, make any arrests, or make any report
of the incident.''

Four months later when one policeman was killed and another
seriously wounded during the New Bethel incident, the events of
1968 were invoked by all sides in the disputes. To the black
community, New Bethel was another indication of the vigilante
mentality of the police and its over-reliance on force. Only Judge
Crockett's intervention had saved an ugly situation from exploding
into a major racial confrontation. On the other side the DPOA took
out a full-page ad calling for Crockett's removal. Carl Parsell
complained that the blue-blood New Detroit Committee was trying
to use the police as a scapegoat. The tone of his speeches and his
general attitude were the same as they had been the previous
December in his editorial for *Tuebor,* the DPOA newsletter, where
he wrote: ''In the 1967 riot when police were restricted in the
beginning from exercising their legal powers, the situation got out
of hand. When proper force was used in the Cobo Hall [incidents]
peace and order was restored.'' Parsell's editorial had also
denounced the Michigan Civil Rights Commission: ''We charge
the civil rights commission with denying constitutional rights to
police officers and denying them due process of law.''

The DPOA failed in its attempt to remove Crockett from the
bench, and an April 16 report of the Detroit Commission on
Community Relations was highly critical of the police department.
The report noted that the *Detroit Free Press* had publicly
apologized for reporting inaccurate information to the public about
New Bethel and that a letter written by a black Detroiter had
characterized the slain Officer Czapski as a fair-minded and decent
man. The report criticized the police reaction as a tragic mistake
that was ''part of the inheritance of the ghetto rebellion in the
summer of '67 in which issues of community policy and response
were never properly resolved. Nor were they clarified in April of
'68, the Martin Luther King assassination aftermath with its
curfew and police mobilization. . . . The DPOA promises of
'support law and order and remove George Crockett' have merged

to symbolize the spectre of the police state and paramilitary government of a colonial people.''

The Community Relations Commission report had just started to circulate when a new flareup occurred over the New Bethel case. This time, the trouble involved Recorder's Court Judge Joseph E. Maher and Kenneth Cockrel, who was the attorney for Alfred Hibbit, one of the men accused of killing Czapski. During the pretrial hearings, Maher abruptly interrupted Cockrel's presentation and ended the proceedings, after doubling Hibbit's bail to $50,000, even though Hibbit had turned himself in as soon as a warrant was issued for him. An infuriated Cockrel stormed from the courtroom and was quoted by the media as calling Judge Maher ''a racist monkey, a honky dog fool, and a thieving pirate.''

Cockrel's words were barely out of his mouth before Judge Maher was calling for Cockrel's disbarment on the grounds of contempt and general unprofessional conduct. Cockrel shot back that he was expressing the sentiments of the black population of the city of Detroit in language congenial to them. The disbarment attempt moved rapidly, and the case was heard in late May. Cockrel's chief counsel was Sheldon Otis, and the Detroit Recorder's Court bench was represented by Michael O'Hara, a former state Supreme Court justice. Wayne County Circuit Court Judge Joseph Sullivan heard the case, since Judge Robert Colombo had disqualified all the Recorder's Court judges from hearing the case. Harry Philo and Justin Ravitz, two of Cockrel's law partners, assisted with the defense. His legal team also included Howard Moore of Atlanta, who had defended Stokely Carmichael and Julian Bond on similar charges, Dennis James of the National Lawyers Guild, Ed Bell of Detroit, who would soon become a judge himself, and Myron Wahls, the President of the Wolverine Bar Association, the professional organization for Michigan's black lawyers.

The first day of the trial, over seventy-five sheriff's deputies patrolled the court and hallways as hundreds of people tried to get into the courtroom. Eventually, a door was broken down, a court reporter fainted, and the court had to be adjourned for one day. The following morning, to the astonishment of the media, the defense said that psychiatrists, psychologists, attorneys, and semanticists would prove that Cockrel's accusations were true. Nationally famous attorneys such as F. Lee Bailey were prepared to fly to Detroit to testify on Cockrel's behalf. Harry Philo indicated the uncompromising view of the defense by stating that the $50,000 bail was "thievery and piracy"; the defense believed that Maher "violated two different statutes several times, that he did it knowingly and that therefore he is a criminal . . . a despicable incompetent who is white." Thus, Cockrel's term "honky dog fool" was correct in a colloquial sense. Sheldon Otis declared, "It is bad enough that our society has made Mr. Cockrel a second-class citizen because of his color. To make him a third- or fourth-class citizen because he is a lawyer would seem to me to be tearing the guts out of the Constitution. Attorneys . . . are obliged *not* to remain silent. It is their obligation to inform the public. Mr. Cockrel would be derelict in his duty if he did not do so." To make it clear that the case could not be hushed up, Cockrel said that he would make daily reports to the public at Detroit's Kennedy Square each day the trial lasted.

In early June, following a six-day recess, the accusations against Cockrel were dropped. Judge Maher agreed to reduce Hibbit's bond to $10,000, and Cockrel issued a statement that saved some face for Maher: "I do not retreat from public statements I have made. I must add I regret that the choice of language employed by me is so widely misunderstood by such a large segment of our population. I have spoken and I shall always speak in the language, colloquial or otherwise, which I believe is understood by the persons to whom I address myself." He told reporters, "This is a vindication of the position we took. I have no regrets for what I said. I think my characterizations were accurate."

4

In each case, Cockrel—dramatic and persuasive
—argued to juries well-populated with the kind of
persons he designs his people's party for—blacks and
workers, the little people he regards as oppressed.

Detroit News Sunday Magazine, October 14, 1973

Cockrel's ability to turn a defense into an offense and to capture favorable publicity in the process was demonstrated over and over again in his struggles with the Detroit police and judicial system. His struggle with Judge Maher proved to be a worthy prelude to his actual defense of Hibbit before Judge Colombo. Assisted by Justin Ravitz, Sheldon Halpern, and Milton Henry, Cockrel took the offensive with a sensational run around left end play by attacking the entire jury-selection system. He charged that in a city which was predominantly working class and in which the population was approaching a black majority, there could be no justice from a jury-selection system that produced only two black jurors and almost no young people or members of the working class. In a series of spectacular and effective legal moves, Cockrel and Ravitz demonstrated that the jury-selection rolls were not fair. Districts with heavy black or working-class populations were slighted in favor of areas with exclusively or predominantly white voters of middle-class background. Young people considered mature enough to vote and to serve in the armed forces were being scratched from lists as immature. One Wayne State University instructor had been disqualified simply because he wore a beard.

The outcome of the Cockrel-Ravitz maneuver was that the original Hibbit jury was thrown out, and a new jury, which was predominantly black, was selected. Hibbit and the other defendants were exonerated at the trial and other subsequent trials.

Even more significantly, the challenge to jury-selection procedures made appeals possible for thousands of Michigan prisoners, and it helped establish new ground rules for Michigan jury selection. The attorneys were pleased with their work, but they did not consider it revolutionary in a pure sense. It was merely a step toward reestablishing basic Bill of Rights guarantees. They felt that ultimately the system would revolt against its own rules rather than allow black and working-class juries to sit in judgment on cases involving laws based primarily on property rights. This revolt would bring about a situation in which class interests would be clearly defined on a mass scale.

The James Johnson case, which came up a year after New Bethel, was a further opportunity for application of the "jury of your peers" strategy. This time, rather than emphasizing race, the defense team led by Cockrel emphasized class. They wanted as many people on the jury with direct work experience in the city as they could get. Their "expert" witnesses included production-line workers who could tell about the dehumanizing effects of working at the Eldon plant. The defense argued that the irrationality which had caused the crime was not a result of some flaw in James Johnson's brain or personality, but of the policies of the Chrysler Corporation. In the contempt case, the judge had been put on trial; in the New Bethel case, the jury-selection system had been put on trial; and in the Johnson case, the Chrysler Corporation was put on trial. In each instance, eloquent and brilliant legal work brought victory in cases which seemed all but hopeless on the surface.

Cockrel had more than the "gift of gab" or "charisma" going for him. His court defenses were meticulously planned and fit into a wider political movement. In each of the celebrated cases, Cockrel broke the bonds limiting the trial to one individual in a specific situation defined by a set of precise circumstances. He enlarged the scope of the cases to involve the interests of a whole community or class, which in turn lent its strength to the particular defendant. As the police continued to gear up their repressive machinery, Cockrel elaborated an anti-repression strategy which became the line of the League of Revolutionary Black Workers. At a January 30, 1970, anti-repression conference organized by the Detroit Newsreel organization Cockrel said that all revolutionary organizations which find themselves in numerous conspiracy trials should look to their own structures, because that should not be happening at all, and never on a wholesale basis if the organization were properly set up. He noted how grand juries and police had failed to jail people like Mike Hamlin, Chuck Wooten, John Williams, Luke Tripp, Ron March, and Fred Holsey. The attempt to dislodge Watson from the *South End* and the attempt to disbar Cockrel himself had also failed, as had attempts to expel high-school supporters of the League. All this and more had been accomplished because local people had been engaged in a local mass struggle. They had not been obliged to call on national celebrities to defend them. Their tactic of defense had not been to complain or moralize but to take the offensive in court and out of court. The ultimate goal was to control the court and police completely. Thus Cockrel declared, ''You do not circulate petitions, write letters to attorney generals, meet with black police assistants, etc. You take over the police department, and you take over the city. This is not reformist. Reformism is what is counter-revolutionary. The content of the particular movement is critical—the overall perspective.''

Cockrel severely criticized many of the participants in the anti-repression conference. In an open attack on the Panthers, he stated that a political organization must do everything in its power to avoid being transformed into defense committees solely concerned with keeping its leadership out of jail. Cockrel may well have had the murder charges leveled against Bobby Seale in mind. Seale's chief accuser was George Sams, a member of the national Black Panther Party who had once been a black gang leader in Highland Park. The League people had considered Sams to be so irresponsible and irrational that they wouldn't even let him be around them, much less be a member of their organization. A related point concerned the uncritical attitude many radical whites

had toward blacks. Cockrel attacked the white chairman of the
meeting: "Is it [your] position that any utterance that is ever made
by any blood at any time is profoundly revolutionary in content and
should not be in any way stifled, stymied, ordered, directed, or
organized? We [the League] regard that as being a wholesale
abdication of the responsibility to use one's time efficiently and to
use the time of other people efficiently." Cockrel went on to say
that much of the work done on "big" national cases was relatively
meaningless because it did not and could not involve the large
mass of working people, who had enormous problems of their own
to deal with. One thread that ran throughout Cockrel's thinking
was the need to concentrate mass power upon a weak point in the
system: "We say that the point of greatest vulnerability . . . is the
point of production in the economic infrastructure of the system.
We say it makes sense to organize workers inside of plants to
precipitate the maximum dislocation and maximum paralysis of
the operation of the capitalist-imperialist system. We say that all
people who don't own, rule, and benefit from decisions which are
made by those who own and rule are workers." In these remarks,
in his practice of law, and in the projects he foresaw for the
League, Cockrel was moving toward building a black and worker
base for a bid for elective office. His main target was the repressive
mechanisms of the state. Cockrel believed that control of the
factories and control of the streets needed to go hand in hand with
control of the courts and the police.

5

*We know that today we have the highly sophisticated
Green Beret STRESS unit roaming our city at will and
killing on whim. . . . It promises to get even better.
General John Nichols is in Germany tonight, studying
police procedures in Munich, Frankfurt, and Berlin.*

*Maybe he'll have ovens for the survivors and witnesses
of STRESS murder. Nichols said he'd tattoo STRESS
on his chest to prove it was staying.*

Sheila Murphy, in a From The Ground Up Book Club
Seminar, March 21, 1973

Detroit had always been known as a violent city, but by 1970 the
situation was clearly out of hand. There were over 23,000 reported
robberies, which meant that at least one out of every sixty-five
Detroiters had been a victim. An army of drug addicts lived in the
remains of 15,000 inner-city houses abandoned for an urban-
renewal program which never materialized. Over a million guns
were in the hands of the population, and union officials estimated
that half the workers came to the plants armed with one weapon or
another. The celebrated police-riot cases of 1968 followed the
pattern of the Algiers Motel case: no cops were convicted. By
January of 1971, the atmosphere of permissiveness regarding
police misconduct and the growing chaos in the streets had
prepared the way for a new police unit called STRESS (Stop the
Robberies, Enjoy Safe Streets). This unit was a secret, elite section
of Detroit undercover assault squads.

The Detroit Police Department never released information on
exactly how many men were involved in STRESS or on their exact
duties, but the unit was estimated to have no more than one
hundred men. The favorite STRESS method was the "decoy"
operation in which one police officer acted as a potential victim in
some area where a crime was likely to occur. As the decoy was
attacked, other STRESS officers moved in for the arrest. STRESS
operated in "high-crime" areas, which invariably turned out to be
areas with overwhelmingly black populations. The difference between STRESS's decoying tactic and patently illegal "entrapment" was soon washed away in a floodtide of blood. During
the first year of STRESS's operation, the Detroit Police
Department chalked up the highest number of civilian killings per

capita of any American police department. The Detroit police in 1971 killed civilians at the rate of 7.17 per 1000 officers. The five closest rivals in killings by police were Houston (5 per 1000 officers), Baltimore (2.93), Chicago (2.54), New York City (1.84), and Philadelphia (1.28). More than a third of the killings in Detroit were done by STRESS, which represented, at most, two percent of the department. The police regarded STRESS as a tough-fisted sheriff's posse dealing with saloon toughs and desperadoes; but to the citizens who suffered an estimate 500 raids without search warrants and twenty deaths by police bullets within thirty months, STRESS seemed more like Billy the Kid run amuck behind the protection of a badge.

The STRESS officers stated that there were more shootings and killings involving their unit because they were doing dangerous work. They were fighting crime in the streets on the only terms criminals understood. They felt that they should be commended for bravery rather than criticized. STRESS Commander James Bannon took a gruff attitude toward the complaints of citizens' committees. He was quoted in *Ramparts* in December 1973 as saying, "No god-damned bunch of intellectual eunuchs is going to tell professional policemen how to do their job."

Bannon's tough talk could not mask obvious problems regarding his men. Critics pointed out that Raymond Peterson had twenty-one citizen injury complaints lodged against him even before he became a STRESS officer and that Michael Ziolkowski was under trial board investigation for mistreatment of a black prisoner at the very time of his appointment to STRESS. The critics wanted to know by what standard these men were picked for jobs which brought them constantly into situations in which their judgments could mean life or death for a citizen. Peterson came to be known as "Mr. STRESS." He was involved in nine killings and three nonfatal shootings during the first two years of STRESS's existence.

Most STRESS killings took place under street circumstances which made judgment in any one case a matter of believing either a policeman sworn to uphold the law or a person accused of perpetrating a street crime. Pressure against STRESS built up through 1971, especially among blacks, but it was not until March 9, 1972, in an affair called the Rochester Street Massacre, that the description of STRESS as a bunch of trigger-happy cops became uncontestable. The Rochester Street shooting differed from others because this time the victims of STRESS were not civilians, but other law-enforcement officers!

The incident began when three black STRESS officers observed a man later identified as a Wayne County sheriff's deputy walk into a building at 3210 Rochester with what appeared to be a gun. The STRESS squad called other police and entered the apartment with guns blazing. Wayne County Sheriff's Deputy Henry Henderson was killed, and three other deputies were seriously wounded. According to subsequent court testimony, all the deputies might have been killed if Patrolman Richard Herold had not arrived on the scene and put a stop to the carnage.

Exactly what transpired at Rochester Street was never made clear. Popular rumor held that the police were "battling for drug turf." Patrolman Herold proved to be a pivotal figure. He had reputedly fought with other police over which heroin dealer worked for which officer. One point beyond rumor was that on January 8, 1973, he was suspended from the force after being arrested in Toronto, Canada, for possession of and dealing in cocaine. This charge was soon followed by a Detroit indictment on similar charges. During the Rochester Street incident, forty-four shots were fired by the Detroit police, forty-one of them by STRESS officers. Deputy Henderson sustained six gunshot wounds as he stood with back to the wall, hands in the air, and ID badge in hand. Three officers were eventually brought to trial, but all were acquitted. On this occasion, Prosecutor Cahalan refrained from making a public statement that black jurors would not convict blacks, as he had after the New Bethel case. What was clear now to everyone was that STRESS could be counted upon to shoot before asking any questions. Constitutional guarantees against illegal search and seizure and police violence were absolutely meaningless should STRESS decide it was a "kill" situation. The

Detroit Police Department learned nothing from the Rochester Street Massacre, for in April of 1973 Police Commissioner John Nichols took Ronald Martin, one of the defendants in the case, to Washington, where Martin informed a House Select Committee on Crime that STRESS was like the United States Marine Corps, "only better."

Even before the Rochester Street Massacre blacks felt that they were in a virtual state of siege. If STRESS cops could kill sheriff's deputies and get away with it, the average citizen didn't have a chance. STRESS's tactics were like the Army's "search and destroy" policy in Vietnam. Eleven deaths occurred between April and August of 1971, and all but one of the victims were black. Cockrel and other radicals working as members of the Black Workers Congress, the Labor Defense Coalition, and the State of Emergency Committee took a leading role in attacking STRESS. On September 23, 1971, more than 5000 people were mobilized by the State of Emergency Committee to demand the abolition of STRESS. The Detroit Commission on Community Relations stated that a broadly based multiracial opposition to STRESS clearly existed. Two more STRESS killings took place in November and December of 1971, bringing the year's total to thirteen. The Michigan Civil Rights Commission was moved to attack STRESS's methods and urged elimination of the decoy technique and better screening and supervision of personnel. The Rochester Street Massacre occurred on March 9th of the following year, and on March 17 Mayor Roman Gribbs and Commissioner Nichols announced "reforms." The death toll had now reached sixteen, but decoy operations were not reduced and lethal force was still justified as long as "reasonable" grounds existed for believing a felony had been committed. The "reform" move was countered on March 26 by a rally of over 2000 people at the University of Detroit stadium in support of a petition campaign to abolish STRESS and a lawsuit against Mayor Gribbs, Commissioner Nichols, and Prosecutor Cahalan. The petition campaign was to gain over 40,000 signatures, and on April 6 the anti-STRESS suit, prepared by Cockrel, Ravitz, and others, was filed in Wayne County Circuit Court. The plaintiffs included the NAACP, Local 600 of the UAW, relatives of STRESS victims, and Local 26 of the Detroit Public Workers union. Judge John O'Hair, who had served as a representative of the police department when he was Assistant Corporate Counsel, placed the case on the regular docket rather than grant an immediate hearing.

STRESS burst back into the headlines on December 4, 1972, when four STRESS men were involved in a shootout with three armed blacks: Mark Bethune, John Percy Boyd, and Hayward Brown. The three young men had been waging a private war against big-time heroin dealers in their neighborhoods. STRESS had staked out one of the dope houses that the three vigilantes attacked. Instead of pursuing the dope dealers, STRESS chased Bethune, Boyd, and Brown. A shootout followed which resulted in the four STRESS officers being wounded, while their prey escaped. Three weeks later, in a second shootout with the vigilantes, STRESS officer Robert Bradford was slain and another officer wounded. The vigilantes escaped once more, and Commissioner Nichols went on television describing them as "mad-dog killers." In the weeks which followed, STRESS put the black neighborhoods under martial law in the most massive and ruthless police manhunt in Detroit history. Hundreds of black families had their doors literally broken down and their lives threatened by groups of white men in plain clothes who had no search warrants and often did not bother to identify themselves as police. Eventually, fifty-six fully documented cases of illegal procedure were brought against the department. One totally innocent man, Durwood Forshee, could make no complaint because he was dead. This 57-year-old unemployed security guard was killed when he fired his shotgun at STRESS invaders whom he believed to be a gang of robbers. On January 12, 1973, Hayward Brown was finally captured. Bethune and Boyd, disguised as a priest and a nun, got out of the city safely but were killed a month and a half later in a shootout with the Atlanta police.

Hayward Brown chose Ken Cockrel to be his attorney, and,

employing his usual tactic of turning a defense into an offensive, Cockrel decided to put STRESS on trial. In defending his client's participation in one killing and several woundings Cockrel invoked the Algiers Motel, Cobo Hall I, Cobo Hall II, the Veterans Memorial, New Bethel, the Rochester Street Massacre, and the whole record of STRESS and the Detroit Police Department. In three bitter and hotly fought trials, Cockrel won total acquittal for his client. The 18-year-old Brown, who was an ex-junkie, came to be a kind of folk hero. He and his two comrades had taken on a job that the STRESS squad, for all its bloody fingers, had not been able to handle. Brown spoke on the radio, on television, and at public meetings and called for the abolition of STRESS. The From The Ground Up organization circulated 8000 copies of an attractively designed sixty-page booklet which gave details on various STRESS killings and pinpointed the political forces supporting and opposing STRESS. During the same period, Raymond Peterson, "Mr. STRESS," was charged with murder when his description of a killing did not hold up against laboratory evidence. The victim in this case was a worker stopped on an expressway by Peterson, who was supposedly on his way to his suburban home. The knife which the worker allegedly used to threaten Peterson turned out under examination to belong to Peterson. Citizens clamored for an investigation of other STRESS killings, but Prosecutor Cahalan seized all the pertinent homicide files and kept them from public view.

The acquittal of Hayward Brown and the charges against "Mr. STRESS" were an indication of a new view of the police shaping in the minds of many Detroiters. Originally, STRESS had been accepted by the inner city as a possible solution to the cycle of violence of which it was the principal victim. The record of STRESS soon proved that the unit meant only an increase in violence. STRESS was a new lethal weapon in the hands of a government which had driven local blacks to violent rebellion twice in thirty years. Black veterans who had banded together to demand jobs and other benefits were victims of midnight STRESS raids. Paroled prisoners working for penal reform reported being followed and threatened by STRESS. Workers said STRESS men had infiltrated the auto plants in order to spy on worker organizations.

The Brown verdicts proved that jurors of all colors were no longer accepting police testimony as automatically more honest than that of ordinary citizens. Jurors were concerned that law officers now viewed themselves as above the law. STRESS obviously regarded itself as a judge, jury, and executioner mandated to deal out instant "justice." Despite the change in public opinion, the Detroit Police Department remained unmoved in its support of STRESS. Police officers rallied around Peterson, saying that he must not be made a sacrificial lamb to a public willing to make a hero out of a "cop-killer" like Hayward Brown. STRESS was renamed the Felony Prevention Squad, and additional "reforms" were made; but to take no chances of having their real power curbed, the police were ready to make a bid for control of the city government itself by running Police Commissioner John Nichols for Mayor. The Detroit Police Officers Association was so sure of itself that it made a thinly veiled threat on the lives of Cockrel and Brown by offering them "one-way tickets to Atlanta."

The prospect of the man ultimately responsible for STRESS becoming Mayor of Detroit unsettled all the forces within the city that wanted to end racial polarization and that were worried about new civil disturbances. Nichols was part of a nebulous hard-line political group which included Prosecutor Cahalan, several former FBI men, and Roman Gribbs, who had been Wayne County Sheriff before becoming Mayor. Nichols was the toughest of the lot. His politics were pure "law-and-orderism," which in Detroit meant among other things, "keeping the niggers in their place." Nichols, like Frank Rizzo, the Philadelphia Police Commissioner turned Mayor, and other police officials seeking elective office around the country, was trying to ride a tide of white fear to political power. In Detroit, a vote for John Nichols meant a vote for STRESS.

Chapter Nine

Mr. Justin Ravitz, Marxist Judge of Recorder's Court

1

Building the kind of power necessary to making more fundamental changes requires the organized activity of large numbers of people willing to struggle for that change. Engaging in the electoral process can be one way to develop such an organization.

Committee to Elect Ravitz Recorder's Court Judge, *The Mini-Manual of Criminal Justice*, 1972

In 1972, Justin Ravitz was elected to a ten-year term as judge of Recorder's Court. The *Detroit Free Press* ran a story on the election headlined "Radical Judge-Elect Ravitz Plans To Shake Up Court"; this was restated on a follow-up page: "New Judge Is A Marxist Who Plans To Shake Up Court." The Ravitz victory was the first materialization of the election strategy advocated by Cockrel and the forces around him. This group was convinced that

Opposite page: Justin Ravitz, moments before his swearing-in ceremony.

the electoral process was a viable means of educating the public on issues, of propagandizing wider solutions, and of winning some limited power. It was a process that could enable them to control some of the weakest links in the power chain of capitalism: its elective officers, its courts, and its legal system. Winning limited power would afford radicals positions from which to launch or to protect future assaults on the strongest links of the system. Elections were not to be substituted for other more radical activities, but to augment those activities with an attack from within basic American institutions.

In an article titled "Toward Our Own Courts . . . & Beyond" published in abridged form in the *Guardian* newsweekly of November 14, 1972, Margaret Borys, one of the principal coordinators on Ravitz's campaign staff, underscored the long-range strategy involved. She noted that the campaign focused on the real causes of violence in Detroit—the disparity between the lifestyles projected on television and the reality of life as lived in Detroit, the desperation of the 200,000 chronically unemployed Detroiters, the heroin problem that caused a million dollars worth of property to be stolen every day by Detroit's victim/junkies, and a police department that behaved like an occupying army rather than a part of the community. She described the basic goals of the campaign in this way:

> The Ravitz Campaign understood that we can neither litigate nor elect our way to liberation, but selective and serious entries into each arena can advance the building of a socialist society. An aggressive, honest, and persuasive campaign helped promote the reality that "radical problems" do indeed "require radical solutions." . . . The political objectives of the Ravitz Campaign are continuing ones: (1) to build class solidarity by organizing a self-conscious and anti-racist white movement (2) to take leadership in the implementation of transitional reforms and demands (3) to achieve a mass multi-racial, independent, radical people's political movement—a movement conscious of the

need and value of victories, unafraid and relentless in its
pursuit of power.

The campaign emphasized Ravitz's record as a radical attorney.
In addition to his role in the New Bethel case, the James Johnson
case, and the anti-STRESS suit, Ravitz had many other impressive
court victories to his credit. He had successfully defended welfare
mothers arrested for demonstrating at the Bureau of Social
Services; he had successfully defended anti-war demonstrators
who were arrested for protesting the bombing and mining of Hanoi
and Haiphong harbor; and he had successfully challenged the
Michigan anti-marijuana law, freeing 130 people from prison. He
had also led the litigation against city and county officials
responsible for the inhuman and barbaric conditions in the Wayne
County Jail, litigation that brought about a reduction in the inmate
population of 50 percent.

Ravitz's campaign literature employed radical populist language to give a revolutionary critique of the system. The major
mass-distribution brochure reprinted a *Detroit News* front-page
photo story showing Ravitz and Cockrel discussing the primary
election returns under a big headline: "Radical Tops Court
Nominees." The brochure's own headline was "Justin Ravitz Is A
Lousy Politician—and that's good." Ravitz's record was
presented with emphasis on his concern for the problems of working people, and he was contrasted to the do-nothing "politicians."
A more substantial piece of campaign literature was *The Mini-
Manual of Criminal Justice,* a 22-page booklet that attacked the
entire legal system in unmistakably radical terms. The booklet
dealt with judges, the money bail system, the Wayne County Jail,
the Detroit Police Department, the Wayne County Prosecutor's
Office, prisons, 24-hour arraignments, the summons system,
pretrial confinement, sentencing, and the heroin problem. The
booklet was prefaced with a militant poem by b. p. Flanigan. A
typical passage began the section "Heroin: Our Analysis":

When we properly understand the role of money in the
American capitalist economy and the dominant control

of monied forces in major government policy decisions and actions, nationally and internationally, then we understand that they purposely have created and maintained conditions that keep hundreds of thousands of people existing in conditions that will force them to fall prey to heroin addiction, just as they keep at least five to six million people, at all times, unemployed.

The campaign was coordinated by a staff of half a dozen, but reached out to involve hundreds of people. On the day of the election, more than 400 unpaid volunteer poll-workers stood in the rain for as long as thirteen hours passing out literature. Several dozen others were organized into support teams that delivered hot food and beverages throughout the day. Almost everyone connected with the organization had had little or no previous electoral experience, yet Ravitz finished second among the seven judges elected with 130,514 votes on a nonpartisàn ballot. Ravitz had received endorsements from some unexpected sources: Council 77 of the AFL-CIO, the *Detroit Free Press,* the Urban Alliance, the Detroit Bar Association, all the district organizations of the Democratic Party, and the UAW. Borys characterized most of these groups as having ''diminishing but real importance, [yet] they shall continue to be a factor in tactical maneuverings until the left wins the continuing allegiance of the masses of people.''

Cockrel's approach had never gotten majority support within the League of Revolutionary Black Workers, and the Ravitz campaign failed to get majority support within the Motor City Labor League. The organization appeared to be solidly behind Ravitz during the primary, but his first-place finish served to disunite rather than rally the organization. A group centered around Frank Joyce brought the whole electoral strategy into question. They felt that MCLL was being transformed into a Cockrel coat-tail rather than pursuing its own independent course. Bumper stickers at Ravitz campaign headquarters were pushing Cockrel for Mayor in 1973, and many MCLL members questioned the viability of a white organization's pushing a black candidate as one of its major activities. Beyond the specific contests, many MCLL members believed, as most radicals of the New Left did, that elections led to reformism. If Detroit's local elections had not been nonpartisan, Ravitz might have had to run as a Democrat to have a serious chance of winning. The Joyce group cited the history of the Communist Party, which had worked in the liberal wing of the Democratic Party and had been instrumental in building the CIO only to be destroyed in the McCarthy era because of its watered-down programs and liberal rhetoric. The MCLL militants also spoke of ex-Communist Jay Lovestone, who had become a key anti-Communist on George Meany's central staff at the AFL-CIO; and they pointed out that Max Schactman, once a firebrand Trotskyist, had ended his long career by supporting the war in Vietnam. Ravitz's candidacy in the August primary had been endorsed by several ministers, a rabbi, Ernest Mazey of the American Civil Liberties Union, numerous doctors, poet John Sinclair, various attorneys, one city councilman, one state representative, and one tate senator. To some people in MCLL, this was the reformist handwriting upon the wall.

The differences within the organization proved irresolvable; and so, in the middle of September, a group led by Sheila Murphy withdrew from MCLL to continue with the election work. In November, they formed a new organization called From The Ground Up. Two summers after the split, it was clear that MCLL had turned decidedly against participation in elections and in favor of intensifying its workplace organizing and deepening its Marxist-Leninist ideology. Among the organization's major concerns was the possible formation of a new communist party involving fusion of various groups in the city and around the country. This was similar to the direction being taken by groups such as BWC and the Communist League.

Cockrel's colleagues and those who had resigned from MCLL were not indifferent to criticism about the dangers of electoral politics, but they were willing to stake their organizational and personal futures on a different line of reasoning. They felt that the ideological purism of many of the radical groups produced an oppositionist mentality incapable of dealing with questions of real power. The STRESS unit was terrorizing half the city of Detroit. Winning a Recorder's Court judgeship meant being able to deliver some measure of protection to the people. Mass popular support from blacks and whites alike would not be won by abstract ideological debates but by extracting concessions from the system. Radicals must head mass struggles so that demands and perspectives could be given a more revolutionary direction. Demonstrating efficient leadership and winning limited victories would strengthen and deepen the popular base. The League had been successful because it had developed many levels and types of power. Reformism was, indeed, a pitfall, but the forces around Cockrel and Ravitz were confident they would avoid it.

Cockrel was not beguiled by his local fame and popularity. The Hayward Brown case required almost all of his legal and organizational talents during most of 1973. New charges were continually brought up, and the case seemed endless. The James Johnson case was similar. Ron Glotta had won workman's compensation for Johnson early in 1973, but in the summer Johnson was charged with assault with intent to murder at the hospital where he was an inmate. Cockrel felt compelled to intervene, and he proved that Johnson had been unjustly accused. It was beginning to seem that a handful of cases could keep Cockrel tied up indefinitely. He told the *Detroit News:*

> I wonder if the time and energy spent on them [the Brown cases] means all that much in terms of furthering the Movement, educating the people, or building up an organization. Much time and energy was spent, a great deal of it to the exclusion of most other things.
>
> And you have to weigh it.
>
> It resulted in the exoneration of an individual. But what was its effect in terms of education and organization? What if the same time and energy had been

devoted toward building an organization? Would the effect have been broader and more important?

Cockrel expressed these doubts in a highly favorable seven-page feature story on him in the *Detroit News Sunday Magazine* of October 14, 1973. The magazine's front cover showed Cockrel standing before a section of the Diego Rivera murals. The headline read: "Revolutionary in a Legal Sheepskin—A Look at Kenneth Cockrel, the Radicals' Courtroom Crusader." An invitation was clearly out for Cockrel to become the black revolutionary tinsel for Detroit's power structure; yet Detroit politics were as deceptive as ever. Behind the glib facade of amity were the lightly veiled death threats delivered by the DPOA. Some people believed that the greatest danger facing the electoral strategists was not reformism but liquidation by the police or right-wing vigilantes. As pressure against STRESS mounted, individual officers were being suspended and disciplined. They and their political allies perceived Cockrel and his allies as their principal nemesis. Many people around Cockrel felt forced to carry weapons lest, in the next Algiers Motel incident or Rochester Street Massacre, they be the victims. They knew only too well that they were actively opposing the military apparatus of the state with limited and underdeveloped forces. Cockrel spoke of cutting down on the number of criminal cases he handled and perhaps concentrating on workman's compensation or other labor-oriented aspects of the law. He also hoped to have more time to think, organize, and travel.

2

I will handle at most approximately 5% of [the] docket. They are, on the one hand, scared as hell of me coming over, and they deserve to be because we're going to fight

*them like hell. But, on the other hand, there's a certain
smug attitude. "Ravitz will be co-opted . . . what can
one judge do" and so on.*

Justin C. Ravitz, speaking at the founding session of
From The Ground Up, November 20, 1972

Justin Ravitz took office early in 1973. In his first year on the
bench, he tried to differentiate himself from the other judges,
while being sufficiently cooperative to achieve the changes he
sought in fundamental practices. One innovation he instituted at
once was to have the courtroom spectators and the judge stand for
the jury, rather than having the spectators and the jury stand for the
judge. The jurors were often visibly confused by this sudden shift
in protocol. Ravitz would explain, "Excuse me; in this court we
stand out of respect for the jury and what you represent. So as soon
as you wish to be seated, please do so and we'll all sit down."
Ravitz did not wear a robe or display an American flag, behavior
that quickly brought about a Michigan Supreme Court ruling
compelling all judges to wear robes and show the flag. The
Supreme Court spoke of a "proper" judicial atmosphere. Ravitz
replied that he too was interested in a "proper" judicial atmosphere, but that his definition of what was proper was somewhat different. He did relent to the extent of putting on a robe and
displaying an American flag next to the water fountain behind a
partition that hid the flag from the jury, although it was in full view
of anyone entering or leaving through the main doorway.

One of Ravitz's major court reforms had to do with the time
people were detained before their cases were heard. The average
holding time was from twelve to twenty-four hours, meaning that
some people were held for a much longer time and some for a
shorter period. In 1972 alone, 23,070 persons had been detained
and never taken to court because there were insufficient grounds.
Ravitz argued that if the police were compelled to take their
prisoners to court immediately there would be many fewer false

arrests and harassments without cause. He set a personal example in his own court and made a series of proposals aimed at getting other judges and the Supreme Court to speed up the system. He threw out all entrapment cases, took the civilian side whenever the situation was questionable, and refused to honor warrants with technical errors. In a move that puzzled some police, he gave them precise instructions on legal definitions of entrapment and technical training in making out proper warrants. He explained that he was not against the police carrying out their jobs but was interested in protecting people's constitutional rights. A further demonstration of his determination to live within the spirit of the Bill of Rights was his acceptance of work-release bonds instead of cash bail. Ravitz stated that the poor should not be denied bail simply because they didn't have ready cash. On one occasion, he accepted a stereo set as bail.

Ravitz did everything in his power to demystify the courtroom, to give political education where the system had miseducated, and to correct the various misconceptions about the judicial system fostered by schools, movies, television, and cheap detective stories. Sensitivity to individual needs, personal informality, and political-education classes all had a role in his perception of what one judge could do. Among his initial efforts was a letter he got another judge to co-sign, which was sent to arrestees informing them that they should not waive their pretrial examinations, a right most of them were giving up, although fully a third of those who did not had their cases dropped. Ravitz took on at least one speaking engagement a week, and he conducted a series of Saturday seminars held in his courtroom, where he explained the judicial system as it actually functioned in the city of Detroit. In all of these activities, Ravitz raised many critical questions. In an article written in 1974 and scheduled for future publication by a Ralph Nader study group on judicial problems, Ravitz wrote:

> Did you ever stop to think why lawyers and judges talk
> in language real people cannot understand? Why nearly
> all people—plaintiffs, defendants, witnesses, jurors,

and indeed, most lawyers—are so frightened when called upon to speak in an American courtroom? Why can't we understand what goes on in our courts, and why are we so afraid in our courts?

. . . The rawness of white racism in this country is only a part of the real message. The law is not only not "color blind," but it more than "tolerates classes among citizens." It is designed to tolerate and perpetuate class division. The law serves the dominant class in a class society.

Ravitz tried to use his radical sensibility in handling every kind of case in order to demonstrate to one and all that a Marxist judge could administer the law more wisely, humanely, and fairly than any other kind of judge. Men convicted of rape were given a pamphlet on rape written by a women's liberation group. They were told to study the pamphlet with other men convicted of the same offense and, when they felt that they had genuinely begun to understand themselves, to contact the judge about the possibility of parole. Ravitz warned them not to "play games with me," as that would result in a closing of communications. Similar tactics were worked out with drug addicts. More overtly political cases were handled with the same tact. In one instance, Ravitz opened his court at night to allow his former law partner Ken Cockrel to get Hayward Brown released without bail. In another case, he gave right-winger Donald Lobsinger a 45-day sentence for a political disturbance that could have netted him a full 90 days. Ravitz gave Lobsinger's supporters some leeway in the courtroom and refused to respond to Lobsinger's "red baiting." He also transformed some apparently routine cases into political ones. One such occurrence was his handling of a case involving the Wrigley's supermarket chain. One Wrigley store had systematically over-priced its meats through false weight measurements. A check showed that 33 out of 40 packages had been priced incorrectly, in favor of the store. The usual procedure in such cases was for the corporation to plead guilty and the charges against any individual to be dismissed. The corporation then paid a nominal fine because a corporation cannot be jailed. Ravitz discovered that this practice had been going on for years. Determined to set new ground rules, Ravitz stated that he was going to punish the supermarket to the maximum allowed by law and that he would hold meat clerks personally responsible for the mislabeling. He noted in court how the Wrigley chain's attorney had tried to instruct him on the "usual" procedure, forgetting who was the guardian of the public trust and who was the criminal. In a test case, Ravitz fined the supermarket $100, the statutory maximum, and ordered payment of $100 more in court costs. He gave the meat clerk one day in jail to serve notice that in the future the old ways could not be taken for granted.

Ravitz's performance in court generated a lot of quiet excitement in the city. His manner was unpretentious. He spoke quietly and repeated his points until his listeners understood, generating an air of mild-mannered fairness. Teachers brought their government classes to observe the radical judge. Individuals wandered into the courtroom to get a look at "the commie judge." Ravitz found that initial hostility was usually overcome when people observed his actual practice. A black worker's comment, "If he's a commie, right on, commies!" was echoed by local news-broadcaster Lou Gordon, who ended a Ravitz interview by saying, "If this is a Marxist judge, we need more Marxist judges." As Ravitz told the authors in February 1974, "We're an aberration, and people want to see what is going on. People who have spent all their lives standing in line waiting to be robbed at cash registers are finding out we're on their side."

A dissident view of Ravitz was voiced by Peter Werbe, who had been a major figure at the *Fifth Estate* for years and who was doing an all-night talk show over WRIF-FM, an ABC affiliate. In August of 1973, he told the authors: "Ravitz gave a guy twenty years the other day. I don't want that kind of power." Werbe was stating frankly what many of the counterculture people of the sixties felt. The Cockrel and Ravitz forces couldn't have disagreed more. They were willing to accept the responsibilities of power, and they were ready to struggle for it whenever they could. They anticipated stretching the political system to its limits, confident that it would ultimately unmask itself in desperate attempts to keep radicals from achieving full power. The very day after Ravitz's election, the Detroit Bar Association spoke of the advisability of having judges appointed rather than elected. Other moves were afoot in the state to limit the kinds of cases that could go before juries at all, to impanel juries of less than twelve people, and to allow majority decisions (8-4 or 9-3) to convict. These moves and others to broaden police powers by negating vital parts of the Bill of Rights could be important issues around which radicals might rally mass support. Cockrel had stated his view in the 1970 Anti-Repression Conference: "We don't engage in bullshit arguments about 'that's reformist' or 'that's not reformist.' That which is reformist is that which is counter-revolutionary. What is not reformist or counter-revolutionary is any action that conduces to the creation of a larger propensity on the part of most people to view revolution as the only course of conduct available to end oppression. That's what we relate to—that's what we understand and see very clearly as being real."

3

I will lead a business resurgence that will produce jobs by the thousands, revitalize our downtown, and our entire city. I will move Detroit forward on a program that includes new port facilities, a stadium, rapid transit, recreational facilities, and housing.

Coleman Young, quoted in campaign literature, Autumn 1973

The election for Mayor in 1973 surfaced many plans for a new Detroit. On the far right stood Police Commissioner John Nichols.

The two major liberal contenders were Mel ("the Other") Ravitz, a pipe-smoking ex-Wayne State University teacher who had served on the city council for many years, and black State Senator Coleman Young. The UAW's endorsement was crucial to their respective chances for election. The Detroit UAW, which was more in touch with political realities in the city, wanted Young; the Wayne County organization, which included the Detroit organization but reflected suburban attitudes as well, wanted Ravitz. The top UAW leadership pushed through an official endorsement for Ravitz, but many powerful local units worked on behalf of Coleman Young, hoping to repeat for a black candidate what they had done for Jerome Cavanagh a decade earlier. The other major candidates were Circuit Court Judge Ed Bell, a black Republican who resigned his office to run, and John Mogk, a political unknown who waged a populist door-to-door walking campaign and ended up getting the *Detroit Free Press*'s endorsement for the primary election.

Cockrel had made it no secret that he was considering entering the race. He was not interested in running for Mayor in 1973 in order to win some other office in the next election, a common practice in Detroit, and he was not interested in running only to educate the public about socialism, as the candidates of the Socialist Workers Party did. Cockrel wanted to run only if he could win. A serious race for the office required large-scale financing and, more important, a broadly based political organization. After considering all factors, the Cockrel forces decided that, in spite of the personal publicity he had received, there were too few primary or secondary leaders for the kind of campaign needed to win the major office in the city government. The pieces needed for a power play were in place, as they had been for the League of Revolutionary Black Workers in 1969; but, once again, there was a lack of the organizational momentum and personnel that could have activated them.

The primary election narrowed the field to John Nichols and Coleman Young. Few elections in modern Detroit history had offered such a clearcut choice. Nichols was the prototype of a white conservative, complete with police credentials—the candidate of the home-owners' associations, negrophobes, and support-the-cops-at-any-cost elements in the city. Young was a black, labor-oriented liberal with a "pinko" past. His camp contained many elements, extending from black nationalists to Democratic Party hacks and UAW liberals. Its lower echelons even included former SNCC people and former League activists such as Larry Nevels and Althea Hankins, both of whom ran regional campaign offices. Cockrel refused to take any active role in the election. Backing Nichols was, of course, unthinkable, and supporting Young would mean promoting the very coalition radicals had been trying the hardest to dismantle. One of the internal contradictions in Cockrel's political outlook was that he had agreed that Ravitz should accept the same sort of coalition support in his race for a judgeship. The major difference was that the radicals set the ground rules in the Ravitz effort with the liberals playing a supporting role, while with Young's campaign the opposite would be true.

In an election marked by severe racial polarization, Young won a narrow victory. Those radicals who opposed electoral struggles believed that this victory showed the weakness of the strategy advocated by Cockrel and his followers. Because of that strategy, all the opposition to STRESS had benefited not the revolutionary forces but Coleman Young, who was just another liberal. They pointed out that, although Young had a radical past, his present political cohorts were Leonard Woodcock and Henry Ford II. These critics brushed aside Young's appointment of 37-year-old Larry Nevels to a $24,000-a-year job as head of the neighborhood city halls as a case of one more black radical being sucked in by the Democratic Party. What appeared to be a major triumph for black Detroiters and progressive forces, especially in opposition to the racist Nichols, was, they insisted, only another instance of prolonging the existing system through liberal reformism. If the city could prove flexible enough to elect its first black Mayor, it was reasonable to assume that STRESS might be abolished and the mass discontent quelled without any real change in the power structure.

The Cockrel forces replied that they had taken the lead against STRESS to stop police-state repression and to build a mass movement, not to win an election. Nichols had been defeated, which was good, and the military situation was thereby more favorable; yet STRESS and the police department remained unchanged. As long as the police ran amuck, a mass movement would be needed to keep them in check. Nevels believed he could use his post as creatively as Ravitz had used his and was angry that radicals had not supported his bid for a seat on the city council. Nevels had lost the primary by only a few thousand votes, and organized radical support could have made the difference between defeat and victory. For his part, Cockrel believed that he could have been elected Mayor had the city's radicals rallied around him from the preceding summer. As it was, if life in the city improved to any visible degree, the liberals would be difficult to dislodge. Cockrel believed, however, that conditions would worsen and that the Young administration might prove to be only the last stand of a failed liberalism. The election proved nothing to Cockrel about the validity of electoral struggle other than that the politics of winning a ten-year judgeship were relatively easy compared to those required to elect the city's chief executive.

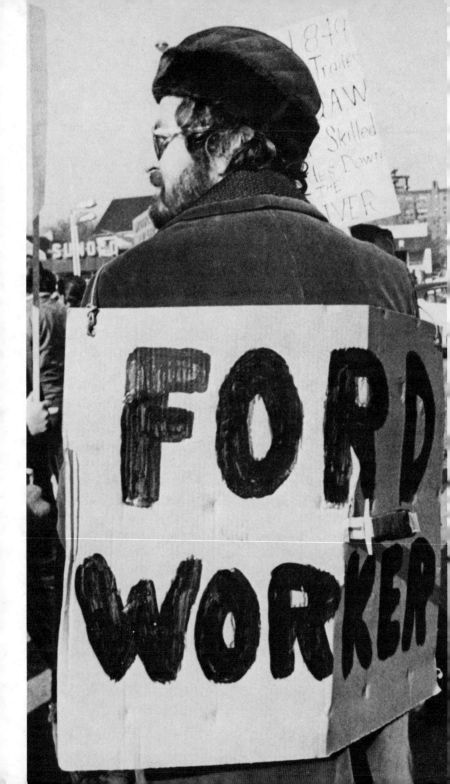

Chapter Ten

The 54-Hour Week

1

*For the first time in the history of the UAW, the union
mobilized to keep a plant open.*

Bill Bonds, WXYZ-TV News, speaking of events at the
Mack stamping plant, August 16, 1973

For Chrysler Corporation, 1973 was a wildcat summer as walkouts
shut down three Chrysler plants: Jefferson Assembly, Chrysler
Forge, and Mack stamping. The wildcat at Chrysler Forge lasted
longer and was more damaging to production than the official
three-day UAW strike, which came in the autumn around model-
changeover time. The problems leading to the wildcats were very
much like those which had led to the formation of DRUM; but this
time the strikers demonstrated a much higher level of racial
cooperation, and their spokesmen talked from a clear class perspective.

The first wildcat occurred at Jefferson Assembly, where 90
percent of the workers in the metal shop were black. The poor
working conditions in the metal shop were aggravated by the
attitude of a white supervisor named Tom Woolsey. Blacks
charged that he was an outright racist. A petition calling for his

*Opposite page: Skilled tradesman protesting "knife-in-the-back" contract at
UAW headquarters, November 7, 1973.*

removal was signed by 214 of the 300 workers in the shop, but the plant management and the union disregarded the workers' petition. On July 24, Isaac Shorter, 26, and Larry Carter, 23, took direct worker action. They climbed into the electric-power-control cage and, by pushing one button, halted the assembly line at the start of the first shift at 6:00 A.M. Not bothering with the union hierarchy, Carter and Shorter negotiated with the company directly from the cage. They said that they would continue the occupation until Woolsey was removed and they were granted an unconditional amnesty. Workers clustered outside the cage with chains in case anyone should try to remove Shorter and Carter by force. Black, white, and Arab workers brought food or stood guard, many of them coming from other departments to demonstrate their support. Thirteen hours later, the two men were carried from the plant on the shoulders of their fellow workers. Chrysler had capitulated on all counts. Doug Fraser, the UAW Director for Chrysler, wondered aloud why the company had set such a dangerous precedent but said that the men deserved ''an A for ingenuity.''

The photo of Carter and Shorter being carried triumphantly out of the plant appeared in all the Detroit papers and in labor-oriented publications throughout the nation. Readers discovered that Shorter was a native of Cleveland, Mississippi, where he had been active from 1969 to 1970 as Chairman of the local National Committee to Combat Fascism, an arm of the Black Panther Party. He later moved to Los Angeles, where he worked in a Chrysler plant until it cut back production. He arrived in Detroit in September of 1971. Carter came from Pensacola, Florida, where he had been fired by a Coca Cola Bottling firm for participating in a unionization effort. He, too, had come to Detroit in 1971. The two men shared an apartment and were good friends. In their statements to the press, they emphasized the class rather than the racial aspect of their actions. Shorter said that he had talked with Woolsey and said, '' 'Hey, man, me and you are in the same class. We are both workers.' But he couldn't understand. And from then on, we started getting into it.'' He told another reporter, ''The black workers in this city could control it. But at the same time, there's no such thing as black control. Because it's not a racial thing. It's the system, which is a capitalist system. It oppresses all people. Blacks, whites, Chicanos, just name it, yellow, brown. And that's the way we should look at it as being."

A few weeks later, on August 28, an even more serious wildcat took place at Chrysler Forge. The plant employed 1100 workers in the making of crankshafts, pinions, and torsion bars. A week before the strike, two workers were crippled by accidents. One had an arm torn off, and another had a finger crushed. Approximately 60 percent of the Forge workers had been working a nearly steady seven-day week for the past six months. The immediate trigger to the strike was the firing of sixteen workers who had been vocal in exposing health and safety violations. The leadership of the strike was primarily white, but leaflets from the *People's Tribune,* the organ of the Communist League, one of the successor groups of the League of Revolutionary Black Workers, were given out the day of the shutdown. One of the wildcat leaders was soft-spoken Jerome Scott, a former member of DRUM and a current member of the Communist League.

The strike at Forge lasted six days and threatened to paralyze all Chrysler production. By the tenth of August, a harried Doug Fraser had said that he would "legalize" the strike if Chrysler did not make concessions. Chrysler then agreed to correct 100 safety grievances immediately and to put 150 more under advisement. In a stormy meeting, over 800 workers decided, by a narrow majority vote, to return to work. In an action not seen for many years, Doug Fraser made a personal appearance at the Forge gates the next morning to urge people to return to work. With a Channel 2 News camera going, Fraser had a verbal confrontation with John Taylor of MCLL. Fraser, a former DeSoto worker, called for a fistfight in the parking lot but backed off when Taylor proved more than happy to accept the challenge. The attempt to blame the strike on "outside agitators" and "radicals" gained momentum when Jerome Scott was charged with criminal acts and civil contempt. What the "red baiting" could not cover up, however, was that working conditions were the main cause of the strikes. Anthony McJennet, a Forge worker, told the *Detroit News,* "Chrysler treats a man like a piece of meat." He might have added that the meat could be black or white. The most significant aspect of the strike was that black radicals had maintained a working alliance with white, mainly Polish workers, something that had not occurred at Dodge Main in 1968, at Eldon in 1969-70, or at the Chrysler Sterling stamping plant where white workers had rebelled in a week-long wildcat in 1969 over working-condition grievances similar to those voiced by DRUM and ELRUM. Doug Fraser put a bold face on his growing anxiety, "Radicals are creating a serious problem at Forge, but we don't feel it is unmanageable."

The day after Forge got back into production, Chrysler was hit at its Mack stamping plant with yet another work stoppage. This time, William Gilbreth, a white member of the Progressive Labor Party, touched off the strike. Gilbreth had been fired for agitation to improve safety and health conditions the day before. He returned to the line at the Mack plant for his regular shift and sat down on the conveyor belt. When the plant protection people came to remove him, he struck a guard with a metal pipe. The plant shut down, as 200 workers in Gilbreth's department sat down with him. Soon Gilbreth was reading announcements to the press which emphasized the demands of the Workers Action Movement, a front organized by his party. Gilbreth stressed that he was an avowed communist and listed various party demands, including the generally popular call for a 30-hour work week. Only a few of the people who remained in the factory belonged to the Workers Action Movement, and many belonged to the International Socialist grouping and the United National Caucus, which were organizational rivals of WAM. Well-known militants, including Isaac Shorter, Larry Carter, Jerome Scott, Jordan Sims, John Taylor, and Pete Kelly, observed the action from outside the plant.

Fraser had said that "Chrysler lost its manhood" in the Shorter-Carter debacle, and what seemed like an unending plague of wildcats was not making the UAW look virile either. The newspapers spoke of "plant hijacking" and played up Gilbreth's overt radicalism. The police and the union sensed that it was a good opportunity for them to make a show of strength. Police Commissioner John Nichols, already a declared candidate for Mayor, personally led a detachment of police into the Mack plant to arrest Gilbreth for striking the guard and to put an end to the sit-down. Fifteen workers, including Gilbreth, were arrested after some minor scuffling. The next morning, workers who wanted to keep the strike going were confronted at the plant gates by Doug Fraser, Irving Bluestone, Emil Mazey, and other top UAW executives backed up by a force of nearly 2000 older or retired UAW loyalists. There was some fighting with local militants, but the sheer size of the union force guaranteed that the strike was over. It was a bitter day for many UAW members around town who remembered the fierce organizing drives of the thirties. The old guard of the UAW had once led the same kind of flying squads to keep factories shut. Now, they had come full circle and saw the task of the union as seeing that the plants remained open. The inspector of the local police precinct thanked Doug Fraser personally for his help and said it was great being on the same side.

The daily media emphasized the role of radicals in each of the wildcats, and the *Detroit Free Press* went so far as to do an article on the various radical groups active in the factories. The sudden visibility of the groups was connected to a process that had been going on at least since the time of DRUM. As the radical white movement turned from a student orientation to a working-class orientation in the late sixties, American radicals spoke of Detroit as being the Petrograd of the Second American Revolution. Virtually every Marxist group in the country sent some members to Detroit to organize workers in the auto factories. By and large, their methods were similar. Some members sold or gave away literature at the gate, while others entered the workforce inside and tried to take leadership roles in local struggles. By the summer of 1973, there were dozens of such groups in Detroit with hundreds of members in the factories.

True to their traditional viewpoints, the newspapers and union officials tried to blame the factory unrest on "outside agitators" rather than on the mammoth problems of safety, health, race, and alienation that faced the American industrial worker. Many of the workers remained confused about the causes of their problems; but some situations, such as the phenomenon of runaway factories, were clearly a result of the structure of American capitalism. Instead of renewing their capital investments in Detroit, the auto companies preferred to find safer surroundings. A few plants were set up in places like Lordstown in what was heralded as a decentralization program; but, far more frequently, new facilities were built in the South, where wages were lower and unionization lagged behind the rest of the country.

A typical example of a runaway plant was the Briggs Manufacturing Corporation. Once an independent giant in the auto-parts industry whose owner also owned the Detroit baseball team and ran the ball park as a kind of civic duty, Briggs was purchased by Chrysler in 1953. Nineteen years later, Briggs workers learned that their factory was to be moved to Tennessee within a year. The workers were told that they were guaranteed a job if they moved to Tennessee too, but their wages would be $2.40 an hour instead of the Detroit rate of $4.30. The stunned workers also learned that Tennessee had a right-to-work law which hampered union activity and that the state was granting Chrysler an interest-free loan of $6.5 million. The Detroit workers discovered that they would lose their pensions, group insurance benefits, job security, workman's compensation claims, and numerous other "fringe" benefits. The affected workers were not the "new" workers written about in scholarly journals, but people whose average age was forty-five and who had an average of twenty years' seniority. Many of them came from white ethnic groups. One hundred and fifty of these workers organized to fight the company. The insurgents could get no action from the union, so they turned to radical labor attorneys John Taylor and Ron Glotta, who promptly took legal action to protect the workers' financial interests.

The workers move to organize themselves and the link-up to the radicals finally drove the UAW to take action. It negotiated a "termination" agreement with the company. This agreement provided for deferred pensions to take effect at age sixty-five for employees with ten or more years' seniority and severance pay ranging from $450 for a worker with one year's seniority to $5000 for a worker with thirty years' seniority. This represented a partial victory, but many of the Briggs workers were willing to take an all-or-nothing chance on going to court. The "termination" agreement negotiated by the UAW was approved only by a slim 39-vote margin, after a long and bitter debate. The courts then dismissed the workers' suit on the grounds that a judge could not interfere with a ratified collective-bargaining agreement between the company and the union.

On May 11, 1973, the Briggs workers voted out the Woodcock slate by a 2-1 margin in an election of local officers. On August 26, the rank and file voted unanimously to condemn the union leadership, particularly that of Local 212, for using a flying squad to break the strike at the Mack stamping plant. On September 5, the UAW's executive board voted to place the Briggs local in receivership, thus removing power from the newly elected shop committee. Forty Briggs workers appeared at Solidarity House, the national UAW headquarters, to back their stewards, but democracy did not prevail. It must have been a particularly sour day for Emil Mazey. Twenty-six years earlier, Mazey had personally led the most popular and forceful of all the union flying squads, the men of Briggs Local 212. Time had wrought many changes. As Gary Kapanowski, a spokesman for the workers whose father had also been a Briggs worker, observed to MCLL news reporters in November, "We at Briggs have received our master's degree in union-company collusion and right-wing politics. We will carry that knowledge with us in our new workplaces."

Wildcat summer and the agitation over the Briggs closing were indications that Chrysler workers were in a fighting mood. The UAW was not. It approached the 1973 contract negotiations determined to hold the line on all the accepted formulas. Once again, the union was more concerned about retirement benefits and other long-term gains than about improving current conditions or dissociating wage increases from higher productivity. Woodcock went so far as to say that a strike most likely would not be necessary. He was only partially correct. The UAW went through a token three-day walkout in late September before the leadership presented Chrysler workers with a contract that represented a fresh step backward with respect to control of the shop floor.

A hundred years after the massive nationwide drive for a 40-hour week, the UAW's major gain was a guaranteed 54-hour week! Legitimating once more the company's insatiable drive for higher production, the UAW agreed that its workers could *only* be scheduled to work nine hours a day, six days a week, with a qualified right to have every third Saturday off, and the absolute right to refuse work on Sunday. Relinquishing the struggle for the 40-hour week for another three years was bad enough, but the contract had numerous loopholes that made even those guarantees the union had obtained meaningless. A "critical plants" clause allowed the company to exempt key plants unilaterally, from the voluntary-overtime rules for as long as three months. The company also won the right to suspend the voluntary-overtime provisions for an entire plant for two weeks if any group of workers disrupted production by refusing overtime. Another clause required a worker to give notice of not wanting to work on a Saturday considerably in advance, and no worker who was absent on Mondays or Fridays was eligible to refuse such work. Thus, the contract actually served the company by helping it to hold down Monday and Friday absenteeism, a growing problem that often significantly reduced production in certain plants. Closely linked to the whole overtime question was the miniscule wage increase of 3 percent a year for the life of the contract. This was considerably less than the constantly rising rate of inflation and meant that workers would need to volunteer for more overtime than they had done in the past just to maintain their existing standards of living.

The UAW boasted that the 1973 contract contained the "thirty and out" clause sought by older workers. According to the contract, a worker with thirty years' seniority could retire with a pension of $550 a month, a figure which would rise to $700 a month for workers retiring after 1978. This long-term retirement benefit, which did nothing to help active workers, was paid for by virtually no action on health, safety, and speed-up problems. The company did agree to more union representatives on the shop floor and to a revised grievance procedure. For the first time, there was formal recognition of Section 502 of the Labor Management Relations Act of 1947, which allowed workers to strike if a job were unsafe. It was this provision that the Eldon Safety Committee had cited to justify its work stoppages in May 1970. None of the men fired in that action were rehired, however; and it seemed unlikely that Chrysler's interpretation of Section 502 would coincide with that of wildcat strikers. The gain was more academic than substantial until tested in court by workers willing to risk their jobs in a confrontation with the company and the union. A major "hidden" defeat involved new workers. To begin with, these workers were to be paid 45 cents less an hour than other workers on the same job. The newcomers could still be fired at any time during the first ninety days, and only after they had worked for six months could they apply for the additional 45 cents an hour, which would be granted as a back-pay bonus. Since more than a third of new workers were generally fired in the first ninety days, the "bonus" was, in fact, a pay cut for thousands of workers, a pay cut negotiated by the UAW, which still collected its initial fee and three months' dues directly from the worker's paycheck.

The established pattern in the auto industry for decades had been that agreements arrived at in one contract were more or less matched in the others. This proved to be the case in 1973, with the General Motors and Ford pacts following the Chrysler pattern. Each agreement was approved by the UAW's general membership, but there was a significant number of "no" votes. Dodge Main ratified the new contract 613-528. At the Jefferson Assembly plant and Eldon a 33-percent "no" vote was recorded. The ratified national contract was backed up by local pacts dealing with individual plant grievances. The effectiveness of these local agreements depended upon the strength and militancy of the local union leadership. The overall pattern was unmistakable. Overtime amid deteriorating conditions and falling real wages remained the norm, as the union pursued a policy of helping older and retired workers at the expense of younger and active workers. Wage gains remained tied to increases in productivity, which, in effect, meant speed-up. The UAW had not gone so far as to volunteer a non-strike pact, but that seemed just around the corner.

The new contract, the election for Mayor, and the murder rate were prime coffee-break topics in the fall of 1973 when Detroit workers got an unexpected boost from black Judge Damon Keith sitting in the Federal District Court. Judge Keith ruled that Detroit Edison had been guilty of discriminating against blacks. He punished the company by ordering it to pay more than $4 million and to change its employment practices at once. The payments ordered included payments to blacks who might have applied for work as well as to those who actually had sought jobs. Detroit Edison took months to rally its forces. While moving to hire and upgrade black workers as fast as possible, the company retained William Rogers, formerly Richard Nixon's first Secretary of State, to represent the utility in the court of appeals and in what seemed an inevitable Supreme Court test. The Keith decision opened the door to attacks on all companies systematically discriminating against any particular group. Just the threat of legal action and fines was sufficient in and of itself to make employers go easy on the "divide the races and rule" strategy that dominated so many American industries.

Auto workers were less excited by the Keith decision than radical activists were. The auto workers were most concerned about conditions in the plants, and the most typical reaction of an angry worker was direct action. At Ford Local 600 a militant union leader shot at a skilled tradesman protesting the contract, and a few months later another Detroit foreman was killed by an irate worker in an incident reminiscent of the James Johnson case. The frustration over working conditions and overtime was suddenly augmented late in the year by even greater frustration over the prospect of no work at all. The energy crisis, which struck the nation so unexpectedly, highlighted the economic dinosaurism of the auto industry. Consumers worried about the shortage of gasoline quit buying large, low-mileage cars like Pontiacs and Oldsmobiles. Sales of those lines fell by over 50 percent, and Detroit automakers began to retool to produce smaller, more economical cars. GM's announcement that it would produce a mini-Cadillac was the clearest sign that the industry was serious about decreasing car size. The auto industry had long depended on high-priced accessories, more powerful engines, and sheer size to maximize profits. Its new tactic was to make money on expensive safety features and anti-pollution devices, using the energy crisis and concern for ecology to keep attention away from prices. The long-term effects of the new emphasis on small cars seemed unlikely to include any basic change in industry profit patterns. The immediate effect on auto workers, however, was disastrous. During most of 1974, official unemployment in Michigan ran to more than 10 percent. In towns like Flint and Pontiac, where large-car production dominated, the unemployment rate was considerably higher and the hardship greater. Unemployment benefits alleviated some economic suffering; but galloping inflation, the prospect of being permanently without work, and the fact that thousands of workers were not eligible for various benefits cast a cloud of gloom over auto workers. Speed-up and the 54-hour week remained the order of the day, in spite of the cutbacks. More profits could still be made by working fewer and fewer workers harder and longer than by any other method.

2

Physically, Detroit has acquired freshness and vitality. Acres of slums have been razed, and steel-and-glass apartments—angular and lonely in the vacated landscape—have sprung up in their place. In the central business district, hard by the Detroit River, severely

> *rectangular skyscrapers—none of them more than five*
> *years old—jostle uncomfortably with the gilded behe-*
> *moths of another age.*

National Observer, July 15, 1963

Detroit had not changed much since the Great Rebellion. Wildcat summer had brought together white and black workers, the skilled and the unskilled, communists and anti-communists, but the mayoral election, street violence, and job insecurity had fed the old antagonisms with fresh fuel. The bleak Detroit winter hit with its usual cacophony of whining engines as the city ended 1973 by establishing several all-time records. Homicides reached a historic peak; car production reached a historic peak; and the earnings of General Motors reached a historic peak. Workers worried about wholesale layoffs just as the prices of fuel, food, and other necessities also reached all-time peaks. The Cotillion Club, an organization of the black elite, gave its 1973 awards to Judge George Crockett, Attorney Kenneth Cockrel, and Judge Damon Keith; yet all the basic problems facing black America festered as lethally as ever.

Carefully picking its way through the Detroit reality, the *U.S. News & World Report* of December 10 was enraptured by the latest plans for building a new Detroit, plans which, like the old plans for a new Detroit, concentrated on buildings, professional classes, and a narrow strip of waterfront. The heart of the new program was a $500 million Renaissance Center with hotels, luxury apartments, office buildings, and quality entertainment facilities to be built on the riverfront, directly to the east of Woodward Avenue. The showpiece of the center was to be a 70-story glass-encased hotel with 1500 rooms. Four 30-story office towers with banks as major ground-floor tenants would share the complex with the hotel. Contributions for the center included $6 million from Ford, $6 million from GM, $1.5 million from Chrysler, $500,000 from American Motors, and smaller contributions from over thirty Detroit firms. The hotel, offices, and projected apartment dwellings were to be serviced by a variety of shops, restaurants, and retail stores. Robert Hastings, a leading city architect, spoke of "recycling" American cities and was quoted in the magazine article as saying: "Detroit has always been thought of as a vibrant, can-do place. If you want to get something done, take this marvelous collection of technical people this city has. . . . Take the people and point them. The problem is to point them. This is what Henry Ford has done."

The enthusiasm of men like Hastings was similar to the enthusiasm that swept most American cities during the days of the New Frontier. In 1964, three years before the Great Rebellion, the Detroit Community Action Program had announced a total assault on poverty: "The overall objective in Detroit is to develop programs which will assist people in becoming self-sufficient and socially responsible citizens, generate participation in community life and the problems of others, and build into the lives of the impoverished the skills and aspirations necessary for useful and rewarding lives."

3

. . . the grayness and the grit, the dirty
funky, hardheavy city, home of greasecake
hands and the baddest right hook you've
ever seen.

detroit.

b. p. Flanigan, "Freeway Series/1"

At 12:01 A.M., January 1, 1974, Detroit recorded its first homicide of the year. Gerald H. Johnson, 46, was killed while standing on a corner, by a bullet fired by someone celebrating the New Year with the Detroit custom of firing a gun. Two more homicides were recorded before the sun came up. Karl Bestman, 73, was shot and killed by robbers as he wiped snow off the windshield of his car. The body of the third victim, Johnnie Harper, 25, was found in an east-side apartment after her neighbors reported hearing gunfire.

Along the darkened streets of the city, the squad cars of the Detroit Police Department passed the 2500 abandoned homes and 5000 empty houses taken over by the Federal Housing Administration, whose program to halt urban decay and abandonment had become mired in corruption and discredited by questionable decision-making. The squad cars passed supermarkets whose huge glass windows had been bricked over ever since the Great Rebellion and whose entrances had been sealed off by metal posts to prevent people from stealing shopping carts. The Goodyear sign by the Ford-Chrysler interchange had already begun to crank out the new year's car production.

During their lunch break the next day, many Detroit workers discussed a new, black-owned professional football team to be called the Detroit Wheels. It was to replace the Detroit Lions, which had moved to Pontiac to be nearer the suburban audience. Later that afternoon, there was an accident at the Eldon Avenue Gear and Axle plant.

A week later, Mayor Coleman Young made a glittering populist debut at an inaugural ball attended by 15,000 people. Diana Ross came back home from Hollywood to be the featured entertainer, and the national media spotlighted Mayor Young as he said, "I issue a warning now to all dope pushers, ripoff artists, and muggers. It is time to leave Detroit. Hit the road!" A photo in the *New York Times* showed a concerned Mayor listening to Leonard Woodcock, President of the UAW, whisper in his ear as a beaming Henry Ford II spoke from a microphone-studded podium about Renaissance Center.

The rebels and revolutionaries you have read about in this book were not involved in the inaugural. Most of them were now in their late twenties and early thirties. They continued to pursue their own vision of a new Detroit.

Index

Abernathy, Rev. Ralph, 191
Absenteeism, 7, 234
Accidents on the job, 9, 103-4, 107-8,
  111. *See also* Safety violations
Ad Hoc, 70, 94, 149, 150, 193
Adleman, Mike, 111
AFL (American Federation of
  Labor), 185
AFL-CIO (American Federation of
  Labor-Congress of Industrial
  Organizations), 39, 214, 215
Al Fatah, 63, 64
Albee, Edward, 133
Aldrich, Dan, 68
Algiers Motel incident, 183-84, 202,
  207, 217
Alinsky, Saul, 91
Amen, Alan, 77, 78
Amen, Karen, 77
Amen, Katherine, 77
Amen, Ron, 77
American Civil Liberties Union, 64,
  215
American Jewish Committee, 96
American Legion, 21
American Motors Corporation, 238
Anti-Semitism, 40, 42, 63-64, 70-71,
  74, 76, 186
Appalachian workers, 4, 37, 187, 188
Arab workers, 4, 37-38; and DRUM,
  50; in 1973 wildcat strikes, 228;
  problems faced by, 76-81
Arabic Community Center for
  Economic and Social Services, 78
Arnow, Harriet, 151
Artists' Workshop, 154
Ashlock, Irwin, 110, 112, 113
Aswad, Barbara, 78
Atwell, Helen Okdi, 77
August, Ronald, 183-84, 188
Automation, 101-2, 104, 124-25. *See
  also* Niggermation

Bailey, F. Lee, 197
Baker, General Gordon, 23, 113, 115,
  146, 152; BEDC and, 97; Black Star
  Productions' activities and, 147; in
  Communist League, 178, 179;
creation of BWC and, 162;
  ELRUM's approach sanctioned by,
  121; Forman compared with, 174; in
  League of Revolutionary Black
  Workers, 84-86; and making of
  Finally Got the News, 138, 141;
  May 1968 wildcat strike and, 24-27;
  Sims on, 177
Bannon, James, 203
Baraka, Imamu (Le Roi Jones), 17,
  133, 134
Battle, Buddy, 43
Bauer, George, 117, 118
Beckett, Samuel, 133
BEDC (Black Economic
  Development Conference), 94-99,
  152, 160, 162, 173; and distribution
  of *Finally Got the News,* 147;
  organizers of, 164-66
Bell, Ed, 196, 223
Bennett, Harry, 187
Bethune, Mark, 206
Bird, Stewart, 137, 138, 139, 143
Bishop, Rachel, 144, 171
Black Art Conference, 146
Black Lake (educational and
  recreational center), 40-41
Black Legion, 65, 186, 188
Black Manifesto (1969), 94-98
Black middle class and the League,
  149
Black Muslims, 22
Black nationalism, 17, 25, 70, 85, 92,
  113, 121, 123, 162, 163, 167, 172,
  176
Black Panther Party. *See* BPP
Black police officers: attitudes of,
  compared with those of white police
  officers, 190; number of, 189
Black Star Bookstore, 82, 152
Black Star Productions, 144-49, 163,
  175
Black Star Publishing, 98, 167, 171
Black Student United Front, 92
Black United Front, 68, 69
Black workers: fight UAW (1941),
  189; jobs held by, 4, 35, 49;
  movement organized by, 4-6 (*see*

also specific organizations; for example: DRUM, League of Revolutionary Black Workers); in 1968 wildcat strikes, 46-47; in 1973 wildcat strikes, 228-33; number of (late 1960s), 34-35; in UAW membership, 40
Bluestone, Irving, 231
B'nai B'rith, 79
Boggs, James, 18, 44, 95
Bond, Julian, 94, 196
Borys, Margaret, 212, 214
Boyd, John Percy, 206
Boyd, Rev. Malcolm, 133
Boyias, Nick, 58
BPP (Black Panther Party), 57, 61, 91, 95, 136, 165, 228; in *Finally Got the News,* 145; problems faced by, 160; support for, 143, 155; tension between the League and, 147
Bradford, Robert, 206
Breakthrough, 21-22, 64, 92
Brickley, James H., 194
Briggs Manufacturing Corporation, 29, 232-33
Broadside Press, 133
Brooks, Charles, 47
Brooks, Gwendolyn, 134
Brown, H. Rap, 15, 165
Brown, Hayward, 206-8, 216, 220
Brown, John, 185
Burns, Eddie "Guitar," 129
Burroughs, William, 73
Butch (union employee), 113
BWC (Black Workers Congress), 159-81, 205, 215

CADRUM (RUM group in Cadillac factory), 85
Cahalan, William L., 67, 204, 205, 207, 208
Cantor, Edith Carroll, 133
Capital investments, post-World War II fluctuations in, 29
Capital study group, 23
Carino, Lawrence M., 1
Carmichael, Stokely, 165, 196
Carpenter, Scott, 184
Carter, Joe L., 130
Carter, Larry, 228, 230
Cavanagh, Jerome, 43, 69, 190, 192, 223
Chambers, Paul, 23
Chandler, Alonzo, 112, 114
Chavez, Cesar, 40, 80
China-Albania Bookstore, 152, 178
Chrysler Corporation, 23-27, 33-39; contributions of, to Renaissance Center, 238; deal made between UAW and, 30-32; DRUM gets aid from, 96; Johnson affair and, 117, 199; and making of *Finally Got the News,* 138, 141; niggermation at, 102-21, 125; 1968 wildcat strikes against, 24-27, 46-47; 1973 wildcat strikes against, 179, 227-31, 233, 235; open letter to, 25-27; organization by the League at, 85; poor corporate record of, 29-30; and *South End,* 57, 66; workforce of, 34-39, 79
CIO (Congress of Industrial Organizations), 215
Cisler, Walker, 2
Clark, Harry, 65
Cleage, Rev. Albert, 146
Cleaver, Eldridge, 145
Cobo Hall I, 191-92, 195, 207
Cobo Hall II, 192-93, 195, 207
Cockrel, Kenneth, 62, 63, 113, 150, 238; as attorney, 10-11, 65, 102, 198-201, 206-7, 216; in BEDC, 95, 97; Black Star Productions' activities and, 147; and creation of BWC, 161-64, 172, 174-75, 181; disbarment proceedings against, 196-97; Dowdell and, 147; on ELRUM, 122; in League of Revolutionary Black Workers, 84, 88-91, 93; and making of *Finally Got the News,* 136, 139, 143; and 1973 mayoral election, 223-25; and Ravitz's election, 211, 213, 214, 216, 217, 220-22; STRESS attacked by, 205
Cockrel, Sye, 89
Cohen, Sam, 132
Colista, Philip, 102
Colombo, Robert, 10, 11, 196, 198
Communism. *See* Marxism-Leninism
Communist League, 164, 178-81, 215, 229
Communist Party, 22, 40, 69, 99, 119, 120, 163, 177, 215
Community Council (Dearborn), 77-78
Community Relations Commission, 70, 192, 195, 196, 205
Community Relations Sub-Committee (Detroit Police Department), 189
Compulsory overtime, 31, 33, 234, 236
Concept East (theatre group), 133
Conyers, John, 94
Cook, Carla, 169
Cooper, Carl, 183-84
CORE (Congress of Racial Equality), 19
Coughlin, Father Charles E., 186

Counterculture, 16, 91, 153-55
Crockett, George, 63, 66-70, 195, 238
Czapski, Michael, 66-67

Daifullah, Nagi, 80, 81
Darrow, Clarence, 183, 186
Davis, Angela, 120, 163
Davis, Rennie, 151
Day, William M., 2
De la Cruz, Juan, 80
Del Rio, James, 67, 69
Dellinger, Dave, 151
Democratic Party, 36, 93, 214
Dennis, Sam, 192
DePugh, George, 137
Detroit Athletic Club, 64
Detroit Bar Association, 214, 222
Detroit Board of Education, 91, 93
Detroit Commission on Community
  Relations, 70, 192, 195, 196, 205
Detroit Community Action Program,
  239
Detroit General Hospital, 17, 58
Detroit Institute of Arts, 100, 101, 134
Detroit Olympic Committee, 19
Detroit Organizing Committee, 94, 99,
  149
Detroit Police Department, 37, 48, 51,
  182-208, 213, 216, 224-25, 240
Detroit Renaissance, 2-4, 238-39
Dodd, Thomas, 99
Douglas, Emory, 143
Douglass, Frederick, 185
Dowdell, Glanton, 23, 145-46
DPOA (Detroit Police Officers
  Association), 10, 66, 68-70, 92, 217;
  and New Bethel incident, 68-69; and
  STRESS, 191, 192, 194-95
Drachler, Norman, 2
DRUM (Dodge Revolutionary Union
  Movement), 28-51, 53, 61, 66, 75,
  190; articles on, 52, 57, 58; BEDC
  and, 96, 97; BWC and, 166;
  ELRUM compared with, 106-7; in
  Finally Got the News, 136, 141;
  formation of the League and, 91;
  formed, 24-25; goals of, 44, 45, 74;
  manipulation of established media
  rejected by, 73-74; and New Bethel
  incident, 68; problems of Arab
  community and, 79, 81; *South End*
  controlled by, 51, 54-55, 59, 63;
  successes of, 83, 85-86, 159-60;
  wildcat strikes and, 229-31; women
  in, 171
DRUM II (Dodge Truck plant
  organization), 85
Dubofsky, Melvin, 180
DuBois, W. E. B., 26, 148

Eastland, James, 99
Eda, Eugene, 135
Education, political, 87-88, 91, 152
Edwards, Eric, 115
Edwards, James, 106, 112, 114, 116-18
Edwards, Nelson Jack, 40
Eldon Safety Committee, 9, 111-14,
  117-18, 235
Eldon Wildcat, 9, 114, 119, 122
ELRUM (Eldon Avenue
  Revolutionary Union Movement),
  9-10, 28, 85, 109, 161, 175; formed,
  106; shortcomings of, 121-23;
  Taylor on, 112-17, 119, 120; wildcat
  strikes led by, 106-7, 230; women
  in, 122, 171
Equitable Life Assurance Society of
  the United States, 3
Evans, James, 193

Factory occupation (1937), 106
Fanon, Frantz, 167, 168
Fanon-Formanism, 168
Felicia, John, 111
Finally Got the News (film), 129, 132,
  134, 136-48, 167
Fisher, Max, 2, 64
Flanigan, b. p., 155-56, 213, 239
Fonda, Jane, 147
Ford, Henry, 31, 42, 105, 134, 187,
  188, 239
Ford, Henry, II, 2, 224, 240
Ford Motor Company: contributions
  of, to Renaissance Center, 238; deal
  made between UAW and, 30-32;
  decentralized operations of, 35;
  1941 strike against, 42; 1973
  contract negotiated with, 235;
  organizing by the League at, 85;
  workforce of, 34, 78-79
Ford Motor Credit Company, 3
Forman, James, 158, 159; in BEDC,
  95, 96, 99; BWC and, 162-69, 171-76
Formanism, 168, 174, 175, 178
Forshee, Durwood, 206
Franklin, Aretha, 131
Franklin, Rev. C. L., 66, 67, 69, 131
Frantz Fanon Institutes, 167, 168
Fraser, Doug, 228-31
Fraser (car manufacturer), 29
Freedom Now Party, 17, 19, 146
Freeman, Ralph, 77, 78
Froines, John, 151
From The Ground Up, 151-52, 207,
  215, 218
From The Ground Up Bookstore, 152
FRUM (RUM group at Ford River
  Rouge complex), 28, 85

Gaidi, Brother (Milton Henry), 67, 198
Garvey, Marcus, 134
Gaye, Marvin, 131
Gelber, Jack, 133
General Motors. *See* GM
General strike, 83, 179
Genet, Jean, 133
German Communist Party, 147
Gessner, Peter, 136-38, 143
Gilbreth, William, 230-31
Gill, Frank, 53
Ginsberg, Allen, 73
Giovanni, Nikki, 134
Glaberman, Martin, 18, 19
Glessing, Robert J., 72
Glotta, Ron, 11, 111, 216, 232
GM (General Motors Corporation):
annual number of grievances at, 33;
contributions of, to Renaissance
Center, 238; deal made between
UAW and, 30-32; decentralized
operations of, 35; manufacture of
small cars by, 237; niggermation at,
124-27; 1956 capital investments of,
29; 1973 contract negotiated with,
235; organizing by the League at,
85; size of, 106; UAW recognized
by (1937), 106; workforce of, 35
GM Technical Center, 39, 44
Godfrey, Joseph, 126
Gordon, Lou, 221
Gordy, Berry, 130
Great Rebellion (1967), 24, 37, 59, 67,
183, 237, 239; background of,
185-88; center of, 15; effects of, 1-3,
14, 15, 189; *ICV* as response to, 16,
20, 21; police officers' opinion of,
190
Greater Detroit Chamber of
Commerce, 1
Greater Detroit Home-Owners
Council, 194
Greenback-Labor Party, 185
Gribbs, Roman, 205, 208
Grievance procedures, 32-33; for
safety grievances, 109-10
Griffen, Betty, 171
Griffin, Robert, 23
Griffin, Rufus, 23, 146
Groppi, Father James E., 17
Guardians, 93
Guevara, Che, 18

Halley, Pat, 130
Halpern, Sheldon, 198
Hamlin, Mike, 23-24, 62, 66, 149-50,
165, 200; as adviser to Black
Student United Front, 92, 93; in

BEDC, 95, 97, 98; and Black Star
Productions' activities, 147; and
creation of BWC, 161-64, 167,
171-73, 175, 177; in League of
Revolutionary Black Workers, 84,
86-88, 91; and making of *Finally
Got the News,* 136; writing for
South End, 55-56
Hankins, Althea, 224
Hankins, Paula, 147, 171, 175
Hayden, Tom, 150, 151
Heaney, James, 194
Henderson, Henry, 204
Henry, Milton (Brother Gaidi), 67,
198
Herman, James, 192
Herold, Richard, 204
Hersey, John, 184, 188
Hibbit, Alfred, 196-98
Hicks, Gregory, 175
Hitler, Adolf, 34, 42, 63
Hoffman, Abbie, 73, 151
Holsey, Fred, 106, 175, 200
Hood, Rev. Nicholas, 194
Hooker, John Lee, 130
HRUM (RUM group of health
workers), 83
Hubbard, Orville (Mayor of
Dearborn), 76-77
Hudson, Joseph L., 2, 29
Hughes, Art, 103

IBA (International Black Appeal;
previously United Black Appeal),
96-99, 176, 178
ICV (*Inner City Voice*; newspaper),
15-27, 54, 55, 61, 87, 112, 190
IFCO (Interreligious Foundation for
Community Organizations), 94, 96,
99
International Socialists, 120, 230
Italian-American workers, 4
Italian Communist Party, 145
Ivory, Marcellius, 40
IWW (Industrial Workers of the
World; Wobblies), 44, 179, 180

Jabara, Abdeen, 75, 78
Jacobs, Jim, 149-50
James, C. L. R., 18
James, Dennis, 196
JARUM (RUM group at Jefferson
Avenue plant), 85
Jenkins, Bobo, 130
John Birch Society, 21
John Hancock Mutual Life Insurance
Co., 3
Johns, Wesley, 121
Johnson, C. G., 153

Johnson, Charles "Mao," 55, 172
Johnson, Gerald H., 239
Johnson, Haynes, 33, 126
Johnson, James, 8-12, 102-3, 117, 119, 216, 236
Jones, Helen, 98-99, 167, 169
Jones, Le Roi (Imamu Baraka), 17, 133, 134
Joyce, Frank, 70, 150-51, 214, 215
Jury selection, 198-99

Kaiser (car manufacturer), 29
Kalimoto, Ernie, 152, 163, 176
Kapanowski, Gary, 233
Keast, William, 2, 58-60, 63, 71, 190
Keith, Damon, 236, 238
Kelly, Pete, 39, 44, 230
Kennedy, John F., 37
Kennedy, Robert F., 37, 78
Kenyatta, Muhammad, 169
King, Martin Luther, Jr., 40, 43, 135, 195
Kirkland, Eddie, 130
KKK (Ku Klux Klan), 37, 186
Knight, Etheridge, 134
Knights of Labor, 185
Kolcheff, Nick, 77
Kotz, Nick, 33, 126

Labor Defense Coalition, 205
Labor Relations Committee (Chrysler), 109
Lateness, 7
League of Revolutionary Black Workers, 9, 82-99, 101, 109, 112, 115, 152, 190; anti-repression strategy of, 200; Black Star Productions and, 144, 147-48; BPP and, 147; BWC and, 159-67, 169-72, 175-78, 180-81; Cockrel supported by, 214; counterculture and, 155; film made by, 132, 136-39, 143; gap between RUMs and, 121; *ICV* and, 19; members of, working on *South End*, 57; 1973 mayoral election and, 223, 224; opinion of, on Sams, 200; Ravitz's bid for judgeship and, 216; white progressive organizations and, 149-50
Lee, Don, 134
Lenin, V. I., 72, 109
Levine, Philip, 144
Lewis, Fulton, Jr., 44-45
Lewis, Sidney, 161
Lichtman, René, 137, 138, 143
Lincoln, Abraham, 34
Liska, Ed, 47
Lobsinger, Donald, 22, 64, 92, 220
Logan, Rose, 104

Lovestone, Jay, 215
Luxemburg, Rosa, 147

McClintock, William G., 2
McJennet, Anthony, 230
McKee, Rob, 112, 114
McKinnon, Frank, 109-11, 115, 117, 120, 123
Madar, Olga, 40
Maher, Joseph E., 196-98
Malcolm X, 18, 63, 134, 135, 145, 160
Mao Tse-tung, 177, 178
March, Ron, 24, 48-50, 139, 200
Martin, Ronald, 205
MARUM (RUM group at Mack Avenue plant), 28, 85
Marx, Karl, 18, 109
Marxism-Leninism, 71-72, 168, 177, 178, 179
Mason, Phillip, 192
Mazey, Emil, 40, 41, 43-44, 79, 215, 231, 233
MCLL (Motor City Labor League; previously Motor City Labor Coalition), 11, 108, 115, 119, 121, 124; formed, 150-52; publications of, 134; Ravitz's bid for judgeship and, 214-15
Meany, George, 39, 215
Medical Committee on Human Rights, 93
Medina, Harold, 69
Medvecky, Nick, 56-58, 63, 71-72, 75, 144
Merrelli, George, 50, 116, 120
MERUM (RUM group at Mound Road Engine plant), 85
Michigan Bar Association, 70, 88
Michigan Civil Rights Commission, 195, 205
Michigan Department of Labor, 102
Michigan National Guard, 1, 15, 188
Michigan Supreme Court, 218, 219
Milliken, William, 3, 68-70
Milner, Ron, 133
Miriani, Louis, 43
Mogk, John, 223
Moore, Howard, 196
Morris, George B., Jr., 33, 126
Morrison, Jim, 136-37
Motown Records, 130-31
Muhammad, Elijah, 22, 129, 135
Murphy, Sheila, 70, 150, 193, 201-2, 215

NAACP (National Association for the Advancement of Colored People), 206
NAC (Negro Action Committee), 19

Nader, Ralph, 125, 219
Nash (car manufacturer), 29
National Association of
  Manufacturers, 39
National Bank of Detroit, 3
National Black Labor Strike Fund, 96
National Committee to Combat
  Fascism, 228
National Conference for New
  Politics, 165
National Institute of Occupational
  Safety and Health, 105
National Labor Union, 185
National Lawyers Guild, 94, 196
National Welfare Rights Organization,
  96
Nevels, Larry, 93, 175, 224, 225
New Bethel incident and case, 10, 11,
  66-70, 181, 195-99, 204, 207, 213
New Detroit Committee, 1-3, 5, 64,
  70, 190, 195
New University Conference, 171
Newark riot (1967), 187
NEWRUM (RUM group at *Detroit
  News*), 83
Newsreel (film-makers group), 136-39,
  143-44, 200
Nichols, John, 201, 205, 206, 208;
  Mack stamping plant wildcat strike
  and, 231; in 1973 mayoral election,
  222, 224, 225
Niggermation, 101-27
Nixon, Richard M., 236
Nunn, Guy, 45

O'Hair, John, 206
O'Hara, Michael, 196
One-String Sam, 130
Otis, Sheldon, 196, 197
Overtime, compulsory, 31, 33, 234,
  236
Ovshinsky, Harvey, 72-73

Packard (car manufacturer), 29
Paille, Robert, 183-84
Paragon Steel (corporation), 85
Parsell, Carl, 66, 191, 194, 195
PASCC (Parents and Students for
  Community Control), 91-93
People Against Racism, 70, 94, 149,
  150
People's Tribune, 68
Perlman, Fredy, 98-99, 167
Peterson, Raymond, 203, 207
Philo, Harry, 89, 196, 197
Police: desegregation of, 3, 4; Detroit
  Police Department, 37, 48, 51,
  182-208, 213, 216, 224-25; DRUM
  harassed by, 47-49, 51; in *Finally

Got the News, 142; during Great
  Rebellion, 1, 155; *ICV* and, 16, 20;
  League infiltrated by, 160; in New
  Bethel incident, 9, 66-68; in strike
  situations, 47, 66, 90;
  unemployment forcing white
  workers to join, 7. *See also* DPOA
Polish-American workers, 4, 36-37
Pollard, Auburey, 183-84
Pollard, Chaney, 184
Powell, Adam Clayton, 135
Production, 1973 automobile, 238
Productivity: hourly, 124; 1946 and
  1970, 101
Profits: GM (1973), 238; post-World
  War II fluctuations in, 29; speed-up
  and increased, 104, 237
Progressive Labor Party, 119, 230
Progressive whites, the League and,
  149-51; Ravitz's campaign and,
  214-15
PSIUP (Italian Socialist Party of
  Proletarian Unity), 61

Race riot (1943), 187
Racism: boycotts to fight, 46; BWC
  and, 160; in Detroit Police
  Department, 190-94; history of, in
  Detroit, 185-87; indifference to, 54;
  institutional, 35-36, 64; UAW and,
  40, 41-44, 47, 112
Radical Education Project, 99
Rallis, Jerri, 77
RAM (Revolutionary Action
  Movement), 17, 23, 160
Ramsey, Carolyn, 146, 175
Randall, Dudley, 133, 148
Ravitz, Justin, 10, 150, 210; as
  attorney for Hibbit, 198; as attorney
  for Sinclair, 155; disbarment
  proceedings against, 196; as judge,
  11, 211-25; STRESS attacked by,
  205
Ravitz, Mel, 223
Reese, Della, 131
Republican Party, 185
Resist (anti-war organization), 171
Retirement, 234-35
Reuther, Walter, 2, 40, 43, 54, 118
Richardson, Elroy, 110, 113, 118
Rivera, Diego, 100, 101, 134, 135, 217
Rizzo, Frank, 208
RNA (Republic of New Africa), 10,
  66, 67
Roche, James, 2, 29
Rochester Street Massacre, 204-5,
  207, 217
Rogers, William, 236
Roosevelt, Franklin D., 34

Roselyn (singer), 130
Ross, Diana, 131, 240
Ross, Doc, 130
Rothschild, Emma, 125
Rubin, Jerry, 151
RUMs (Revolutionary Union
  Movements), 51, 92, 120, 132, 170;
  Communist League and, 179;
  creation of BWC and, 161; in
  Finally Got the News, 142; gap
  between the League and, 121;
  spread of, 74-75, 85-86; writers of,
  compared with Forman, 174. *See
  also* DRUM; ELRUM
Russell, Jack, 152
Russell, Michelle, 152, 171, 175

Sabotage, 7
Safety grievances, Taylor on, 109-10
Safety on the job, 11, 12, 101-5,
  109-13, 115-20
Safety violations: at Chrysler (1970;
  1971), 101; grievance procedures to
  remedy, 32-33; leading to refusal to
  work, 111-12. *See also* Accidents
  on the job
St. Bernard's Church, 128, 129, 135
Sams, George, 200
Sanchez, Sonia, 134
Saroyan, William, 133
Schactman, Max, 215
Scott, Jerome, 229, 230
Scott, John, 110-13
SDS (Students for a Democratic
  Society), 40, 54, 99, 151, 153, 177
Seale, Bobby, 200
Senak, David, 183-84
Serrin, William, 29, 32, 40, 41
Sheffield, Horace, 43
Sherman, Jannette, 34, 105
Shop Stewards' Committee
  (Chrysler), 109
Shorter, Isaac, 228-30
Sims, Jordan, 44, 106, 230; on Baker,
  177; defeats McKinnon, 123;
  ELRUM's attitude toward, 122;
  reputation of, 109; and safety
  problems, 110-12, 115, 118
Sinclair, John, 91, 154-55, 215
Sirhan, Sirhan, 78
SNCC (Student Non-Violent
  Coordinating Committee), 17, 19,
  95, 165, 166, 224
Socialist Workers Party, 19, 120, 223
Solidarity Committee for the League,
  146
Sostre, Martin, 145
South End (Dearborn), 76-79

South End (newspaper), 52, 53, 55-60,
  62-66, 68-72, 74-75, 87, 190
South End Revolutionary Union
  Movement, 75
South Vietnamese National
  Liberation Front, 61
Southern Land Bank, 95
Spark (radical organization), 37
Spearman, Ted, 175
Speed-up, 237; niggermation and,
  101-27; 1968 wildcat strike
  concerning, 46-48; systematization
  of, 30-31
Spreen, Johannes F., 69
Stalin, Joseph, 177, 178
State of Emergency Committee, 205
Stevenson, Denise, 101
STRESS (Stop the Robberies, Enjoy
  Safe Streets), 182-208, 213, 216,
  224-25
Strike: general, 83, 179; in 1941, 42; in
  1970, 31-32, 124-25; in 1972,
  124-25; in 1973, 227, 234; against
  UAW (1971), 41. *See also* Wildcat
  strikes
Sullivan, Joseph, 196
Sutherland, Donald, 147
Sweet, Ossian, 135, 183, 186

Tabor, Derrick, 194
Taylor, John, 108-21, 229, 230, 232
Temple, Fred, 183-84
Thomas, Bill, 174
Thomas, Danny, 76
Thomas, J. C., 110, 118
Thompson, Faye, 130
Thompson, Gary, 103, 104, 111, 116,
  119
Thompson, Russell, 116
Thornton, Clarence, 111, 117
Tojo, Hideki, 34
Toussaint L'Ouverture, Pierre
  Dominique, 18
Townsend, Lynn, 2
Travelers Insurance Co., 3
Trevellick, Richard, 185
Tripp, Luke, 61, 152, 178; in BEDC,
  95; Black Star Productions'
  activities and, 147; creation of BWC
  and, 162; Dowdell and, 147; in
  League of Revolutionary Black
  Workers, 84, 90-91; police
  repression and, 200; writing for
  South End, 52, 55-56, 58, 75
TULC (Trade Union Leadership
  Conference), 42-43, 190
Turner, Mabel, 171

UAW (United Auto Workers), 21-22, 115, 189; Al Fatah article and, 64, 66; archives of, at Wayne State University, 54; black workers fight (1941), 187; Chrysler recognizes (1937), 106; conservatism of, 40-43, 45; DRUM opposes, 46-50; funds for IBA and, 97; job discrimination and, 35-36, 39; Johnson affair and, 10-11; Mack stamping plant wildcat strike and, 230-31; negotiates termination agreement for Briggs workers, 232-33; and New Bethel incident, 70; 1973 contract negotiated by, 234-36; 1973 mayoral election and, 223, 224; 1973 strike led by, 227, 234; post-World War II deal made by, 30-33; problems of Arab community and, 79, 80; and racism, 40-42, 47, 112; and safety on the job, 11, 12, 102, 103, 105, 119; STRESS attacked by, 206; supports Ravitz's bid for judgeship, 214

UHURU, 17, 19, 23, 172

Unemployment: in 1972, 212; in 1974, 237

UNICOM (community organization), 93, 175

United Farm Workers, 80-81

United National Caucus, 39, 44, 123, 230

Unstabled Coffeehouse (theatre group), 133

UPRUM (RUM group of United Parcel Service workers), 83

Urban Alliance, 214

Utter, Lloyd, 102

Veterans Memorial incident, 193-95, 207

Wages, 105-6, 234

Wahls, Myron, 196

Walker, Bill, 135

Wall of Dignity, 134-36

Wallace, George, 37, 142, 192-94

WAM (Workers Action Movement), 230

Washboard Willie, 130

Washington, Booker T., 148

Watson, Edna, 93, 171

Watson, John, 50, 61-62, 132, 150; in BEDC, 95, 97; Black Star Productions and, 144-47, 149; characteristics of, 19-20; on control of means of production, 46; and creation of BWC, 161-64, 166, 167, 170, 172-75; as editor of *South End*,

55-60, 63-66, 71-75; on extent of on-the-job accidents, 107; in League of Revolutionary Black Workers, 84, 87-88, 91, 93; and making of *Finally Got the News*, 136-39; and New Bethel incident, 70; and publication of *ICV*, 22

Watts riot (1964), 187

Wayne County Induction Center, 19

Wayne State Fund, 64

Wayne State University, 53-55, 58-60, 71, 77

WCO (West Central Organization), 91, 96, 146, 150

Weaver, Joe, 65, 70

Weber, John, 135

Weiner, Lee, 151

Wells, Mary, 131

White Panther Party, 155

White workers: effects of black workers' movement on, 6-7; ELRUM and, 117; in Great Rebellion, 188; in 1968 wildcat strikes, 46-48; in 1973 wildcat strikes, 228, 230; Sims and, 112-13

Widick, B. J., 43-44

Wieske, Richard, 124

Wildcat (group), 106

Wildcat (newsletter), 9, 114, 119, 122

Wildcat strikes, 7; in 1968, 24-27, 46-48, 66; in 1969, 106; in 1970, 9, 110-11; in 1973, 179, 227-31, 233, 235; to oppose safety violations, 111-13, 116-20, 235

Williams, John, 61; in BEDC, 95; and BWC, 162, 175, 178; in League of Revolutionary Black Workers, 84, 90-91, 93; police repression and, 200

Williams, Mamie, 104

Williams, Robert (exile in China), 18, 143, 178

Williams, Robert (League leader), 178

Williams, Tennessee, 133

Wilson, Chuck, 175

Winkelman, Stanley J., 2

Wolfe, Sidney, 34, 105

Wolverine Bar Association, 196

Women: BWC and, 160, 170-72; in ELRUM, 122, 171; in MCLL, 151; in UAW, 40

Woodcock, Leonard, 39, 40, 54, 79, 224, 233, 240

Woolsey, Tom, 227-28

Wooten, Chuck, 49; in BEDC, 95; and Black Star Productions' activities, 147; ELRUM's approach sanctioned by, 121; in League of Revolutionary Black Workers, 84,

Wooten, Chuck (continued)
  85; loses job, 161; and making of
  Finally Got the News, 139; and
  on-the-job safety, 113, 115; police
  repression and, 200
Workers' control, 46, 49, 160; DRUM
  demands for, 44; general strike to
  achieve, 83
Workforce: at Ford, 34, 78-79; general
  composition of, 38-39; number of
  Arab workers in (1973), 78;
  percentage of national, employed in
  auto industry, 1, 30

Working conditions. *See* Accidents
  on the job; Safety on the job;
  Safety violations; Speed-up
Workman's compensation, 108
Worobec, Richard, 66-67

Young, Coleman, 69, 192, 222, 240
Young Socialist Alliance, 57
Yousseff, Zakhour, 78

Ziolkowski, Michael, 203
Zwerdling, Abe, 93